MODEL BUILDING IN ECONOMICS

The failure of the models used in the run-up to the 2008 financial crash raised questions regarding the dependability and suitability of modeling, heightening concern about its role and its limits. In this book, Lawrence A. Boland provides an overview of the practices and problems faced by model builders to explain the nature of models, the modeling process, and the possibility for and nature of their testing. In a reflective manner, the author raises serious questions about the assumptions and judgments that model builders make in constructing models. In making his case, he examines the traditional microeconomics-macroeconomics separation with regard to how theoretical models are built and used and how they interact, paying particular attention to the use of equilibrium concepts in macroeconomic models and game theory and to the challenges involved in building empirical models, testing models, and using models to test theoretical explanations.

Lawrence A. Boland has been teaching at Simon Fraser University since 1966. He has also taught at the University of Wisconsin–Milwaukee and was a visiting professor in the department of economics at Boston University. At Capilano College and Vancouver Community College, he taught introductory sociology. He is a Fellow of the Royal Society of Canada. Dr. Boland has published six books on economic methodology, including *The Foundations of Economic Method: A Popperian Perspective* (2003), *The Principles of Economics: Some Lies My Teachers Told Me* (1992), and *The Methodology of Economic Model Building: Methodology after Samuelson* (1989).

Model Building in Economics

Its Purposes and Limitations

LAWRENCE A. BOLAND
Simon Fraser University, Canada

CAMBRIDGE
UNIVERSITY PRESS

32 Avenue of the Americas, New York NY 10013-2473, USA

Cambridge University Press is part of the University of Cambridge.

It furthers the University's mission by disseminating knowledge in the pursuit of education, learning and research at the highest international levels of excellence.

www.cambridge.org
Information on this title: www.cambridge.org/9781107032941

First published 2014

A catalogue record for this publication is available from the British Library.

Library of Congress Cataloguing in Publication data
Boland, Lawrence A.
Model building in economics : its purposes and limitations / Lawrence A. Boland.
pages cm
ISBN 978-1-107-03294-1 (hardback)
1. Econometric models. 2. Economics. I. Title.
HB141.B64 2015
330.01′5195–dc23 2014009762

ISBN 978-1-107-03294-1 Hardback
ISBN 978-1-107-67347-2 Paperback

To Meghan Trentin, the world's greatest granddaughter

Contents

PART III TESTING AND MODELS

PART IV METHODOLOGICAL CONSIDERATIONS

Preface

At one time I mistakenly thought it would be a good time to produce a second edition of my 1989 book on the methodology of economic model building. As I will explain, I changed my mind after I conducted a simple survey of my colleagues and learned that most economists today see model building very differently than I did twenty-five years ago. It became apparent to me that the planned second edition of my 1989 book would be a big mistake. So, instead, I decided to write a different book – one more appropriate for today's economists and students of economics. It might also serve as a lesson for methodologists.

The 1989 book (*The Methodology of Economic Model Building: Methodology after Samuelson*) was directed at methodologists and economic model builders who think they know something about methodology. Actually, the only thing the latter seemed to know at that time was that for one to be taken seriously, one's model must be testable. So in the 1989 book – using some examples of very simple Keynesian models – I set about demonstrating that for all practical purposes an empirical test would require far too many more observations than are possible. For example, for any non-stochastic model that includes a Cobb-Douglas production function, a non-stochastic test using a logical conjunction of exact observations of the variables involved might require a quarter-million observations! That is, the conjunction of observation reports would form a compound statement that constitutes just one possible counter-example – one that would logically refute that model. Of course, a stochastic model would take even more observations.

My original intention for conducting an informal survey of my colleagues was simply to do a little market research. So, I created a set of simple survey questions and went door to door seeking responses. I wanted to know what my colleagues saw as model building in their respective research fields. At the time I thought this would be a simple matter of asking them about the kinds of techniques used to produce models in their fields and the purposes and limitations of those techniques. My older colleagues seemed to have no trouble understanding what I was getting at, but my younger ones could not figure out what I was talking about, making it difficult to complete my survey. That was 'Plan A' and it turned out seemingly not to be very informative.

So, I moved on to 'Plan B': I retooled my survey by first showing each of my survey subjects a quotation from page 886 of Richard Nelson and Sidney Winter's famous 1974 article on evolutionary economics. Specifically (after adding bold emphasis):

> In economics (as in physics) what we refer to as a **theory** is more a set of basic premises – a point of view that delineates the phenomena to be explained and modes of acceptable explanation – than a set of testable propositions. The **theory** points to certain phenomena and key explanatory variables and mechanisms, but generally is quite flexible about the expected conclusions of empirical research, and a wide class of **models** is consistent with it.

I asked my survey subjects if they understood what this quotation said. And again, my older colleagues said they understood perfectly what was being said, but my younger colleagues said they had no clue what Nelson and Winter were trying to say. From what I could figure out (with a little bit of Internet research), the younger-older designation seemed to be centered on whether the subjects did their graduate work in economics after or before about 1980.

I am glad I did this survey because it indicated to me that the planned second edition of my 1989 book would be a complete waste of time. I needed to write a very different book – not one directed at methodologists or at methodologically minded model builders worried about testability. Instead, I decided that I needed to try to bridge this apparent generation gap. But first, I needed to know why the gap exists.

The idea of this gap turns out not to be my discovery. Had I read some recent work by my friend Axel Leijonhufvud [1997, 2006], I would have already known that the words 'model' and 'theory' mean something very different today from what they meant when I was a graduate student. At least I can claim that my informal survey results add support to Axel's empirical claim, which is that model building today is a very different enterprise from what it was thirty or forty years ago. However, I don't think Axel has provided any explanation for this generational gap.

I also found that there is an extensive literature discussing 'theories *versus* models'. Most of it is critical and is almost always complaining about the dominance of mathematical formalism. As Axel says, the common notion among model builders is that mathematics is just a language – but as he says, so is English, and it too can be useful. Most critics of today's model building go much further and blame mathematics and formalism for what they see as the downfall of modern economics and why they think modern economics is useless. The critics may be right, of course, but their literature is not likely to have any effect on the younger generation. In addition, the obstacle is not the differing meanings of the word 'model' but rather the differing meanings of the word 'theory'.

Coincidentally, during the time I was conducting the survey interviews, a famous game theorist came to my university to give a seminar on his current research. During his talk, he did refer frequently to models and theories, but he did so interchangeably. It seemed that, to this famous model builder, different models were different merely by including *additional* behaviour elements in the form of a new mathematical object or element. In addition, model building seems usually to be done with explicit formal elements – not explicit *representations* of existing non-mathematical elements of a theory, as I discussed in my 1989 book. For a while I had difficulty understanding what he was saying since I was trying to interpret his view in terms of my 1989 book. Surely, I thought, such a famous economist would understand model building as I do. But, clearly, my expectations were wrong. At first this was puzzling until I investigated when he got his PhD and discovered – surprise! – it was after 1980. Of course, this apparent confirmation of my empirical conjecture requires further investigation, but in any case, it appears that my younger colleagues are not so strange after all. That is, today, economists commonly use the words 'theory' and 'model' interchangeably, so it is easy to understand why the younger generation has difficulty understanding the Nelson-Winter quotation and the idea of 'theories *versus* models', as there is apparently no 'versus' possible.

I think I can explain the observed generation gap, but first let me informally review the relevant history. Mathematical economics has, of course, been around a long time. However, in the 1950s and 1960s, model builders saw model building as a project of explicitly *representing* existing theories with the use of mathematics. Paul Samuelson's *Foundations of Economic Analysis* was devoted to demonstrating the usefulness of such a project. And much of his research was devoted to building mathematical models of various theories from our history in order to show how useful mathematics can be. But in the 1970s, things seemed to change. Young economists of the day would call anyone using mathematics 'a theorist'. Moreover, the distinction was no longer between models and theories but rather between theoretical and empirical research. This is probably a result of the elevation of econometrics to be an essential part of graduate economic education. This generation of new teachers, who may have seen a difference between models and theories but no longer saw it as an important methodological idea, became the teachers of the young generation I am discussing here.

So, to explain the generation gap when it comes to discussing theories versus models, I suspect that it is the teachers and textbooks of the late 1970s that should be blamed. If so, just what is it that these teachers and textbooks did that was different from what was done by the older generation of teachers and textbooks?

Thinking back over all the students I taught in my literature-based graduate classes (which some of my colleagues considered 'philosophical'), I seem to remember that the textbooks they were using in other classes had something in common. All of their theory textbooks had mathematical problems to solve at the end of the chapters – except for those classes taught by my Chicago-oriented colleagues. What were missing in the textbooks were the usual verbal problems that we had been given when I was a student. That is, we always had as our first task to translate a verbal problem into a mathematical problem and only after that to solve it. This younger generation seems to never have had to engage in this first step, but instead to set about just solving the mathematical problems they are given.

If my conjecture is right, we should be able to examine the textbooks before and after 1980 and find different types of study problem, but a little thought suggests this will not be easy. Even if the assigned textbook had study problems of one type or the other, one cannot be sure what kind of problem any given teacher would use. Nevertheless, today, there are really only two or three key textbooks used in graduate microeconomic theory classes. And if you open any of them to the problems or exercises at the end of a chapter, you will find nothing but mathematics-oriented problems. For example, here is a typical exercise that one can find on page 38 of Mas-Colell, Winston, and Green's 1995 textbook:

> Suppose that $x(p, w)$ is homogeneous of degree zero. Show that the weak axiom holds if and only if for some $w > 0$ and all p, p' we have $p' \cdot x(p, w) > w$ whenever $p \cdot x(p', w) \leq w$ and $x(p', w) \neq x(p, w)$.

And from the 2006 textbook by Frank Cowell, page 47:

> For any homothetic production function show that the cost function must be expressible in the form
>
> $$C(\mathbf{w}, q) = a(\mathbf{w})\, b(q).$$

Interestingly, Cowell's book has an introductory chapter all about models and model building with no mention of theories, although there is a reference to 'theoretical models' (as opposed to 'empirical models', presumably).

Graduate textbooks today are probably more a symptom than the cause of the generational gap. As suggested earlier, the switch began in the 1970s when the perspective changed to theoretical-versus-empirical rather than theory-versus-model. But, I think this in turn is the symptom of the increased emphasis on the use of mathematics in undergraduate intermediate-theory textbooks. If we look at how those textbooks changed during the 1970s, we will find an increasing proportion of the problems and exercises being framed as mathematical problems. For comparison, let us consider C. E. Ferguson's 1969 intermediate textbook, which is the one I often used when teaching intermediate micro theory. In Ferguson's book there were only a handful of problems, and these would involve a table of values with which the student was to calculate averages or margins. Of course, at the ends of chapters there were lists of questions – such as this one from page 72:

> In year one, your income is $2,000; in year two, it is $4,000. The goods you bought in year one for $2,000 cost exactly $4,000 in year two. (*i*) You are better off in year two. (*ii*) You cannot be worse off in year two. Select the proper answer.

Or this one from page 216:

> In the late 1950's, the development of trilevel 'rack' cars for carrying new automobiles substantially lowered the costs of hauling such traffic. This represented (*a*) a change in demand for railroad services, (*b*) a change in supply of railroad services, (*c*) a change in supply of trucking services for new automobiles, (*d*) all of the above.

Interestingly, the only mention of models occurs in a short introductory section on methodology where theoretical analysis is said to precede model analysis.

This observation is not to deny authors promoting the use of mathematics. My colleague, the late Cliff Lloyd, was one of many activists promoting the use of mathematics in economics textbooks, as evident in his intermediate textbook published in 1967. It had no study problems at the end of chapters; instead, he put mathematical analysis in appendices to almost every chapter. The word 'models' appears only in the first paragraph of the introduction and with no explanation of any kind. His book seems to be intended to show how to discuss intermediate theory using mathematics, not to characterize model building. To him, models are just mathematical representations of basic theoretical notions. One can see textbooks such as this as seeds planted that bore fruit in the perspective seen in the post-1980 view that no longer sees a distinction between theories and models. Yet, in textbooks by other similar activists, such as in Robert Clower and John Due's 1972 textbook, even though microeconomic theory is presented only in mathematical terms, the problems and questions at the end of the chapters still were always verbal problems or questions, for which the task for the student was to transform the verbal problems into mathematics so as to use the mathematical analysis they learned in the chapter. Interestingly, in the case of Clower and Due's book, there is a discussion of models in chapter 1. However, consistent with the pre-1980 perspective, models were the result of a two-step procedure [p. 3]. Specifically, one begins with

> the preliminary statement of a problem to be investigated together with a provisional description of a set of phenomena that are thought to be relevant for analyzing the problem ...
>
> Having settled on a problem, the next step in the formulation of a theoretical model is to designate as *unknowns* certain variables whose values are provisionally assumed to describe salient features of the (actual or hypothetical) economics system to which the problem relates. We then seek to impose restrictions on these unknowns, usually in the form of explicit or implicit functional relations.

Now, let us by comparison look at a problem that can be found in a post-1980 intermediate textbook such as Hal Varian's [2006], page 70:

> Which of the following are monotonic transformations? (1) $u = 2v - 13$; (2) $u = -1/v^2$; (3) $u = 1/v^2$; (4) $u = \ln v$; (5) $u = -e^{-v}$; (6) $u = v^2$; (7) $u = v^2$ for $v > 0$; (8) $u = v^2$ for $v < 0$.

Exercise questions such as this are often followed by an appendix of more detailed mathematics. Perhaps less surprising, let us consider an 'exercise' from Varian's more advanced 1992 textbook, page 39:

> Let $f(x_1, x_2)$ be a production function with two factors and let w_1 and w_2 be their respective prices. Show that the elasticity of the factor share (w_2x_2/w_1x_1) with respect to (x_1/x_2) is given by $1/\sigma - 1$.

And like Cowell's book, models and model building are discussed but with no mention of any relationship to theories. However, Varian does specify on page 1: 'By a model we mean a simplified representation of reality.'

As I am not sure examining textbooks tells me as much as I would like, I went back to my younger colleagues and discussed my conjectured explanation for the generation gap. They all agreed that in their graduate education they never had to do the old first step of translating a verbal problem or question into mathematics to solve or answer it. They were usually given problems or questions in mathematical form, such as the ones from Varian's books I mentioned earlier.

Somewhat arbitrarily, I have put 1980 as the watershed, but the current notions of theories and models began much earlier. I remember attending a 'theory conference' at Queens University in 1977. I was there replacing my late friend, the aforementioned Cliff Lloyd. It became clear that, among the participants at the conference, the use of the term 'theory' merely meant any mathematical model. I thought that was strange at the time but dismissed it as merely a sign of immaturity that would soon go away.

As I said at the beginning, I am abandoning my original intention to produce a second edition of my 1989 book. Ironically, I always tell my students that they must always be clear about their intended audience when writing their papers or giving a seminar presentation. Looking back after my recent survey results, I am now wondering who I thought the audience was for the 1989 book. If I thought I was going to enlighten the younger generation, I am sure I failed. Clearly I was not practicing what I preached.

Still, I am convinced that the old way of looking at theories versus models is correct, makes sense, and is certainly more intellectually informative – that is, more about economics *ideas* than about the latest modeling techniques. Nevertheless, one proceeds with the cards one is dealt. So, I have written this book such that it does not matter whether or not a reader would understand the quotation from Nelson and Winter. Throughout, however, I will not pass over any opportunities to discuss the theoretical ideas that lie hidden behind the various models discussed. After all, it is how our theoretical notions change as a result of successful model building that should be the most important thing we should be learning.

Acknowledgements

I wish to thank my colleagues and friends who provided a significant amount of critical feedback from reading early versions of the various chapters. In particular, I much appreciate the help I received from Brian Krauth, Ken Kasa, Aris Spanos, Luba Petersen, Chris Muris, Erik Kimbrough, David Colander, Shih En Lu, Jack Knetsch, and Irene Botosaru. I also wish to thank those who answered my questions early on, in particular Ken Arrow, Marcel Boumans, David Hendry, Kevin Hoover, John Duffy, Pedro Garcia Duarte, Dick Lipsey, David Laidler, Songzi Du, David Andolfatto, David Jacks, David Hammes, David Levy, Fernando Martin, Geoff Hodgson, June Flanders, and Andrew Jewett.

Prologue: Model building yesterday versus today

> An econometrician's job is to express economic theories in mathematical terms in order to verify them by statistical methods, and to measure the impact of one economic variable on another so as to be able to predict future events or advise what economic policy should be followed when such and such a result is desired.
>
> This definition describes the major divisions of econometrics, namely, specification, estimation, verification, and prediction.
>
> *Specification* has to do with expressing an economic theory in mathematical terms. This activity is also called *model building*. A *model* is a set of mathematical relations (usually equations) expressing an economic theory. Successful model building requires an artist's touch, a sense of what to leave out if the set is to be kept manageable, elegant, and useful with the raw materials (collected data) that are available.
>
> Stefan Valavanis [1959, p. 1]

As beginning economics graduate students soon discover, most of their time will be spent learning about model building. As James Heckman observes, 'Just as the ancient Hebrews were "the people of the book", economists are "the people of the model"' [2000, p. 46]. But, students will also discover that there will be little explicit talk about how best to go about building models. Instead, they are seemingly expected to learn inductively by example. Over the last fifty or sixty years of educating modern economists, most things have not changed much. However, what one is supposed to think constitutes a model and what one is supposed to think a model can or should do has changed dramatically. Originally, the idea was that common principles of economics could be illustrated with physical models, but later it was that they could be represented by mathematical models.[1] Representative models were

[1] See, for example, Stefan Valavanis [1959].

spearheaded mostly by the work of Jan Tinbergen in the 1930s.[2] In the last two or three decades, the representative notion of models seems to have been lost. Today, models are objects of research on their own, without explicit recognition of any underlying principles that someone might wish to discuss without reference to a specific model. Stated another way, models today are easily viewed as simple instruments to be used to measure the economy and hopefully to learn about the economy in a trial-and-error manner.[3] Unfortunately, by viewing models as mere instruments, students have been cut off from the origins of ideas underlying the models and hence from an opportunity to learn about those ideas.

1. Representative models of yesterday

Until the 1980s (or in some cases, the late 1970s), almost all graduate students were taught to think of models as particular representations of more general theories – for example, the ISLM model of John Maynard Keynes's *General Theory* or Paul Samuelson's models of Ricardian economics. That is, models were always models *of a theory*. The mechanics of such representations involve three separate decisions that the model builder would have to make: (1) choose the basic behavioural principles or theory that one is going to build a model of, (2) choose how each principle or element of a theory is to be represented (usually, this is a choice of the mathematical tools to use) and (3) choose how to specify or 'calibrate' the model's elements if it is to be applied to observable data.

1.1. Choosing basic principles or a theory

Before the 1980s, it was common for students at all levels to be assigned study and exam problems (or questions) in a verbal or literary form that required the students to begin by deciding how to translate the verbal problem into a mathematical problem to solve. In other words, they had to begin by building a model of the problem such that, should they obtain a solution to the model, they would thereby have solved the assigned verbal problem or answer the assigned verbal question. As such, the model *represented* the verbal problem or question. This way of looking at models was very common in other fields as well. In particular, economics students were being taught to look at models in

2 See Marcel Boumans [2005].
3 See Mary Morgan and Margaret Morrison [1999].

the same way that most engineers used models. For example, designing an airplane or an automobile, the engineer might choose to build a scaled-down model to test in a wind tunnel. Doing so would necessarily involve selecting those attributes to ignore as being unimportant and those that are important (and usually, the latter are ones that also do not depend on size whenever it is a scale model). For wind tunnel tests, it is usually just a matter of accurately representing the shape. Today, of course, design engineers would more likely use a computer model and test it based on programmed physics principles. In either case, the test model involves simplification (e.g., using clay rather than metal in the case of wind tunnels). If carefully done, one can learn whether some new innovative idea has a chance of working and thus producing the desired aerodynamic results. No conclusions can be reached for attributes left out, of course.

In economics, things are usually more intellectual than mechanical, but models still involve selection and simplification. At minimum, the first step is to decide what variables in the theoretical explanatory principle are to be quantified and then which of those are to be endogenous (i.e., to be explained) and which are to be exogenous (i.e., not explained but considered to play an important role, perhaps as constraints).

Keeping things as simple as possible at this early stage – and in order to illustrate how model building was done in yesteryears – let us consider an elementary textbook example, one about explaining supply or, more particularly, the output of a single-factory firm that produces standard-size garbage cans. Let us say we are interested in the extremely simple explanatory principle that says the volume of output depends directly on how much labour it employs. To build a model, then, we first say that the daily output of cans will be represented with a scalar number X that stands for the number of cans that go out the door each day. Producing the cans, let us say, takes an input of a quantity of homogenous labour (no special skills possessed by anyone); this will be represented by the scalar L that stands for the number of man-hours worked each day. The simplest explanatory principle would be to say that these variables are positively correlated. Of course, there may be other factors that matter as possible constraints – such as the size of the factory, the number of tools available, and so forth. However, for the purposes of this very simple explanatory principle, these factors will not be explained but are still assumed to matter and hence will have to be recognized. The factory size will be represented by a scalar Z that identifies the square meters of the factory, and the number of tools will be represented by a scalar K. So far this is a fairly weak explanation since it only claims that the relationship is a positive correlation. However, it does claim implicitly that if the size of the factory or the number of tools available were to change, then output X could change without any change in the number of labour-hours utilized, contrary to our initial explanation.

Although it is not trivial, all that is said with such a simple behavioural theory of the daily supply of one firm is that *if* the factory size and the number of tools utilized do *not* change, we would expect the daily output to *not* change – but *only if* the quantity of labour employed does *not* change. Those wanting to say something more might choose to build a model of this behavioural theory or they might instead just recognize more variables. For example, ordinary labour is obviously not homogenous regarding skills; there can be more than one type of tool needed to produce garbage cans, and while factory size is important, the configuration of that size might matter, too. However, including these would involve adding more variables and would thus change our original explanatory principle – and as such, we would no longer be building a representative model of the original simple explanation. That is, it would not be just a different model; it would represent a different explanation. For now, let us stick with the very simple explanation with which we began.

1.2. Choosing tools of representation

If we do continue to keep things very simple (i.e., maintain homogeneous labour and one type of tool, etc.) and want to build a representative model, the usual first step is to express the basic input-output relationship as something like $X = f(L, K, Z)$ with $\Delta X/\Delta L > 0$ (a simple expression of a positive correlation). This would not say much more than the verbal statement at the beginning of this example, of course. To say more, we would need to add assumptions about the nature of the $f(\bullet)$. We could assume it is a simple linear function, such as $X = \alpha L + \beta K + \gamma Z$ with $\alpha > 0$. Most important, as long as every quantity recognized here is positive, it does still represent the verbal idea of the simple explanatory principle with which we started.

More interesting theories that one would more likely want to go about representing with models would usually involve many different relationships between the variables in question (e.g., simultaneous or lagged) and hence many more functions that would also have to be included in the representative model. For example, K could be considered an endogenous rather than exogenous variable and explained rather than taken to be a given. Going further, one might like to consider production technology to be a matter of choice. This choice might be a matter of changing the tools used or the way the tools are used.

1.3. Specifying or calibrating the functional elements of models

One important thing to keep in mind about mathematical functions used to represent economic relationships – such as the one discussed earlier concerning the supply output of one firm – is that some of the quantities represent observable variables (e.g., X, L, K and Z) and others are not observable because they are mathematical artefacts of the type of equation used. That is, in the simplest case, the coefficients α, β and γ are there because we have assumed a linear relationship. Had we assumed the relationship to be quadratic, many more coefficients would have to be dealt with, even though the number of observable variables would be the same.[4] The coefficients usually represent presumed *parameters* of the relationship being modeled, and thus there is always the possibility that they are themselves either Nature-given or, in the case of the supply function, technology-given. If at some time in the future the technology dramatically improves, some of these parameters might increase or decrease.

Sometimes we have independent knowledge of the size of such parameters. Perhaps we know that, given K and Z, an individual worker will produce twenty cans in one day. At other times we do not know exactly the values of the parameters, but we can guess. In this case, depending on the purpose for building the model, we might make several observations of X and L over several days and try out our guess to see if it fits the observed data. Doing this amounts to a form of calibration [see Kydland and Prescott 1991, 1996] and is much like what is done in some branches of engineering where measuring instruments need to be calibrated. Sophisticated engineering aside, even more mundane cases would be the calibration that always has to be done to make sure a magnetic compass points to the real North Pole rather than the magnetic north pole, or the calibration of a thermometer by setting its 0°C where it reads when inserted into ice water and its 100°C where it reads when inserted into boiling water.

2. Theoretical versus empirical models today

In what follows I will restrict the use of the word 'model' just to empirical models based on data from an actual economy. Such models will often be distinguished from information in the form of what may be called theory. In this simplistic

4 For more on this, see chapter 6 of Boland [1989].

> viewpoint a theory starts with a set of consistent assumptions and then produces logical consequences from them in a form relevant to economic questions. On some occasions this theory is best expressed using very sophisticated mathematics, 'best' here meaning the most rigorous and compact although not necessarily the easiest to understand. To have something easier to use and to interpret a simple version of the theory can be formed, an approximation, and this is sometimes called a theoretical model. However, I will call all such constructs just 'theory'. I will take the attitude that a piece of theory has only intellectual interest until it has been validated in some way against alternative theories and using actual data.
>
> Clive Granger [1999, p. 6]

So far I have been discussing how models were viewed before 1980 when students were usually expected to translate their verbal study questions into mathematical questions. Today, judging by the most popular theory textbooks, few students are expected to do such a translation (except, perhaps, those being trained in the old, 1960s–1970s Chicago School tradition). And so, all this so far might seem strange to some readers since, when opening articles in the major mainstream journals, there is often no discussion of non-mathematically presented explanatory principles.

What students today are taught is to distinguish between 'theoretical models' and 'empirical models'. Theoretical models (which will be discussed in Part I) are basically what one would get if one were to follow the step-by-step process discussed earlier, but usually for such models the process has not been explicitly stated – only the final result is revealed. How they were constructed is now rarely discussed. That is, a theoretical model is implicitly representative of some verbal explanatory theory, but that verbal theory is not at issue and so is rarely separately discussed.

Empirical models (to be discussed in Part II) can range from simple linear or log-linear single equations (where the coefficients are estimated with the available data) to more elaborate multi-equation models. While simple empirical models have been developed for more than seven decades, more elaborate versions began to appear in the 1970s and 1980s, which were focused on the readily available labour or financial data. Today there are many more sources for data and many different types of data available. Representative empirical models are usually designed to represent either some behavioural theory or just available data – rarely do they do both, but it is not impossible.

Today, representative empirical and theoretical models still have a common first step. Both begin with the identification (if only implicitly) of a list of relevant variables. Although the theoretical models will always have their list separated into those variables that are endogenous and those that are exogenous, some empirical models may let the question of exogeneity be determined with an appropriate test of the data. However, they can differ in terms of how the list of relevant variables is arrived at.

Representative theoretical models are already focused on or limited by one or more explanatory principle or behavioural theory that as such asserts causes and effects and thus identifies which variables are exogenous versus which are endogenous. Builders of representative empirical models need not be so limited. Their first step is usually to examine a body of data and then decide what to identify as relevant variables. This may be guided by *a priori* principles or theories but need not be. As Clive Granger [1999, pp. 16–17] puts it:

> One can find advocates at [two] extremes, some saying that theory contains the only pure truth and so has to be the basis of the model, even to claiming that all 'residuals' have to have theoretical explanations, leaving little place for stochastics, uncertainty, or exogenous shocks to the system. At the other extreme, some econometricians have thrown up their hands in despair when trying to find a use for theory and so build 'atheoretical' models based just on examination of the data and using any apparent regularities and relationships found in it. Most applied economists take a middle ground, using theory to provide an initial specification and then data exploration techniques to extend or refine the starting model, leading to a form that better represents the data.

He goes on to note [p. 18], however,

> If no theoretical basis is used and if a complex modeling situation is considered, with many possible explanatory variables and plenty of data, the possibility of 'data-mining' or 'data-snooping' becomes a problem, particularly now that computing is both fast and cheap. Clearly evaluation procedures need to be applied using data sets that were not involved in the model selection and estimation process, either 'out-of-sample' in cross-section or panel analysis, or 'post-sample' in time series. It is not sufficient to merely show a statistic that indicates that one model performs better than others; a correct hypothesis test is required...

What is important in any representative empirical model is to keep in mind the purpose for the model. Some empirical models are intended to help with forming policy formation. Others are intended to be tests of competing behavioural theories or principles. Some think the purpose of building empirical models is to learn inductively from the data, but if strictly interpreted, this notion is based on a false theory of learning.[5] In any

[5] For more on this, see chapter 1 of Boland [2003].

of these ways of using models, it is easy to see them being used as research or policy instruments.

3. Models as instruments

> While theoretical principles . . . have to form a consistent system, instruments are built on the basis of a compromise of often incompatible theoretical and empirical requirements. Theories should be true, or at least not false, but models have only to fulfill their goal satisfactorily.
>
> Marcel Boumans [2005, p. 20]

While it is hard to deny that economic models can be used as instruments; whether that is profound is another matter. That models are often used as instruments does, however, seem to divorce them from the old (pre-1980s) view of the theory-model relationship. That is, today, models are no longer thought to be merely designed to be simplified representations of some given theories – instead, they might be designed from the start to be instruments. For this reason, such models will be of interest on their own, and behavioural theories may play what seems a secondary role in the design of the instrument-model.

3.1. Building models to serve as instruments

One does not build tools or instruments only for the sake of building tools or instruments; one must have a purpose or goal. But, of course, theoretical and empirical model-instruments will usually have different purposes. That is, which type of model one would build depends on one's purpose. Let me explain.

3.1.1. *Theoretical models as instruments:* Beginning in the mid-1970s (as I noted in the Preface), 'theoretical' became synonymous with 'mathematical'. Of course, it is easy to see that empirical models also use mathematics – so, today, 'theoretical' merely indicates that a model's intended purpose may not necessarily involve previously observed data – and in some cases, it may mean not having anything to do with observable data. There are many possible purposes or aims for building theoretical models. One suspects that in the early days, particularly after World War II, building theoretical models was done for purely mathematical reasons. That is, for the purposes of showing that, by mathematizing one's preexisting verbal theory, the theorist would be able to more easily prove the various theoretical claims being made with that theory regarding policy or simply being made for our understanding. Historically, perhaps since the time of Léon Walras and the later promotion of his general-equilibrium analysis in the late 1930s, there has been a continuing effort to prove that Adam Smith was right. Most of this effort involved building general-equilibrium models and proving the theoretical existence of an equilibrium set of prices [cf. Hahn 1973]. This involved so-called existence proofs that were based on the axiomatization of Walras's general-equilibrium analysis. In this case, the purpose of the model building would be to create a logical tool to perform the intended proof.

Today, an obvious purpose for building some theoretical models is to try out new mathematical techniques.[6] In many cases, the purpose is just to develop an alternative to an existing theoretical model using a different technique (perhaps one more aesthetic or less demanding or more rigorous, etc. to prove the same theoretical proposition). In recent years, the primary new mathematical technique has involved game theory. Fifty or sixty years ago, the new technique being promoted was ordinary set theory. Critics often complain that this changing of techniques is only an issue of the latest changing fads – but, of course, it need not be.

In a more practical way, some theoretical model building is done to figure out a policy for governments to employ to achieve desired aims. How can the government reduce unemployment, inflation, and so forth? What damage might be done with some proposed policies? What are the relevant constraints on any particular proposed policy? What are its limitations? Such questions have been at the core of economics since before the time of Adam Smith and long before theorizing was focused on building theoretical models.

A considerable literature has developed in recent years concerning the history of building models to serve as instruments for economic measurement.[7] The instruments can range from the theoretically simple consumer index number or national income accounts measures to the possibly more sophisticated measure of such a thing as the elasticity of demand for a particular product. The purpose in all cases is to have an autonomous (uncalibrated) instrument – that is, one that makes sense before being

6 See the survey results in my 1986 article with Herbert Grubel for how such use of mathematics was critically viewed then.

7 For example, see Mary Morgan [2001] as well as the remainder of the *Annual Supplement* to Volume 33 of *History of Political Economy* journal.

applied to empirical data. Few graduate courses spend much time on the issue of developing measures – too often it is simply taken for granted.

Now, the most obvious use for theoretical models is as tools to simulate an economy for the purpose of deriving, say, optimal fiscal or monetary policies. In this case, one would, for example, represent notions of aggregate demand and supply functions – including notions about the labour market and demands for investment or liquidity preference, and so on. With such a model and its identification of significant parameters, one could try to calibrate these parameters so that one could plot the effects of various changes in the exogenous policy variables that a government might be able to control, such as the interest rate, the tax rates, and so on.

The common factor in all of these theoretical models is that their development usually comes before any consideration of data for the purpose of specification or calibration. Questions about what should be the optimal governmental policies need to be addressed before attempting to simulate an economy for the purposes of evaluating the policies. Obviously, calibration based on empirical data is the last step in the development of a simulation model that might be used for what Finn Kydland and Edward Prescott [1996] call a 'computational experiment'. One question that still might be asked is whether consideration of empirical data should come before or after one develops a theoretical model. On the one hand, some think one must always consider data before forming a theoretical explanation. On the other hand, theoreticians will counter that, even when looking at data, one will implicitly, if not explicitly, be presuming some existing theoretical model. I will not try to resolve this dispute here, but in Chapter 12 it will be used as a case study concerning how one goes about choosing a model-building method in macro-econometric studies.

3.1.2. ***Empirical models as instruments:*** Those who think consideration of empirical data should come before theory development have been around for a long time – perhaps going back to the seventeenth century, the days of Galileo or Francis Bacon. The basic notion is that one would examine the available data and look for patterns and then form a conjecture as to the causes of the pattern. For some, it is merely a matter of identifying patterns. Critics, however, point out that one can be a little too selective in identifying patterns and see only what one wants to see. Or, in a similar vein, one could just be engaging, as Granger said, in 'data mining' – perhaps to justify one's prior prejudices.

Surely, however, empirical data have to matter if one is to advocate particular government or corporate economic policies or if one is claiming to explain the real world or maybe forecast the future state of the economy in order to make investment or policy decisions. In this regard, large models designed to represent or display large bodies of data began being developed in the mid-1930s. The most famous early large models were the input-output models created by Wassily Leontief to summarize and categorize economic data from the year 1919 for the trade between 41 sectors. Interestingly, the NBER[8] began collecting statistical data – National Income Accounts – for the same period. A major leader of this activity was Wesley Mitchell, who was not satisfied with the economic theories of the day and thought we should begin by looking at the data concerning national income and how it is distributed. During the 1950s and 1960s, econometricians began developing very large models designed to describe and represent much more of the available data. By 'very large', I mean models with a very large number of equations that are econometrically estimated using the available data. In the 1950s, there was the so-called Klein-Goldberger model, which had 25 equations; in the 1960s, there was the Brookings model, which had 400 equations. Eventually, many central banks began producing similar national models and today there are even commercial models for many countries. Commercial econometric models, such as the well-known DRI/McGraw-Hill models, can have more than 1,000 equations. Models such as these are intended to be used to produce forecasts of financial and economic indicators for use in strategic planning. Such commercial models are used today primarily as short-term forecasting instruments by Fortune 500 corporations and policy analysts for governments and regulated industries. Unlike in the 1960s and 1970s, today few graduate courses are devoted to discussing such large-scale econometric models.

From the beginning, the purpose of these large models was primarily to be instruments for producing short-term forecasts as well as producing evaluations of effects of possible policy proposals. The growth in the size of the models was due mostly to the growth of the body of data – starting with aggregate annual data and later quarterly data and specific data for more and more sectors and sub-sectors. These models are often claimed to be data-driven, as if theoretical considerations were not needed. Of course, theory does play a role, but it is always limited by having to be tailored to fit only the data available.

[8] The National Bureau of Economic Research.

Some empirical models are explicitly related to theoretical models. These are empirical models developed to test particular chosen theories. In some cases, experiments are conducted to produce data to be used to test theories or theoretical claims. In either case, empirical data is used to test the theories or answer questions such as: Does the theory in question truly explain the observable data? Does the theory truly represent the available data? To these questions I now turn.

3.2. Testing with models: its purpose and its limitations

Interestingly, the methodological question of whether one's theory or model is testable has been asked for many years. Originally, it was thought necessary to ask because, in the late 1930s, critics of the growing practice of mathematizing economics claimed that mathematics-based models could only produce tautologies, but Samuelson [1947/65] easily proved this criticism to be in error. Today, the issue of testability, if it is ever raised, is merely about whether the theory or model is 'informative'.[9] Model builders rarely raise this issue today, so I will postpone considering it until later.

To understand how models can be seen as a means of testing theoretical explanations, one has to look back at the pre-1980s view of the relationship between a theory and its model. Specifically, a model of a theory was thought to involve adding to the basic assumptions of the theory by assuming specific representations of each of the elemental assumptions of the theory. Earlier, I gave an example of this where the model builder would have to choose how to represent the elements. In that example of a firm's input-output relationship (one for which the output depends on the input of labour, given the firm's amount of tools and factory space), the question I addressed was, does the model builder choose to represent that relationship with, say, a linear or a quadratic function? My main point is that the decision to assume the input-output relationship can be empirically represented by a linear (or quadratic, etc.) function is an *additional* assumption. Obviously, any calibration of the parameters of the assumed relationship may also involve additional assumptions.

With the older view in mind, let me now discuss the various problems with using models as instruments to test theoretical explanations. First,

[9] As I explained in chapter 6 of my 1989 book, the greater the number of conceivable observations being denied (should the theory or model turn out to be true), the more informative it is.

there is the logical problem that philosophers call the Duhem-Quine thesis. It recognizes that, should one be able to find evidence that if confirmed would constitute a refutation of the test *model*, one would not thereby necessarily have provided a refutation of the more simple basic *theoretical* explanation that is presumed in the model. In the simple example of the form of a production function, one may have only confirmed that the added assumption of linearity was false, and thus the evidence does not necessarily refute the basic (positively correlated) input-output relationship. That is, perhaps the model builder should have instead assumed a quadratic function, and so on (this consequence of the Duhem-Quine thesis will be discussed much more in Chapters 8 and 9). At minimum and most important, the Duhem-Quine thesis shows that one cannot easily or simply use a model as an instrument to convincingly test a theoretical explanation. However, it still may be argued that this may be due only to the application of the strict true-vs.-false criterion. If one instead allows for the less severe criterion of confirmation or disconfirmation, convincing test are still possible, but they nevertheless require some care (as I will explain in Chapter 9).

Second, though, there is still the problem of confusing 'non-confirmed' with 'disconfirmed' – a confusion that has plagued empirical testing for many decades. Simply stated, one criterion does not fit all tests. That is, without a true-vs.-false test, whichever statistical criterion is used in order to be able to say a hypothesis or assumption is not confirmed will not be equivalent to a criterion of whether the statement is disconfirmed; failure to confirm can only indicate that it is not confirmed. Of course, this does not apply to the non-stochastic criterion of absolutely true or false where not-false equals true and not-true equals false. Moreover, the use of statistical criteria still requires that the statistical adequacy of the data and model be assured (as I will discuss in Chapter 10). At this stage, it is enough to point out that using models as instruments to test theoretical explanations is faced with logical obstacles that must be dealt with. I will postpone further discussion of the logic of testing with models until Part III.

3.3. Instrumentalism: it purpose and its limitations

Although it is not always stated explicitly, viewing models as instruments is really saying that such models should never be considered absolutely true or false but only better or worse in performing their intended task. The idea of considering theories or models as instruments rather than as intended true explanations of observable phenomena goes back at least to the early eighteenth century. Specifically, this was when the famous Bishop Berkeley advocated interpreting Newton's physics as only an instrument to predict the movement of planets rather than as a claimed true theory because the latter interpretation would compete with the authority of the Church on such matters. Philosophers might spend a lot of time arguing over such issues, but we will not do so here. Rightly or wrongly, model builders in economics are less concerned with whether their models are absolutely true than whether they are an improvement over what has been built so far. The only things to keep in mind here is that a useful instrument for one task might not be useful for another and what works today may not work tomorrow. The only area where all this might come up is when considering alternative modeling methods. Discussion of the more philosophical aspects of this issue will be postponed until Chapter 11.

4. Outline of book

Above all, I want to stress that this book is not intended to be a textbook on how to build models or how to apply particular mathematical methods such as game theory. Instead, it is, metaphorically speaking, more concerned with the *Forest* than with the *Trees*. Hopefully, all readers will find this helpful.[10] In this regard, the reader will undoubtedly notice that most chapters and many sections and subsections within the chapters begin with a few quotations. I invite the reader to see each of these as discussions between participants in a virtual seminar – usually one with differing positions about the topic at hand.

With the Forest-vs.-Trees perspective always in mind, the first chapter of Part I begins by examining the traditional micro-macro separation with regard to how theoretical models are built, are used and possibly interact. The next three chapters give particular attention to the use of any equilibrium concept in general as well as the equilibrium concepts used in macroeconomic models and in those based on game theory. Part II begins with a chapter that discusses building empirical models in terms of the historical separation between microeconomics and macroeconomics. And given that, until relatively recently, most empirical model building in

[10] For those readers not familiar with the latest technical economics jargon, occasionally (as I have done already), I will also provide a note or two to explain some of the terminology or important concepts.

economics seems to have involved macroeconomics, the next two chapters focus on the purposes of building empirical macroeconomic models and the problems that must be solved in doing so. Part III addresses the many problems of testing models as well as using models to test theoretical explanations, which I discussed earlier. Part IV addresses some of the methodological and sociological problems discussed in recent literature. The closing Epilogue will raise a concern about focusing on the technical problems and decision at the expense of inadvertently producing models that serve only one ideological perspective even when that perspective may not be desired by the model builders themselves.

PART I

THEORETICAL MODELS

1

Microeconomic versus macroeconomic theoretical model building

When we approach the study of business cycle with the intention of carrying through an analysis that is truly dynamic ... we are naturally led to distinguish between two types of analyses: the micro-dynamic and the macro-dynamic types. The micro-dynamic analysis is an analysis by which we try to explain in some detail the behaviour of a certain section of the huge economic mechanism, taking for granted that certain general parameters are given ...

The macro-dynamic analysis, on the other hand, tries to give an account of the fluctuations of the whole economic system taken in its entirety. Obviously in this case it is impossible to carry through the analysis in great detail. Of course, it is always possible to give even a macro-dynamic analysis in detail if we confine ourselves to a purely *formal* theory.

Ragnar Frisch [1933a, p. 2, emphasis in original]

One of the functions of theoretical economics is to provide fully articulated, artificial economic systems that can serve as laboratories in which policies that would be prohibitively expensive to experiment with in actual economies can be tested out at much lower cost. To serve this function well, it is essential that the artificial 'model' economy be distinguished as sharply as possible in discussion from actual economies. ...

Any model that is well enough articulated to give clear answers to the questions we put to it will necessarily be artificial, abstract, patently 'unreal'.

Robert Lucas [1980, p. 696]

It should be noted that before the 1936 publication of Keynes's *General Theory*, economic textbooks made no distinction between microeconomics and macroeconomics. If there were any differences, they would have been either between 'value theory' and 'money' chapters or between partial- and general-equilibrium models. But even general-equilibrium models would have not been widely considered – at least not until the late 1940s, and even then the consideration was limited to the minority of economists interested in mathematical modeling. General-equilibrium analysis – such as that of Léon Walras – was not openly promoted in English theoretical literature, although that was the intention with the publication of John Hicks's *Value and Capital* in the late 1930s. Of course, Adam Smith's *Wealth of Nations* could easily be seen as macroeconomics, as it has a lot to say about the growth of whole nations, although the analysis is usually about the effects of individuals doing what is best for them – that is, Smith's work can be seen as a mixture of micro and macro. So why is the distinction prominent in modern economics and if not in all modern research then at least in all undergraduate economics curricula? Before eventually launching into a detailed discussion of theoretical model building, I would like to lay out some critical notions about the basic ingredients at the foundation of micro and macro economics.

Leaving aside the opinion of some macroeconomic theorists, from the beginning macroeconomics was to be studied separately from the economics that was based primarily on Alfred Marshall's *Principles of Economics* [1890, 1920]. One argument for this shift from a Marshallian-dominated economics might be that Keynes's work occurred in the midst of ideological disputes over the role of government in the economy and particularly in the recovery from the Great Depression of the 1930s. Those economists who saw the need for a government role in the economy became critics of those who saw enlightenment in Marshall's *Principles*, which was based primarily on partial-equilibrium analysis[1] and for the most part devoid of a major role for the government.

By the late 1940s, separate macro- and microeconomics classes began to appear in major university programs[2] and spread to almost all departments by the late 1950s. Before such classes began to appear, economics departments surely had members of both camps (i.e., followers of Keynes or of Marshall), so clearly the potential for curricular disputes would have been obvious. One possible way to avoid having the opposing camps 'fighting in the hallways' – between those who focused on what we now call the macro economy and those who continued in the Marshallian partial-equilibrium tradition – would be to create separate courses. This separation was auspiciously facilitated by the 1948 publication of Paul Samuelson's subsequently popular undergraduate textbook *Economics*. Interestingly, this book did not initially refer to 'macroeconomics' although the distinction between macro and micro was implicitly promoted by virtue of its organization. It also

1 By a 'partial equilibrium', economists distinguish, say, the equilibrium of one market (regardless of the state of other markets) from that of a general equilibrium where all markets are in a state of equilibrium – or, at least, demand equals supply in all markets.

2 Kenneth Arrow, for example, told me he taught an explicitly macroeconomics course for the first time in 1948.

promoted a role for what became known as Keynesian economics by giving an explicit role to the government in a nation's economy.

While the micro-macro distinction may persist in today's economics curricula, there are critics of continuing this distinction when it comes to graduate education. These critics fall into two separate groups: those who say macroeconomics is merely a way of interpreting general-equilibrium economics (after all, any general equilibrium concerns the whole economy) and those who simply demand that (as a matter of methodology) any macroeconomic analysis must have a microeconomic foundation. In some ways, these two groups are saying the same thing because general-equilibrium analysis presumes that individuals, if viewed separately, behave in accordance with Marshallian analysis – that is, individuals are presumed to be maximizing profit, utility, and so on. Fortunately, while ideological disputes may have precipitated the creation of separate micro and macro courses, ideological disputes do not play as big a role in mainstream economics today as they once did. Nevertheless, the distinction between micro and macro courses and research still exists in most economics departments.

1.1. The nature of theoretical microeconomic models: the necessary ingredients

Modern theoretical microeconomic models have a long history that roughly began with Marshall's *Principles of Economics*, first published in 1890. Marshall was a trained mathematician but felt that the math should be suppressed or at least relegated to footnotes or an appendix at the end of his economics book. His mathematics of choice was simple calculus since this was all that was needed to model the basic notions of his economics. His economics was focused primarily on the decisions made by individuals and in particular the decisions that affected a single market. If one can explain each and every individual participant's decision in a market for particular good, then one thereby will also have explained the market as a whole. Similarly, if one can explain every individual's decisions for all goods in all markets and for every individual in the economy, then one will have explained what we call the macro economy. In this sense, clearly the micro-macro split seems artificial. Nevertheless, Marshall did not have much to say about what we call macroeconomics in his book's first five parts (which, by the way, Marshall called 'Books' in his 'Volume', as was the custom of his day). However, in the (commonly ignored) Book VI of his *Principles*, he did discuss the distribution of national income. Of course, if one has explained the decisions of all individuals, one might think that there really is no need to say more.

Marshall's basic notions in his *Principles* involved the logically necessary conditions for maximization (or minimization), which are discussed in the first four parts of his book. The main topic of Book V is the various neighbourhood properties of an equilibrium. Today, most microeconomics courses and microeconomic theoretical models conform to his basic principles that he explained in this fifth part. Some model builders have extended their models to 2- or 3-period models, such as the basic so-called Fisher models.[3] Such Fisher models are not really considered dynamic models as they are usually mere applications of what most think of as Marshall's short-run vs. long-run type of methodology for modeling.[4]

1.1.1. The primary basic principle for theoretical micro models

Anyone who has taken even just a beginning course in economics will be familiar with the concepts of maximization (or 'economic rationality'), equilibrium, and so forth. Unfortunately, some of these basic concepts are not well understood even by teachers, as is evident in today's standard economics textbooks. So, as things proceed, I will occasionally critically examine these concepts and hopefully clear up some lingering confusion – particularly since many textbook characterizations can be the source of confusion when building models.

Let us begin with the first and main principle at the foundation of every microeconomic model – namely, the explicit assumption of constrained maximization (or, more generally, optimization, since a firm for example might wish to minimize costs). Economists have gotten into the habit of

3 Such as models with one agent that lives two or three periods with certainty.

4 Without going deep into this here, it should be noted that too often teachers and textbooks misunderstand the temporal aspects of Marshall's short runs and long runs. His 'runs' or 'periods' are not referring to how far in the future to extend time considerations, but how much transpired time has been allowed for in the explanation of a decision being made. For Marshall, a short-run decision is limited to a year or a harvest period because in his day a change in machinery might take a much longer period of time, the amount of machinery or tools (namely what we refer to as capital) is thus considered fixed – see Marshall [1920, pp. 302–15]. Of course, the fixity of the amount of machines or tools is used to define the short run in textbooks. His main point was that, to explain a variable of choice, it must be possible to change its value (he called this the Principle of Continuity). If one is thereby only considering the previous year, there may not have been enough time to change the amount of machinery. For more about how time is used in Marshall's partial-equilibrium analysis, see Boland [1992, chapter 2].

calling this the assumption of 'rationality', which is not as informative. All that rationality assures is that one can provide a logically valid argument that explains the action of an individual where the provided argument consists of a set of assumptions with which one can deduce that action as a logical consequence and thereby explain the action as being 'rational'. Maximization is more than this. What is assured by a sufficient rational argument are just two things: (1) *universality* – specifically, that *anyone* who accepts each and every one of an explanation's assumptions as a true statement logically must accept the truth of any logically derived statement such as that which represents the action being explained; and (2) *uniqueness* – specifically, that the action in question is the only action that can be so deduced – that is, it is a singularly unique (or 'well-defined') action given the assumptions.[5] Note that, as such, rationality says nothing about the goal of the action or about any constraints that might prevent reaching that goal. Stated this way, it is easy to see that an assumption of maximization is a narrow, special case of behavioural rationality. As such, for anyone not trained in the jargon of economists, the assumption of rationality is actually vague [cf. Lagueux 2010], but the assumption of maximization is never as vague.[6]

In order to implement the constrained-maximization assumption, the model builder must always identify what is to be maximized (utility, profit, wealth, sales, etc.) as well as the constraints (income, technology, available resources, etc.). Next, the model builder would usually need to identify constraints that must be overcome or dealt with – usually with microeconomic models this involves existing prices, income, resources, available supply, existing demand, and so forth. Skeptics [e.g., Richardson 1959] might say that the decision maker's knowledge or source of knowledge also needs to be identified. Or, going further, the model builder should identify how the decision maker learns and, in particular, learns from errors [see Clower 1959]. Basically, some of us think that the model builder ought to go much further and explain *how* the decision maker decides which option will maximize [see Boland 1986, chapter 11 and 2003, chapter 16; as well as Samuelson and Robson 2010].

5 Note well, uniqueness in this sense should not be confused with the equilibrium uniqueness usually associated with the explanation of prices and quantities in general-equilibrium models, although they are not totally independent considerations. Equilibrium uniqueness will be discussed in the next chapter.

6 For more about distinguishing rationality from maximization, see pages 49–55 of Boland [2003].

1.1.2. The commonly stated secondary basic principle of theoretical micro models

Textbooks often state a second basic principle, namely the assumption of the existence of an equilibrium. Usually textbooks would claim that this assumption is about a price or quantity where the amount demanded of some good in question is equal to the amount of its supply – in game-theory-based models, it is about an outcome in which all players are making optimal choices given the other players' logically optimal choices. This seems a simple matter, but it needs to be critically discussed to appreciate what is being assumed. However, for now, it is enough to be explicit about what this principle claims.

Few graduate or undergraduate microeconomic textbooks, let alone their models, adequately explain the process for how the price reaches the equilibrium level. What should be recognized is that any state of equilibrium must involve dynamics. This is not true for a state of balance. A balance may be temporary, accidental, stable or unstable. A claim that a state of balance exists is a static claim unless there are reasons for why it exists *and why it will persist.* In the case of a market, the equality between demand and supply may be an accidental balance that, if disturbed, would not return – for example, whenever the demand curve is steeper than the supply curve and both are negatively sloped. To ensure that the balance is not accidental, one would need to explain why instead the supply curve is necessarily steeper than the demand curve[7] – that is, we must explain why it is a stable *balance.*

In the 1950s and 1960s, the question of stability was often discussed by builders of equilibrium-based models. Specifically, the discussion was in terms of what was called stability analysis. In terms of the explanation of prices, stability analysis would ask of a claimed market balance or, in the case of models, a claimed solution: What would happen if the price for some reason were higher (or lower)? Would it return to the previous balance if the higher (or lower) price were not the result of permanent or ongoing exogenous changes or shocks external to the market? Since most models today rely only on the assumed or derived existence of an equilibrium or, in the case of game-theoretic models, on whether the solution is a Nash equilibrium, stability analysis does not seem to be as much of a burning issue as it once was [see Boland 2003, chapter 3]. Since today most textbooks and microeconomic theorists simply ignore the distinction between

7 For more on this, see chapter 7 of Boland [1986].

equilibrium and balance, let us for now drop further consideration of this distinction until the next chapter's discussion of equilibrium-based models, where I will return to a more detailed discussion of how the equilibrium concept is used today in model building.

There is another, somewhat confusing distinction involving the equilibrium concept. If we are providing a generic explanation of a single consumer's choices based on the assumption of constrained maximization, as seems to always be the case in textbook analysis as well as Marshall's *Principles*, can we also claim to be explaining *all* consumers' choices? Similarly, if we provide a generic explanation of a single supplier, have we thereby explained all suppliers? If the answer to both of these is yes, then surprisingly, there is no need for the additional, secondary (equilibrium) principle! This seemingly elementary point turns out simply to be the result of the textbook definitions of the demand and supply curves. That is, the demand curve is what we get when we (perhaps hypothetically) confront each and every consumer with a price and ask how much they would demand.[8] When we then add up all these individuals' demands at this price, we get a point on the market demand curve. By (hypothetically) repeating this for all possible prices, we then plot the market's demand curve. Of course, we can do a similar thing for the suppliers to get the supply curve. Given our maximization-based explanations, the individual's answer is always a quantity that would maximize utility of the consumer and profit of the supplier. In other words, the demand curve is the locus of price-quantity points for which *every* consumer is maximizing utility. Similarly, the supply curve is the locus of price-quantity points for which *every* supplier is maximizing profit. This means that if demand equals supply, then at *that* market-clearing price, everyone is maximizing – both consumers and suppliers. And if every consumer and every supplier are maximizing, then all markets are at least in balance. If the stability of every state of balance is assured – usually in textbooks by assuring that all demand curves are negatively sloped and all supply curves are positively sloped – then universal maximization guarantees an equilibrium in every market, so long as there are no changes to constraints, and thus there is no reason for anyone to change their demand or supply decision. Hence, there is no need for *additionally* assuming the secondary principle of equilibrium. A corollary is that if we assume universal and persistent maximization, there can never be a disequilibrium – or even an unbalanced market.

8 Textbooks usually state this as an assumption involving all suppliers and demanders being 'price takers'.

1.1.3. The alternative route of behavioural theoretical micro models

Although most behavioural and experimental microeconomic models are more empirical than theoretical, their purpose is at root theoretical. Experimental economics is obviously empirical, but not all experiments are directed at testing traditional economic models. Behavioural economics is usually directed more toward utilizing psychological literature and as such will put such model building outside the scope of my discussion in this chapter. However, as we will see later, the early work of Herbert Simon will be relevant when it comes to discussing alternatives to the 'rationality' presumed in traditional equilibrium-based microeconomic models. The empirical aspects of behavioural and experimental economic models are important, nevertheless, and thus are subsequently discussed in a later chapter. In particular, the testing aspects of behavioural and experimental economic model building will be the primary focus of Chapter 8.

1.2. The nature of theoretical macroeconomic models

Macroeconomic theorists usually offer two different ways to distinguish macro from microeconomic models. On the one hand, one can claim that the recognition of dynamics distinguishes macro from micro theory. On the other hand, one can claim that macro analysis can be distinguished from micro analysis by whether it is based on Walrasian general-equilibrium or Marshallian partial-equilibrium analysis.

The general question of dynamics in macroeconomic models is considered fairly straightforward as it merely involves recognizing how maximizing agents deal with decisions over time. It is claimed that macroeconomic theory involves situations where agents face dynamic problems or face questions that include expectations. Examples might be questions of growth, business cycles, inflation, stabilization policies, or almost any situation where agents – perhaps interactively – are repeatedly making choices over time.

The other perspective that some macroeconomists use for the distinction would also seem straightforward, even elementary, but we need to be careful, and to do so I will keep things as simple as possible. As I have already suggested, partial-equilibrium analysis is the primary methodology at the center of Marshallian economics. It is what one learns in any elementary principles class, but rarely, if ever, do teachers or their textbooks mention Marshall, even though his view of economics, and in particular that of his fifth part (Book V), is implicitly the sole basis of elementary textbook microeconomic analysis. Marshall's economics focused on explaining how an individual makes a decision. As I noted earlier, any decision in question is explained by characterizing it as resulting in a partial equilibrium as a result of constrained maximization. As always, the maximizing choice is made facing fixed constraints, such as endowments, tastes and given prices in the case of the utility maximizing consumer and, in the case of the profit maximizing supplier, technology, available resources and given prices. Of course, one can claim in the case of Marshall's supplier, the firm, that it faces two different decisions depending on whether one is explaining a short-run decision, such as deciding how much labour to employ with the fixed amount of available capital (i.e., a fixed number of machines or tools) and hence how much product to supply, or one is explaining a long-run decision, such as how much capital to acquire or which industry to operate in. In Marshall's long-run, technology is still a fixed factor, and thus even the long-run equilibrium of the firm is still, in one sense, just a partial equilibrium.[9]

Now, from the perspective of the macro model builder, it can always be claimed that, when explaining the decision of one agent using Marshall's economic methodology, all other agents are ignored (although, more correctly, the equilibrium actions of all others are embodied in the going prices and thus can be ignored as supposedly no additional information is needed). In contrast, one can claim that Walrasian general-equilibrium analysis requires the simultaneous recognition of all agents and thus goes well beyond Marshallian considerations. For this reason, many might easily see general-equilibrium analysis as a form of macroeconomic theory, *But this concept of macroeconomic theory is problematic* – particularly if we are also to claim that, unlike microeconomic models, macro models are fundamentally dynamic. This is because usually – and perhaps by Walras' design [see Walker 1996] – Walrasian methodology does not involve decisions over time, as the issue addressed by Walras was primarily a static mathematical question: Can there exist a vector[10] of prices for all goods that would allow all markets to clear simultaneously by having all agents maximizing? That is, Walrasian economics is fundamentally a static mathematical analysis. As such, Walras thought the main issue is a matter of counting equations and unknowns and assuring their number is the same,[11] but, as

[9] For more on this, see further chapter 2 of Boland [1992] and chapter 6 of Boland [2003].

[10] Where a 'vector' is merely a list of prices consisting of one price for each good to be bought or sold.

[11] Which is usually considered necessary for solving a set of simultaneous equations.

Abraham Wald [1936/51] explained, this requirement turns out to be an inadequate guarantee for the existence of an equilibrium price vector. Note that while the role of time was not a major issue for Walras, subsequent critics of Walrasian general-equilibrium model building pointed out that without an explicit role for time one cannot expect to include money in a Walrasian general-equilibrium model, as money would be needed if, for example, long-term contracts are to be recognized [see Shackle 1967, chapter 9; Davidson 1977]. Any consideration for a role for money in any general-equilibrium model muddies the micro-macro distinction if that distinction is also to be based on the static-vs.-dynamic distinction. All this notwithstanding, and as will be discussed in Chapter 6, empirical macroeconomic models based on a dynamic stochastic general equilibrium (DSGE) continue to be a mainstay of current macroeconomic research today even though the dynamics of these models only involves a recognition of time rather than a clear role for time in the dynamics.[12]

I come back to these various methodological approaches to distinguishing between micro and macro a little later. In the meantime, let us look at other, less methodological ways of distinguishing micro from macroeconomic theory.

1.2.1. It is a matter of what questions are asked

Let us consider some questions that few people will undeniably consider to be macroeconomic issues: Why is unemployment rising or not falling? Why is there inflation? Why was there a major recession in 2008 and 2009? Why might the income disparity between wealthy landowners and the working poor be increasing? Although one might try to answer such questions using only what they learned in their undergraduate microeconomics textbook with its predominantly Marshallian partial-equilibrium model, it would be difficult.

Note that even in this short list of macro-type questions, there are two separate aspects being recognized. On the one hand, they are all about effects of the dynamic behaviour of the participants in the economy; on the other hand, while most are about the holistic behaviour of an aggregation, the last question is about the behaviour of a heterogeneous collection. Interestingly, both questions would be the most difficult to answer with Marshall's partial-equilibrium-based microeconomic methodology, so some might see a clear need for a macro alternative to microeconomics. If

[12] For more about the role of time in dynamic models, see Boland [1978] and [2003, chapter 10].

Marshall's Book V is to be the sole basis for consideration of dynamics, it must be kept in mind that this fifth part of his book was solely about neighbourhood properties of an equilibrium and, as such, can only be used to explain the role of variables of choice. And for this reason comparative statics analysis is the only directly useful application of Book V. Discussion of any questions involving the distribution of heterogeneous behaviour are difficult, too, if they are to be based on his Book V as marginal variations about an equilibrium are virtually impossible to extend to questions of distribution. A distribution is a macro concept[13] discussed only in his Book VI, which today, as I said earlier, is the one part of his book that hardly anyone sees a need to read or discuss. Moreover, except for a few recent macro models that try to incorporate heterogeneous agents, the distribution of heterogeneous behaviour has been primarily relegated to game-theoretic models and, in particular, evolutionary game theory models.[14] I will return to the discussion of such models in Chapters 3 and 4.

1.2.2. Do micro-foundations matter?

For now, let us leave aside considerations of macro questions that involve matters of distributions within an economy and instead confine our discussion to dynamic aggregate behaviour, which almost everyone today sees as what characterizes modern macroeconomic theory. That is, let us here consider macroeconomic theory as being solely about explaining the behaviour of aggregates (e.g., GDP, employment levels, aggregate price levels, money supply) – of course, there will still be a minimal degree of heterogeneity since we will always need to distinguish between demanders and suppliers or between consumers and producers.

From the beginning, critics of macroeconomics in general and of Keynes in particular would claim that there is an 'aggregation problem' [e.g., Leontief 1936; 1947]. Can we talk about such objects as aggregate demand or even of savings and capital as aggregate phenomena? Much mathematical ink was devoted to specifying the necessary conditions to ensure that one could consistently aggregate production or consumption functions. For example, it is commonly understood that one can easily aggregate

[13] Textbook discussions of distribution have always been somewhat ambiguous and do not always indicate that it is a matter for macroeconomics rather than microeconomics. This is likely because distribution was discussed long before textbooks began explicitly recognizing a separate macroeconomics after the publication of Keynes' *General Theory*.

[14] For more on evolutionary game models and heterogeneous behaviour, see chapter 9 of Boland [2003].

individuals' consumption if all individuals' preferences are identical and homothetic. Of course, many critics argued that such conditions are too demanding to be useful – that is, this may demand too much of truly heterogeneous macro economies. But more generally, there is a problem with aggregation even if we think we could consider using a Walrasian perspective so as to provide us with micro-foundations. Many critics will say there still remains an obstacle for doing so – namely, what is understood to be the Sonnenschein-Debreu-Mantel theorems,[15] which, as Alan Kirman [2011, 116] puts it, 'showed that it is not possible with only the standard assumptions on individuals, to show the convergence of an adjustment process to an equilibrium' and thus [pp. 125–6],

> If we adhere to the basic tenet of the Walrasian General Equilibrium model that macro or aggregate behaviour must be derived from underlying rational micro foundations then we have to explain how the characteristics of the aggregate are determined by those of the individuals. It is here that the General Equilibrium model has let us down because we can say very little about aggregate behaviour in that model. This is what we have learned from the [Sonnenschein-Debreu-Mantel] results.

A major implication of the Sonnenschein-Debreu-Mantel theorems would seem to be that there is no guarantee that using the assumption of a 'representative agent' to provide the aggregate implications of general-equilibrium theory would also represent all the individuals in general-equilibrium-based micro-foundations.

As to the aggregation problem, Franklin Fisher [1987] summarized it by focusing on only aggregating consumption or production. About consumption he says [1987, p. 54]:

> In general, the only consumer-theoretic restrictions obeyed by aggregate demand functions are those of continuity, homogeneity of degree zero, and the various restrictions implied by the budget constraint.

And about production he says [p. 55]:

[15] This refers to theorems in three articles published in the 1970s (viz, Sonnenschin [1972], Mantel [1974] and Debreu [1974]). According to Robert Solow [2008, p. 244], the Sonnenschein-Debreu-Mantel theorems say 'that the only universal empirical aggregative implications of general equilibrium theory are that excess demand functions should be continuous and homogeneous of degree zero in prices, and should satisfy Walras' Law'. Note that when model builders talk about 'excess demand functions' they are just referring to a composite function about how the difference between the quantity demanded and the quantity supply varies with the price.

> In general, aggregation over any set of inputs or outputs requires separability[16] in each firm's production function. Further, under constant returns[17] . . . aggregation over firms requires either that the aggregator functions applied to the firms all be the same (no specialization) or, if not, that the *only* difference in production functions be the nature of the aggregator function (generalized capital augmentation).
>
> Abandoning constant returns does not provide practical help. Most non-constant returns cases do not permit aggregation even if all firms have the *same* production function. The cases that do are very restrictive.

Fisher concludes that the results he discusses 'show that the analytic use of such aggregates as "capital", "output", "labour" or "investment" as though the production side of the economy could be treated as a single firm is without sound foundation' [ibid]. Unfortunately, as he points out, 'This has not discouraged macroeconomists from continuing to work in such terms' [ibid].

For reasons such as this, many critics will say that macroeconomic theorems will only be accepted if they can be shown to have microeconomic foundations – that is, that any claimed macroeconomic behaviour needs to be explainable as the result of microeconomic analysis of the individuals participating in the economy. In other words, any macro behaviour is nothing more than an interpretation of microeconomic analysis. For some, this was easy since, as I have already noted, macroeconomics can always be seen as a way of interpreting Walrasian general-equilibrium analysis. But the problem remains, as aggregation *over time* would seem to require the absence of distributional changes – or even of changes in relative prices – to be useful analysis.

1.2.3. Representative agents versus micro-foundations

> The object of representative-agent micro-foundations is ultimately to eliminate macroeconomics – to derive all results from microeconomic theory. Distinctively macroeconomic phenomena on this view are . . . merely epiphenomena. In contrast, the object of the aggregation and general-equilibrium programs of micro-foundations was to push towards an understanding of how genuine macroeconomic phenomena arise out of microeconomic behaviors.
>
> Kevin Hoover [2012, p. 52]

16 Usually, one of the mathematical requirements for aggregation either for explaining how utility is obtained in the case of consumption or of multiple outputs or inputs in the case of production is that of separability. That is, for example, the utility derived from the consumption of multiple goods is just the simple sum of utility obtained by each good independently.

17 'Constant returns' simply means that if *all* inputs are, say, doubled, output will also double.

Kevin Hoover [2012, p. 21] identifies three different micro-foundations programs. The first is Lawrence Klein's 1940s 'aggregation program' that was concerned with the compatibility between behaviour evident in aggregative data and the individual behaviour we usually would use microeconomic theory to explain. The second was the 'general equilibrium program' of John Hicks, who was promoting Walrasian economic theory in the late 1930s and was concerned with whether it could generate what today we would recognize as macroeconomic theory. The third program Hoover calls the 'representative-agent program' as advocated by Robert Lucas in the 1970s and 1980s. The most important aspect of these three programs is whether they would continue to see macro-and microeconomics as separate approaches to explaining economic phenomena. As Hoover notes, the aggregative and the general-equilibrium programs do not seek the elimination of macroeconomics, but the representative-agent program does.

The early criticisms of macroeconomics based on the 'problem of aggregation' were to some extent directed at the rise of Keynesian economics. Of course, aggregation has been a part of economic theory since long before Keynes. Specifically, even in microeconomic theory the market demand curve is, after all, an aggregation of individuals' demand curves. Nevertheless, in macroeconomic theory, having to assume that every individual has the same preferences or that all production functions are in some way identical is, for some, an unacceptable stretch whenever the quest for realism requires the recognition of the heterogeneity of all factors of production and of all consumers.

In Book IV of his *Principles*, Marshall faced heterogeneity directly when he wanted to compare industries with regard to increasing and decreasing returns. An industry, of course, is an aggregation of possibly heterogeneous firms. The firms can differ in their ages, their sizes, and maybe even their production functions. To deal with the existence of heterogeneous firms, Marshall eventually introduced the 'representative firm' [1920, Book IV, chapter 13, §2, p. 264] and went on to say that it 'in a sense is an average firm' [p. 265]. Marshall even suggested a metaphor; he said that we should see an industry as one would see a 'virgin forest', where some trees are much older than other trees [1920, Book V, chapter 5, §2, p. 305]. In the case of firms, some young firms may be facing increasing returns as they learn the business, while older firms have long passed their optimum size. The plausibility of this metaphor is partly because there is presumed a direct monotonic correlation between the age and the size of a firm.

While a representative firm may be acceptable if it is representing only the average age or size of firms, it runs into difficulty if it is to represent something simple like unit costs since unit costs are not monotonically correlated with size. A 1928 article by Lionel Robbins was a prominent early critical attack on Marshall's representative firms and focused on the size of the representative firm. But, Marshall's representative firm was instead intended to focus on unit costs [Maxwell 1958] and this may be why his representative firm was eventually relegated to being only a firm in long-run equilibrium. As John Wolfe noted [1954, p. 437], by the mid–1950s, Marshall's representative firm was purged from the textbooks. So, why among macroeconomic model builders do we today see so much discussion and use of representative firms or consumers or agents in general?

In James Hartley's 1997 book about modern macroeconomics, *The Representative Agent in Macroeconomics*, he identifies three basic – but non-mutually exclusive – reasons for the return of the representative agent [p. 20]. One rationale is that it is a way of dealing with either the *Lucas Critique*, concerning the false presumption of stable 'deep' parameters governing the behaviour of individuals in response to any macro policy change, or the Thomas Sargent and Neil Wallace [1976] critique of Keynesian-policy ineffectiveness. Another is related to reasons for using Walrasian general-equilibrium models as a basis for macroeconomics. And the third is to facilitate providing micro-foundations for macroeconomics. Not explicitly included in his list is the obvious methodological fact that representative-agent models are far simpler and more convenient than full-blown general-equilibrium models. About this, Hartley says [p. 27]:

> There are far too many agents in the economy to model each one individually. It thus becomes impractical, if not impossible, to study the effects of policy or market imperfections without some simplification. At this point, the representative agent comes to the rescue. By using a representative agent framework, we need only specify a small number of functional forms.

He then notes that Sargent [1979, p. 371] had suggested just this early on.

Although Hartley does not mention them, there may be two other rationales (also non-mutually exclusive). One is the 'new Classical' macroeconomic program and its old Chicago school's laissez-faire ideological predisposition in favour of market-friendly microeconomics as opposed to government-friendly Keynesian models. The other is the simple fact that almost everyone trained in economics is predisposed to understanding microeconomic explanations. Probably equally important is that, at the level of basic ideas (as opposed to modeling techniques), basic microeconomic explanations have not changed much since the 1930s, while, until recently, macroeconomics had been all over the map.

Hartley does acknowledge [pp. 124–6] that some think the demand for micro-foundations and the acceptance of the representative agent in this regard exists at root because of a commitment to the philosophy of 'methodological individualism' – where this philosophy is the view that only *people* decide, *things* cannot decide [see Hoover 2001, pp. 69–74; Boland 2003, chapter 2]. Such a view would seem to preclude accepting non-individualist things, such as macro variables. In this sense, to some macro theorists, the representative agent looks like an acceptable individual or person rather than a thing.

In all three of Hartley's cases, the objective of using the representative agents is to build 'models in which macroeconomic equations are rigorously derived from consumer and firm optimization problems' [p. 23]. Building a macro model in the form of a representative-agent model indirectly provides micro-foundations and thereby avoids the parameter instability and policy ineffectiveness critiques. By explicitly positing one agent as representing all agents, it is thought that heterogeneity is not being ruled out and hence the old aggregation problem would seem to be also thereby avoided.

Interestingly, while the 1987 edition of the *New Palgrave Dictionary of Economics* contained Fisher's entry on the 'aggregation problem', there was no entry for the representative agent. For the 2008 second edition, the aggregation problem did not even have an entry, and the representative agent still did not get an entry even though it plays prominently in modern macroeconomic model building. If there is ever to be an entry in some later edition, it surely will have to mention the various criticisms of the modern reliance on representative-agent modeling.

Criticism of the reliance on representative-agent modeling is not difficult to find. Hoover has published more than one book about the history of macroeconomic model building, which include critical observations about the use of representative agents [e.g., Hoover 1988, 2003]. And, of course, there is Hartley's 1997 book [p. 18], which explicitly argues that:

> The most devastating criticism of Marshall's limited use of the representative firm also applies to its modern counterparts. By their very design, representative agent models conceal heterogeneity, whether it is important or not. Economists who would never automatically assume that the important characteristics of all policy regimes are homogeneous routinely assume that heterogeneity among agents is unimportant.

Eventually, he goes further to conclude [p. 194]:

> There is no theoretical reason for insisting that all of macroeconomics is reducible to microeconomics, that microeconomic theory yields explanations for macroeconomic regularities, or that the direction of causality is solely from

> microeconomics to macroeconomics. There is no empirical justification for this insistence. In fact, there is every reason to believe that macroeconomic regularities are not derivable from standard microeconomic theory. There is in sum no reality in the myth of microfoundations.

Kirman's widely cited[18] 1992 article 'Whom or what does the representative individual represent?' stands out as a solid critical examination of representative-agent modeling. He begins by asking a basic question [p. 119]:

> If macroeconomists are interested only in certain basic macroeconomic problems which do not directly involve considerations of distribution or coordination, why do they bother to construct representative individual models?

As he notes [pp. 121–2], by deriving individual demand curves using the textbook consumer with standard indifference curves and budget endowments for all goods being considered available in the economy, we can subtract the endowments from the demand curve for each good to get the individual consumer's 'excess demand' curve. Assuming, of course, we are dealing with a finite number of consumers and goods, we can sum over all consumers for each good to determine the excess demand curve for the whole economy. Doing so obtains excess demand curves for the whole economy that would satisfy such things as Walras's Law, which (as discussed in an earlier note) is needed for any model of an economy in general equilibrium. As Wald [1936/51] had already shown, even if at the individual level all individuals' preferences were consistent – that is, their preferences satisfy the Weak Axiom of Revealed Preference, meaning that whenever choosing between two bundles[19] of goods, say A and B, and bundle A is chosen when both can be afforded, to be consistent, B would be chosen only if A cannot be afforded[20] – at the aggregate level, the same consistency is not assured. At the aggregate level, it is possible that even when both bundles are affordable, sometimes A is chosen and at other times B. Such inconsistency in preferences is ruled out in the microeconomics textbook's consumers' choices. If a representative textbook consumer could actually represent all consumers, Wald's observation would be of no concern. But it would be of no concern only because of the Sonnenschein-Debreu-Mantel results[21]

[18] But as Hoover notes, it is cited usually by critics and not by users of the representative-agent methodology.

[19] The consumer is assumed to be choosing how much to buy of say two goods (maybe potatoes and tomatoes), and a pair of quantities of those two goods is a bundle.

[20] Perhaps, as the result of a change in relative prices of the goods in question. Today we commonly say such behaviour amounts to a revealed preference for bundle A over B.

[21] See note 15.

[Kirman 1992, p. 122]. So, if micro-foundations must be provided, perhaps the representative agent is the only option for macroeconomic model builders.

With this in mind, Kirman then proceeds to argue [p. 134]

> that well-behaved individuals need not produce a well-behaved representative agent; that the reaction of a representative agent to change need not reflect how the individuals of the economy would respond to change; that the preferences of a representative agent over choices may be diametrically opposed to those of society as a whole.

On the basis of these arguments, he concludes [ibid.]:

> [I]t is clear that the representative agent should have no future. Indeed, contrary to what current macroeconomic practice would seem to suggest, requiring heterogeneity of agents within the competitive general equilibrium model may help to recover aggregate properties which may be useful for macroeconomic analysis.
>
> Yet, despite these arguments, I suspect that the representative individual will persist for as long as economists focus on a framework of anonymous individual maximization. Only if we are prepared to develop a paradigm in which individuals operate in a limited subset of the economy, are diverse both in their characteristics and the activities that they pursue, and interact directly with each other, will economics escape from the stultifying influence of the representative agent. Within such models there can and should be considerable aggregate regularity. However, the fact that behavior at the macroeconomic level exhibits regularities does not mean that it is useful or appropriate to treat the economy as a maximizing representative individual.

1.2.4. Methodological justification of using the representative agent

> Most of dynamic general-equilibrium macroeconomic theory relies heavily on the representative-agent abstraction; it is assumed that the economy behaves *'as if'* it is inhabited by a single (type of) consumer. At the same time, this macroeconomic theorizing attempts to take micro-foundations seriously; the parameters of the models are typically selected on the basis of existing empirical and theoretical knowledge, and the models are then used to generate quantitative statements. At first glance, the representative-agent assumption appears to be inconsistent with a serious treatment of micro-foundations. There are two circumstances, however, under which the representative-agent construct would be a reasonable modeling strategy. First, it is possible that the theoretical assumptions needed to justify the use of a representative consumer are roughly met in the data. This view, however, is hard to defend. . . . A second possibility is that the aggregate variables in theoretical models with a more realistic description of

> the microeconomic environment actually behave like those in the representative-agent models.
>
> Per Krusell and Anthony Smith, Jr. [1998, p. 868]

If the macroeconomic model builders who do rely on representative agents are asked to justify their use given the growing list of criticisms of the realism of models produced using such agents, there is only one way they can do so. If they are explicit, that way will be to call on the views of Milton Friedman's famous 1953 methodology essay that defends 'as if' assumptions against any criticism of the realism of those assumptions by in effect asserting that models are mere instruments.[22] As such, rather than requiring demonstrable realism of assumptions, all that is required is that the model works for the intended task. Recognizing heterogeneity may not be part of the intended task and hence, they would say, such a criticism is not relevant.

Nevertheless, for some time, macroeconomic model builders have recognized the need to recognize heterogeneity. And one can expect that there will be many attempts to deal with heterogeneous agents in a macro model that makes a more realistic attempt to provide micro-foundations. There are certainly many macro model builders today who recognize the importance of differing knowledge and dispositions toward risk and expectations of individuals that can have significant impacts on macro dynamics and thus need to be addressed. For these and other reasons, there now are appearing models claiming to recognize heterogeneous agents [e.g., Chang and Kim 2006, 2007; Honkapohja and Mitra 2006; Krusell and Smith 2006], but it is not at all clear that all such recent attempts overcome Hartley's critical observations.[23]

1.2.5. Can the many published critiques of representative-agent methodology be ignored?

Today the need for the recognition of diversity or heterogeneity in macro models may be a motivation for some macro model builders, but Kirman's and Hartley's criticism or challenges will continue to remain obstacles that will always need to be addressed. Of course, such criticism can be ignored, but what is the methodological cost? Obviously, one would have to face up to the criticisms based on recognition of the aggregation problem as well as the implications of the Sonnenschein-Debreu-Mantel results. But most

[22] For more about Friedman's 1953 essay, see Boland [1979] and part I of Boland [1997].

[23] For a discussion of the difficulties and a demonstration that such an attempt might need non-standard assumptions, see Sungbae An, et al. [2009].

importantly, any questions involving heterogeneity are put out of bounds. It is not clear how one would address the claim by some new Keynesian macroeconomists that recessions are the result of coordination failures (including wage rigidities and the like) if one relied only on representative-agent models.[24] For a single (representative) agent, there is nothing to coordinate. Similarly, for a single agent, there is nothing to be distributed. Of course, proponents of building macroeconomic theoretical models can simply say that such questions are uninteresting and thus there is no need to abandon representative-agent methodology.

1.3. The static-versus-dynamic basis for distinguishing micro from macro

As Hicks noted in his *Value and Capital* [1939/46, p. 115], the 'definition of economic dynamics (that much controverted term) which I have in mind here is this. I call Economic Statics those parts of economic theory where we do not trouble about dating; Economic Dynamics those parts where every quantity must be dated'. This brings us here to one last issue that must be critically addressed. It has to do with the general notion of dynamics when it comes to distinguishing macro from micro theoretical models. Are the 'dynamics' in question real or apparent? Are dynamic actions taken by decision makers over time proactive or reactive? Or, more generally, is the notion of time in dynamic macroeconomic models (or micro models, for that matter) real or just logical? Let me explain.

First I wish to return to the point I raised earlier – namely that Walrasian general-equilibrium models as they are used today do not involve a *role* for (real) time. This may be a surprising claim since many model builders continue to see the Arrow-Debreu model [1954] as the paradigm *dynamic* general-equilibrium model. This model, contrary to common opinion, is not dynamic in the sense that a macroeconomic theoretical model is claimed to be dynamic [see Kirman 2011, pp. 110 and 114–15; Boland 2003, chapter 10]. Like Walras, Kenneth Arrow and Gerard Debreu were seeking a proof for the existence of an equilibrium price vector. As such, as once advocated by Hicks, their use of time as a variable was limited to being just an index on goods sold in different markets such that, as an index, it can just as easily be interpreted as a spatial location index instead of a time location index. That is, while as an index for markets at two different points

[24] For a possible exception to this claim but one that does so with non-standard assumptions, see Farmer and Guo [1994].

in time, they could just as easily be markets at two different locations. Thus, contrary to early Hicks' notion of time [1939/46, p. 115], but consistent with his later view [1976], the Arrow-Debreu model does not really involve dynamics since the difference between two different points in time is mathematically indistinguishable from two points in space. For example, in the Arrow-Debreu model, a hamburger bought today is a different hamburger than one that may be bought next year – these two hamburgers are considered different products in two different markets, today's versus next year's hamburger markets. But instead of today's versus next year's markets, we could just as easily be talking about London's versus Geneva's hamburger markets! Let us look at this issue of real time a little closer.

1.3.1. Time in economics versus economics *in* time

> My subject here . . . concerns a principle which has come up, in several ways, in the work of Professor Georgescu . . . It is a very simple principle: the irreversibility of time. In space we can move either way, or any way; but time just goes on, never goes back.
>
> John Hicks [1976, p. 115]

Given my earlier observation, it might be asked, so what is 'real' time as opposed to the 'apparent' time that I am accusing Arrow and Debreu as well as the early Hicks of employing? The simple answer is, real time is irreversible, but apparent time need not be. Like so many topics in economic model building, the issue is not a new one but one easily forgotten. Many, many years ago, the famous physicist Arthur Eddington put the main issue concerning time as one of recognizing 'time's arrow', and in this light he said [1928/58, pp. 68–9]:

> The great thing about time is that it goes on. . . . I shall use the phrase 'time's arrow' to express [the] one-way property of time which has no analogue in space. It is a singularly interesting property from a philosophical standpoint.

Specifically, time goes on, not back, but *we* can go back and forth in space. And with this in mind, in 1978 I published an article surveying all the ways economists include time in their models up to that time (sorry!). A detailed discussion can be found in my 2003 book [chapter 10]. Here I will only list and briefly discuss them.

In addition to the Hicks-Arrow-Debreu time-as-a-subscript approach, there is the 'economics of time' approach. The paradigm of this approach was the Austrian economist Eugene Böhm-Bawerk's model of the average production period – which was designed to answer the question of the optimum time to cut trees down or when to bottle a barrel of wine. In his model, the dynamics are external and are invested entirely in a biologically given growth trajectory of a tree or an aging profile of a barrel of wine. The time-based trajectory is just an *exogenous* constraint that the optimizing tree farmer or wine merchant reacts to. In modern times, Gary Becker's allocation of time [1965] model is an obvious example – in his case, the decision maker faces the constraint of a limited amount of time (per week: 168 hours). His model was designed to answer a question about the allocation of time between competing activities. As such his model merely involves a static allocation of a commodity and in no way represents an explanation of dynamics. And in both Böhm-Bawerk's and Becker's models, no dynamics are being explained; that is, there is no *endogenous* dynamic variable involved – only a static allocation, in the case of Becker, or a statically given growth function, in the case of Böhm-Bawerk.

Another approach is the 'variable givens' or 'lagged variables' approach, which in pre-1980 macroeconomics is usually attributed to adaptive expectations-based models. With this approach, one might attempt to determine the *time-path trajectory* of the endogenous variables. Given that the solution of a model represents its explanation, the only way the endogenous variables can change over time is either by one or more of the exogenous variables changing, or by some of the parameters of the logical relationships autonomously changing, or both. The population's growth rate in Nicholas Kaldor's growth model [1957] is an example of the former, and what Hicks [1976] called an 'autonomous invention' or a non-neutral change in technology might be an example of the latter.[25] However, in 'new Keynesian' macroeconomic theoretical models, the *relationships* (or the 'deep parameters' that characterize the relationships with regard to tastes or technology) are usually presumed not to change over the relevant time-period – the presumption that the Lucas Critique challenged. The entire explanation of historical change is usually invested in the exogenous changes of the givens and sometimes only in external shocks. Some changes in the givens can be represented by movements along their fixed trajectories. Thus, if some of the static givens of a typical Walrasian model are replaced by time-path trajectories for a specified time period, the result will be derivable equilibrium trajectories or paths for the endogenous variables over the same time period. However, with this method of including time, we have only replaced a point in time with a static sequence of corresponding points in a fixed period of time. The solution will be a fixed sequence of

[25] For more on this, see Boland (1971).

changing values and the 'dynamic' actions are completely reactionary and not a matter of autonomous choice.

Obviously one does not necessarily have to assume that the time period of the exogenous variables is the same as that of the endogenous variables. One could assert that some of today's exogenous variables may be yesterday's endogenous variables.[26] A classic example of this approach is the John von Neumann [1937/45] balanced growth model. With this 'lagged variable' approach, we are also able to derive a time-path trajectory for the endogenous variables. However, the position of the trajectory over a given time period will depend only on the initial set of values for the exogenous givens. The initial values of the givens are essentially the only exogenous variables of the model over the whole time period, and again no autonomous dynamic choices are being made.

On the surface, the direct approach of including an exogenous time-path for the givens, or the indirect approach using lagged variables, looks like a solution to the problem of explaining dynamics. But a closer examination will show this to be an illusion. In the exogenous trajectory approach, the endogenous variables are changing *only* because the exogenous variables are changing. In the case of lagged variables, the position of an endogenous variable on its trajectory is uniquely determined merely by the length of time that has transpired since the initial givens were established. The position of the trajectory itself is uniquely determined only by the initial values of the exogenous givens. In both cases the trajectories of the endogenous variables are exogenously fixed. The only 'dynamics' in the model are either exogenous shocks or reactive changes along an exogenously given trajectory. Hicks [1976] refers to this as the economics *of* time rather than economics *in* time. Since exogeneity of any model results from an explicit choice to not explain the givens or their behaviour, we have not explained the dynamic changes within the model. In other words we are still relying on either random shocks or a statically given time-path trajectory which is fixed over the relevant time period. Random shocks, of course, are never explained and we would also not explain why a given trajectory exists in some form rather than some other.

Note well, in the case of a trajectory's path, we could, for example, assume the given path was such that the exogenous variable grew at a constant rate. If we should be asked why we did not assume an increasing rate, we cannot justify our assumption solely on the grounds that it yields the observed

[26] Macroeconomists might refer instead to 'state variables' or just 'initial conditions'.

time-path of the endogenous variables. The truth of our assumptions regarding exogenous givens must be independent of our conclusions regarding endogenous variables.[27]

The last way to address dynamics I will consider here is the 'flow variables' approach. The criticisms raised against the approaches that add time by appropriately defining certain variables can be extended to those approaches that add a time-differential equation to an otherwise static model. One of the problems with using equilibrium models to explain prices is that observed prices may not yet have reached their equilibrium values. Thus, as everyone seemed to agree pre-1980, we need an explanation of the disequilibrium behaviour of the endogenous variables [e.g., Barro and Grossman 1971]. Judging by the dominance today of the DSGE model among many macro model builders, the need is no longer an urgent issue. Those model builders who do think dynamics must be about economics *in* time, as Hicks advocated, will not be satisfied with just relying on some variations of the DSGE model, which typically consider only equilibrium time paths rather than explain how prices, for example, adjust to the equilibrium prices.

1.3.2. Ad hoc dynamics in microeconomic models of equilibrium prices

It was once thought that a theory of price (or quantity) adjustment could simply be attached to microeconomic equilibrium models. The basic approach was once to add a differential (or difference) equation which gives the rate of change of the price as a function of the amount by which the two sides of one of the equilibrium equations deviate from equality prior to reaching equilibrium [e.g., Frisch 1936; Samuelson 1947/65; Arrow 1959]. In market demand and supply analysis this usually would be an equation of the following form:

$$(dp_t/dt) = h(S_t - D_t),$$

where $dh/d(S_t - D_t)$ is negative and $h(0) = 0$. But unless this additional equation is explained, the dynamics are purely improvised and arbitrary. Just stating what is mathematically necessary for a complete model or explanation is not enough.[28] A make-shift differential equation for the 'dynamics' of the market does not even say who changes the price or why

[27] See chapter 6 of Boland [1986].

[28] For more on this, see chapter 9 of Boland [1986].

it is being changed by the needed amount. Obviously, this would be difficult with a model based only on a representative consumer or firm. Until we can say why the price has changed (rather than describing how much it should change), we have explained neither the process of disequilibrium change nor the equilibrium dynamics of the market.

1.3.3. One route to including endogenous real time in macro models based on the representative agent

Again, as Eddington pointed out, the issue for a real dynamics is that the time in question must be irreversible (i.e., 'it goes on', not back). For economics, the question is what time-based action taken by a decision maker is irreversible by its nature – that is, not because one chooses not to change it. The problem with most models that invest their dynamics in exogenous (i.e., unexplained) changes is that, logically, changing the exogenous variables back to their original values before the change would restore all the endogenous variables to their state before the exogenous change.[29]

Hartley raises these issues when discussing the Lucas Critique and the extent to which the representative-agent models can actually avoid it. The point of the Critique seems to be that government policy changes can change how individuals make decisions, and hence the government is not warranted to expect the effects that their policies are intended to create – some may think that this depends on whether one is expecting the effects based on a purely macroeconomic model or on one with adequate microfoundations, one where only tastes and technology are exogenously given, as in the case of a Marshallian long-run equilibrium model. So, some may think, to avoid this Critique, the model builder must provide microeconomic explanations for the deep parameters of the relationships underlying the individuals' decision processes – such as those that would explain how the individual responds to the changed policy environment. Hartley's argument [1997, p. 53] is that this would also be the case for the representative agent, and hence its use does not overcome the Lucas Critique. One suspects that there is an infinite regress lurking here. If fundamental circular arguments are to be avoided, every explanatory model must have at least one exogenous variable. Even when one thinks the deep parameters have been explained, someone can still demand that their underlying exogenous variables or parameters be explained, too, and this merely requires different

[29] Which, at least, violates the Second Law of Thermodynamics [see Georgescu-Roegen 1971].

exogenous variables – which in turn can be questioned, and so on. Perhaps, it might be critically and boldly said that the demand for micro-foundations is itself an invitation to an infinite regress!

The alternative to all this is to find an endogenous variable that is inherently non-reversible. My suggestion has always been that learning and the knowledge of the decision maker must be explicitly dealt with. And for the purposes here, we need only note that learning is inherently non-reversible – one cannot unlearn.[30] Now, having said this, surely it will be said that is exactly what the assumption of rational expectations is intended to do. But, unfortunately, how the expectations are learned is not explained. They are only presumed to conform to an ideal model that is the true description of the current state of the economy. As critics of the presumption of rational expectations have often observed, the only learning of correct expectations is the result of all decision makers being presumed expert econometricians [B. Friedman 1979]. Apart from the heroicness of such a presumption, it also begs a question concerning the process of learning. Unfortunately, too often the presumed process of learning (which I will discuss in Chapter 11) is the one invented almost 400 years ago and was refuted by David Hume more than 200 years ago.[31] But worse, even if we ignore this philosophical point, while the learning in the presumed rational expectations may be irreversible, it is so only because of the presumption of the truth of the underlying model of the current state of the economy. All this can be avoided if one recognizes that all knowledge is fallible and thus one is always having to actively learn. For example, one might learn that the underlying model is not true.

1.4. The purposes of building a theoretical macro model versus a micro model

This brings us to a basic question. Given all the continuing push to require any macroeconomic theoretical model to have a micro-foundation – whether it is general-equilibrium-based or representative-agent-based – why bother with building macro models?

Keynes was quite explicit in stating his purpose. He said that he would build a model of the *whole* economy – distinguishing his model from Marshall's individualist approach. Keynes also rejected the presumption

30 Of course, one can forget, but that is not unlearning.

31 Most of chapter 1 of Boland [2003] is devoted to explaining how this presumption also affects mainstream economics.

of Marshall's Book V, which was concerned only with the neighbourhood properties of an established equilibrium. Keynes wanted to talk about an economy where not all markets are in equilibrium. Most important, he explicitly recognized the heterogeneity of the economy. For example, in his 1937 article where he was defending his book from its critics, he explicitly said there is no reason to assume there is only one way to deal with decisions that would affect a future situation – he actually identified three different ways [1937, p. 214]. Of course, this viewpoint precludes the assumptions of both the representative-agent approach and the rational expectations approach. However, Keynes was willing to recognize that there are circumstances where nobody would respond to monetary policies designed to stimulate the economy – for example, when everyone is extremely pessimistic about the future – but, contrary to the claims of the Lucas Critique, Keynes did explain why such circumstances sometimes exist.

Keynes was also quite explicit in identifying how his approach differed from 'classical' theory (he includes neoclassical theory such as Marshall's in this category). For example, he says [p. 219]:

> My next difference from the traditional theory concerns its apparent conviction that there is no necessity to work out a theory of the demand and supply of output *as a whole*. Will a fluctuation in investment . . . have any effect on the demand for output as a whole, and consequently on the scale of output and employment? What answer can the traditional theory make to this question? I believe that it makes no answer at all, never having given the matter a single thought; the theory of effective demand, that is the demand for output as a whole, having been entirely neglected for more than a hundred years.

Hartley, having quoted this paragraph from Keynes's 1937 article, concludes [1997, p. 176], 'If Keynes is right, if it is *necessary* to work out theories of *aggregate* demand and supply, then the microfoundations story is a myth'. But this does not require a rejection of microeconomic models, just the recognition that they do not, perhaps cannot, go far enough to be a sufficient basis for understanding the whole economy.[32]

[32] One can even argue that, rather than demand micro-foundations for macroeconomics, Keynes [1937] was arguing for macro-foundations for microeconomics [see Boland 1982, p. 83; 1986, pp. 166–7; 2003, p. 143].

2

On the limitations of equilibrium models in general

> [T]he direction economics, and particularly theoretical economics, took in the 20th century was to a great extent due to Walras' influence. This was not so much the result of his own results but rather a reflection of his vision. He was convinced that economics should have 'sound mathematical foundations' and his concern for this is reflected in his correspondence with his contemporaries such as [Henri] Poincaré. However, his specific vision of the nature of equilibrium became the benchmark for modern economic theory and led us to the Arrow-Debreu model which is characterised by its lack of institutional features, and the lack of any proof of stability under adjustment, as later to be shown by Sonnenschein, Mantel and Debreu. Above all there is no place in this framework for out of equilibrium dynamics. Whilst Walras is to be lauded for his insistence on the interdependence of markets, we should also be aware that he set us on a path towards economic models which, while admirably internally consistent, seem to be unable to match the empirical evidence.
>
> Alan Kirman [2010, abstract]

> Can we learn anything about the efficiency of real world market economies by studying the efficiency of Arrow-Debreu-style general equilibrium models?
>
> Richard Lipsey [2012, §II]

In simple terms, Walras's general-equilibrium models are intended to explain all prices and quantities simultaneously. They would do this by positing a set of objective functions for each and every individual demander and supplier. Usually, this is a set of utility functions for the demanders and a set of production-based profit functions for the suppliers. Universal maximization subject to constraints is assumed, as well as assuming all participants in all markets are price takers. As such, there are a few logical requirements. One must just be able to deduce a singular vector of prices given all the assumptions.

As we would say today, as an explanation, a general-equilibrium model must have at least one solution, of course, but to be an explanation, the solution must also be unique. That is, if our model is to explain why prices are what they are, we must also explain why they are not what they are not (as Hukukane Nikaido put it many years ago [1960/70, p. 268]) – that is, our explanation must not allow the logical possibility of any other equilibrium prices, or otherwise we would need to explain them away. If such uniqueness is assured by the assumptions provided in the model, most general-equilibrium model builders will be happy. Unfortunately, as Ragnar Frisch [1936] long ago argued, not only must there be a unique vector of prices in equilibrium, but we must also explain *how* the vector came about. Such a 'how' issue is a matter of dynamics. And again, Walras did not actually provide an explicitly dynamical process other than possibly to say, as we do today, that if for any product there is an excess of demand over supply, then the demanders will bid the price up (or suppliers will bid it down if supply exceeds demand), and the explanation for their price-bidding behaviour is simply that at the going price they are not maximizing. At least this provides an explanation for why any non-equilibrium price would not persist and thus provides the needed explanation for why prices are not what they are not. But as I noted in Chapter 1, unless we explain how much the price is bid up or down, this is nothing more than a logically necessary condition of assuming that all markets are being cleared (i.e., that demand equals supply in every market) or equivalently, as also explained in Chapter 1, assuming that all decision makers are maximizing. It definitely is not an explanation of the dynamics. And, as Arrow [1959] explained, we need an explicit assumption about how demanders respond to an excess demand. Do they raise the price 1% or 10%? And, who bids the price up or down? Moreover, is the answer to these questions also a matter of some type of maximization? Price adjustment is a matter of explicit dynamics, and this is a matter of recognizing time explicitly in the general-equilibrium model. That most economic theorists and model builders do not recognize the kind of question Arrow addressed – as I briefly discussed in Chapter 1 and will further explain later in this chapter – is mostly due to a common confusion about how an equilibrium differs from a balance.

2.1. Time in economic models or economic models *in* time?

The Hatter was the first to break the silence. 'What day of the month is it?' he said, turning to Alice: he had taken his watch out of his pocket, and was looking at it uneasily, shaking it every now and then, holding it to his ear. . . .

'Two days wrong!' sighed the Hatter. 'I told you butter wouldn't suit the works!' he added, looking angrily at the March Hare.

'It was the *best* butter', the March Hare replied.

Lewis Carroll

As noted in Chapter 1, the question in the title of this section was addressed in Boland [1978], and I will not repeat myself here other than to indicate again what is required for a truly dynamic model and why just putting time in a model does not always make the model dynamic. And as I also noted, the widely used 1954 Arrow-Debreu model is a primary example of a falsely dynamic general-equilibrium model. Rather than explaining a vector of today's prices as a unique set, Arrow and Debreu proposed to explain all market prices for today and for all future markets up to a defined horizon. They do this simply by putting time as a subscript on each product and each price. And again, they do this by assuming that a hamburger sold in today's market is a different product than a hamburger sold in next year's hamburger market. I say this is a false dynamics because, again, the subscripts could just as easily represent different points on the planet – for example, the hamburger market in New York is different from the hamburger market in Beijing. And so, there is no explanation for how the prices adjust to the equilibrium state that would make a point in time formally different from a location on the planet, and hence there are no real dynamics. For a model to be truly dynamic – that is, *in* time – there must be an endogenous change in one or more of the endogenous variables recognized in the model. This is what Arrow's 1959 call for a theory of price adjustment is about. Obviously, one can identify a few articles where endogenous change is recognized, such as Paul Romer's [1986] model of 'endogenous growth', which invests the endogeneity in the growth of technical knowledge rather than the usual treatment where technological change is deemed to be exogenous. Knowledge in this case is treated as a quantity (a 'stock' [loc. cit., p. 1003]), one that can produce increasing returns, and making it an object for economic maximization analysis. But there is little explanation for this growth or accumulation of knowledge except to say, 'Knowledge is accumulated by devoting resources to research' [p. 1007]. This does not avoid the problem of explaining the dynamics; it just asserts that dynamics exist.

2.2. Equilibrium versus balance

As I promised in the previous chapter, a main point to be addressed here is one not always appreciated by economic model builders. Specifically, that equilibrium is a dynamic concept but balance is a static state. Physicists and chemists are almost always puzzled when economists talk about an unstable equilibrium. What confuses these natural scientists is that they take for granted that by definition an equilibrium is stable. Nevertheless, one commonly hears economics teachers saying something about an 'unstable equilibrium' even though this is really an oxymoron. What they are really talking about is an 'unstable balance' – a balance can be unstable (think of a coin balanced on its edge) but a true equilibrium cannot (think of a marble at the bottom of a round-bottomed bowl).

Fundamentally, the assumption of a market equilibrium should be claiming something more than the existence of a balance between demand and supply in the market. That is, the concept of an equilibrium – as opposed to the concept of a balance – involves a minimal form of dynamics. Again, most textbooks fail to make this distinction since they often treat the balance and equilibrium concepts interchangeably, and this failure to distinguish between an equilibrium and a balance continues to occur despite Arrow's widely recognized 1959 article pleading for a theory of price adjustment. In this regard, he explained why in microeconomics our explanation of prices for when demand equals supply will necessarily differ from our explanation of prices for when demand is not equal to supply. That is, he said that while we can validly assume that decision makers are price takers in the former case, in the latter case we cannot be assuming all decision makers are price takers but instead must explain how and why prices are adjusted to the equilibrium level. In short, there must be someone who is not a price taker and instead changes the price.

So, again, natural scientists would likely claim that the economist's alleged 'unstable equilibrium' is an oxymoron. But without going into the intricacies of physics or chemistry, we can see this in simple terms. Specifically, consider again a coin on edge on a table. So long as we do not shake the table, the coin can remain on its edge, but if we bump the table the coin will fall over. About this we would thus say that such a coin on edge is in an *unstable balance.* Now consider a marble in a large, round-bottomed bowl. If we put the bowl on the table, bump and wait, the marble will eventually settle at the bottom of the bowl, and if we bump the table again, the marble will roll up one side or the other of the bowl but eventually resettle at the bottom. Together, the marble, the bowl, and gravity means that the marble's eventual resting at the bottom of the bowl says that the marble in this bowl is in a state of equilibrium.

In economics, when we talk of a stable market we are necessarily talking about dynamic forces. If something changes in a market such that demand exceeds supply, the act of a demander (one who is suffering the excess demand) bidding up the price is a force restoring the balance of demand and supply. However, to say this presumes that excess demand occurs when the price is below the market-clearing price (such that a rising price reduces excess demand until the balance is restored). Of course, this will always be the case if demand curves are negatively sloped and supply curves are positively sloped. If for some reason the demand curve for some good were positively sloped – as in the case of Giffen goods[1] or a Veblen effect[2] – and the supply curve were negatively sloped – such as when there are quantity discounts – then excess demand could occur at prices above the market-clearing price such that any bidding the price up would make things worse (i.e., create a greater excess demand). Thus, in this latter case bidding the price up would not produce a market-clearing price. So, saying that a market is stable is saying more than either that demand and supply curves are correctly sloped (viz. excess demand occurs below the clearing price) or that demanders respond to excess demand by bidding prices up. It is saying that both are the case.[3] Thus, when someone says only that the equilibrium price equals the one where there is an equality of demand and supply, this is not enough. Specifically, demand can equal supply (perhaps accidentally) in the case where the curves are incorrectly sloped, but (like the coin on edge) this only assures the existence of a possible balance since any disturbance of the market that creates either excess demand or excess supply would cause the price to move away from the balancing price, thereby indicating an unstable market.

All this may seem very elementary to some readers, but I raise this to illustrate in simple terms what it means for the existence of a state of equilibrium and why some critics such as Arrow claim there are problems with merely assuming the existence of an 'equilibrium' state without making explicit assumptions about the dynamics needed to assure the achievement of an equilibrium – particularly, whenever there are possibilities of shocks to the market or the economy.

2.3. Consistent and complete explanations

One of the great insights of the early economists was that, given the appropriate institutional structure, an economy based on free-market transactions is self-organizing. The key to explaining this market behaviour is that agents respond to the same set of prices, which are determined in markets that tend to reflect the

1 A good for which demand goes up when the price does.

2 The result of choosing a higher priced good because it would impress one's neighbours.

3 For a more detailed discussion about this, see chapter 7 of my 1986 book – particularly, section 3.

> overall conditions of scarcity or plenty. ... [E]conomists had long assumed, although often just implicitly, that an economy composed of such markets would have a unique overall equilibrium and that it would be unique. But they had not, in spite of the heroic efforts of Léon Walras, been able to prove that gut feeling until Kenneth Arrow and Gerard Debreu took up the problem. Using some mathematics hitherto unknown to most economists, they proved the existence of an equilibrium for a model of an entire competitive economy. The conditions that their general equilibrium model required were quite special and many were not found in the real world. ... [I]t was shown that a general equilibrium could exist in a model that did mirror at least some aspects of real economies. One of the most basic of the many necessary conditions is that firms be price takers operating in competitive markets, not price setters operating in oligopolistic markets.
>
> Richard Lipsey [2012, §II]

Much of the hard theoretical work done in the 1950s and 1960s was devoted to axiomatizing[4] Walrasian general-equilibrium analysis. The central issue was first whether such an explanation of prices and transacted quantities was consistent. The primary way to establish consistency was to build a model that consisted of a set of simultaneous equations and to solve it for a vector of prices and a vector of quantities based on the behavioural assumptions of maximizing either utility or profit. Axiomatization involves rigorously specifying an explicit set of assumptions about the nature of the assumed utility functions and production functions as well as about the posited constraints, such as the limited amounts of labour and capital. If successful, one would be able to solve for vectors of prices and quantities, but it is always possible that there is more than one solution, which raises an important methodological problem for anyone who thinks their model can be used to explain observable prices and quantities. While an observed vector of prices can be consistent with the assumptions of the model, when there are multiple solutions it means that the model is also consistent with non-observed prices and thus, as already noted, while it may be used to explain why prices are what they are, it does not explain why all other logically possible price vectors are not observed. That is, as an explanation of prices and transacted quantities, the model is incomplete.

Just to be clear here, all I am saying is that, for an explanation of prices to be complete, one must not only explain why prices are what they are but also

[4] Axiomatization refers to a style of formal mathematical model building that is explicit about identifying assumptions as axioms (and thus not in question). Such axiomatization resembles the formalities that we once saw in high school geometry classes – particularly those that were designed primarily to teach logic and thus taught about axioms, postulates, hypotheses, etc.

why they are not what they are not. Obviously, to the extent that one has a complete solution to a system of equations (such as the contents of a general-equilibrium model), one must be sure that multiple solutions are not possible. But, also obviously, the set of equations must be consistent (i.e., not entail contradictions). The burning question is, of course, how does one assure that one's model is both consistent and complete?

In the language of the 1950s and 1960s, if one is using a general-equilibrium model to explain prices, providing this needed assurance requires at minimum proving the *existence* of a solution for the set of equilibrium prices so as to prove at minimum the model's consistency. To prove completeness of one's general-equilibrium-model-based explanation of prices, one needs to prove the *uniqueness* of the equilibrium price vector represented by the solution. But if we are going to claim that our general-equilibrium model explains prices (and transacted quantities), the existence of a unique equilibrium set of prices is not enough. That price vector solution must be stable. Stability analysis in the 1950s and 1960s was in effect the Holy Grail. The main point here is that using the solution of an equilibrium-based model to explain anything is not enough. If it is to be an explanation, the solution must not only exist and be unique, it must also be stable, and that stability must also be explained. This was the motivation behind both Arrow's plea for a theory of price adjustment in 1959 and the persistent complaints about the lack of real dynamics in the 1954 Arrow-Debreu general-equilibrium existent-proof model. Let us now turn to these aspects of equilibrium solutions of general-equilibrium models.

2.4. Existence versus uniqueness

[T]he equality of the number of equations and unknowns does not prove that a solution exists, much less the uniqueness of a solution, as can already be seen from quite simple examples such as the equations

$$x^2 + y^2 = 0 \text{ and } x^2 - y^2 = 1$$

which have no solutions for the unknowns x and y. On the other hand, there are systems of equations where, despite the agreement in the number of equations and unknowns, there are many, even an infinite number, of solutions. For example, the equations

$$\begin{aligned} x^2 - y^2 &= 0, \\ x + y - z &= 0, \\ xz &= 0 \end{aligned}$$

have an infinite number of solutions for *x*, *y*, and *z*.

Abraham Wald [1936/51, pp. 369–70]

When Walras was thinking about assuring the existence of an equilibrium set of prices (i.e., prices for which all markets are clearing), he thought that one just had to make sure the number of equations equaled the number of endogenous variables. This would have usually been an elementary case for solving a set of simultaneous equations. But Walras was wrong, as this equality is neither necessary nor sufficient. As Abraham Wald [1936/51, pp. 369–70] explained in the quotation at the top of this section, the equality of the number of equations and unknowns does not prove either the existence or the uniqueness of the solution to a system of simultaneous equations.

One way to look at the questions of existence and uniqueness in general-equilibrium models is to see them both as essential aspects of what are called fixed points and fixed-point theorems. For a given model M (e.g., a general-equilibrium model) that is used to explain y (e.g., an equilibrium price vector), a fixed-point $\bar{y}$ implies that $M(\bar{y})=\bar{y}$. If we think about a general-equilibrium model of a market economy, the basic notion is that everybody is a price-taker, but those prices are being determined in the market. When we plug in specific values for a set of prices, those prices induce demanders and suppliers to transact quantities that are consistent for allowing all demanders and suppliers to be maximizing. From the perspective of general-equilibrium models that explain prices, fixed-points are obviously relevant. And of course, any disequilibrium set of market prices cannot be a fixed-point because someone is not maximizing either profit or utility. To be a fixed-point, the market prices must cause demanders and suppliers to be maximizing and, as such, to not have any reason to change their demand or supply quantities. To prove the existence of an equilibrium set of market prices for the general-equilibrium model M, depending on the form of the equations being used in the model, one would invoke a fixed-point theorem such as Brouwer's, if the mathematics used to model the general equilibrium is calculus-based, or Kakutani's, if it is a set-theory-based model. Either fixed-point theorem specifies what assumptions are necessary and sufficient for a consistent explanation for why the prices are what they are. But note well, proving the existence of a fixed-point set of equilibrium prices says nothing about dynamics – that is, fixed-point theorems are static devices saying nothing about the dynamic processes that would be needed to move the prices to the fixed-point. Nevertheless, a fixed-point would be a minimum condition for assuring the existence and uniqueness of an equilibrium set of prices by whatever dynamic process that might be considered – that is, a fixed-point is a necessary but not a sufficient condition for a unique, stable set of prices.

2.5. Equilibrium stability analysis

> [I]t cannot be denied that there is something scandalous in the spectacle of so many people refining the analyses of economic states which they give no reason to suppose will ever, or have ever, come about. It probably is also dangerous.
>
> Frank H. Hahn [1970, p. 1]

Despite the plea of Arrow's 1959 article and the large number of articles published in the 1960s that addressed the need to provide some sort of stability analysis for any model that would explain prices using some form of general equilibrium, hardly anyone today seems concerned. One obvious reason might be that nobody succeeded in providing the needed stability analysis using a model with plausible assumptions and so there seems to be nothing to talk about.

There were attempts to address the need in the 1960s – notably Frank Hahn and Takashi Negishi (1962) and subsequently a book by Franklin Fisher (1983). Given the absence of a plausible equilibrium model, it is not clear whether stability analysis was dropped because everyone agreed that it was a failure or simply because everyone involved lost interest in formally axiomatizating economic theories. I suspect these possible reasons are not mutually exclusive. Whatever the reason, we are left with a vulnerability that can too easily be exploited by critics of economic models and economic model building.

2.6. Money and time in equilibrium models

> Money is technologically equivalent to a primitive version of memory.
>
> Narayana Kocherlakota [1998, p. 250]

As discussed here and Chapter 1, putting time into a model by simply including time subscripts on variables or by recognizing a time lag will not satisfy most critics of allegedly static general-equilibrium models. What some critics have in effect demanded is that the model must be *in* time – that is, any recognized time variable must obey 'time's arrow'. What is not often recognized is that failure to properly recognize a role for time has made it difficult to also recognize a realistic role for money. Again, this is not a new problem but was one that concerned the axiomatic model builders in the 1960s [see Hahn 1965]. That is, money must be something more than a numeraire to express prices or, as it is usually stated as the 'Hahn Problem': can we construct a general-equilibrium model where money has value even though it has no intrinsic use or direct utility?

Paul Davidson [1972, 1977] and George Shackle [1972] have told us what we must do to give money a significant role other than just a numeraire. Money can have a significant role if we put our general-equilibrium model *in* time – not just putting time in our models. Specifically, the usual characterization of a Walrasian general-equilibrium model treats transactions as if they are all barter type without requiring money. In the 1960s, money was presumed only to be a static store of value, unit of account or medium of exchange. That is, money's role in an equilibrium model was to serve as a means of expressing prices so as to avoid having to list all possible relative prices. Shackle and Davidson separately argued that the existence of money in an economy is a direct consequence of the importance of real time. Specifically, contrary to transactions in a barter economy, actual market transactions sometimes require placing an order at one point in time and acquiring the goods at a later point in time. Usually, this involves a contract. A contract can specify the consequences of failure to deliver the goods or otherwise fulfill the contract. The penalty for failure is almost always expressed in monetary terms. This means that for any general-equilibrium model that claims to be dynamic, the possibly necessary existence of contracts means there is an additional role for money that goes beyond the accepted static role. In other words, in the Davidson-Shackle view, money makes real-time contracts possible. Moreover, without essential processes that involve the passage of time (e.g., tool manufacture, tree growth, wine aging, etc.), contracts would be unnecessary.

Obviously, it could be said, the Davidson-Shackle view does provide the essential endogeneity of dynamics – particularly in the case of investment with its recognition of the role of 'expectations'. In Shackle's view, the formation of expectations needs to be recognized because decisions such as investment or future sales involve 'uncertainty'. Moreover, since we cannot know for certain that our expectations are true, the Davidson-Shackle view would make contracts (and money) an essential part of an explanation of 'rational' decision making. But unfortunately, it is all too easy for clever equilibrium model builders to argue that the recognition of uncertainty, expectations or contracts merely leads us to explain why certain contracts are better than others, thereby simply bringing the contracts and expectations into the typical microeconomic research program as additional endogenous variables.

2.7. Expectations and knowledge in equilibrium models

What is not often recognized in general-equilibrium models is the knowledge that an individual would need for any decision making being modeled. Too often model builders confuse information with knowledge, not realizing that this presumes, as mentioned in Chapter 1, the theory of learning that the philosopher and economist David Hume refuted more than 200 years ago – that is, there is no valid logic that allows someone just to make observations and with them alone *prove* some general proposition is true [see Boland 2003, chapter 1]. Expectations are formed simply because, by itself, any quantity of information available today is never a sufficient logical basis for one's knowledge of the future.

As I explain in chapter 8 of my 1986 book, unfortunately, whenever economic model builders think there may be a problem with expectation formation, they usually attribute it entirely to inadequacies of the 'information set' (which is shorthand for a collection of the available observation-based information), rather than to the reliability of the individual's method of learning. That is, whenever it is possible to form two different sets of expectations given any one information set, it is presumed that such a possibility is evidence of the insufficiency of the information set rather than of any inadequacy of the learning method. This interpretation of such a possibility is really a symptom of the particular theory of learning that is always employed. It is the theory of inductive learning that Hume showed was false. In simple terms, it is the theory that says 'facts speak for themselves'. Given this theory, any uncertainty in the message of the facts is presumably not to be attributed to an inability to process the information. And it is presumed that it does not matter who perceives the information set, the conclusions reached are the same. The inevitability of the model builder and the individual decision maker reaching the same conclusion regarding the individual's optimum is the basis of the modern use of the Rational Expectations Hypothesis [e.g., Lucas and Prescott 1971 and Sargent and Wallace 1976].

If we ignore Hume – that is, ignore that there is no logically valid way to form guaranteed true generalities based solely on observations – it is easy to see why modern macroeconomic model builders can so easily assume that individual decision makers base their plans on rationally formed expectations. Even though perfect knowledge is not presumed, there is still a presumption of a perfect method of learning, albeit a slow method. Whenever all individuals are presumed to be processing the same information set, it does not matter whether the model builder is explaining the ultimate general equilibrium or is explaining an aggregate variable which no single individual could ever determine. By concentrating on aggregate variables, one does not have to worry about explaining any individual's expectations or learning method, since any single individual's decision based on an inadequate learning method is presumed to have little effect on the values of the aggregate variables. Of course, one would have to worry about this whenever a representative agent is invoked to provide microfoundations. Otherwise, the only obstacle in the way of avoiding the microeconomic problems about how the individual makes a choice based on expectations of a future equilibrium is the troublesome question of how we can be sure that no individual's errors will cause a disequilibrium or prevent an equilibrium.

As they were originally defined by John Muth [1961, p. 316], who introduced them as an explicit hypothesis, rational expectations, 'since they are informed predictions of future events, are essentially the same as the predictions of the relevant economic theory'. There are two reasons why the individual's expectations would be 'essentially the same'. One is that the 'sameness' is based on the innocent appearing presumption that 'facts speak for themselves' – which means, without any help from possibly erroneous *a priori* knowledge. The other is that the 'sameness' is based on a belief that the 'relevant economic theory' has a solid and sufficient foundation of empirical facts which can be observed by anyone. These reasons are contradicted by popular criticisms, such as Benjamin Friedman's [1979], which claims in effect that Muth's so-called Rational Expectations Hypothesis lacks an adequate learning theory for how expectations are formed. The belief in a solid foundation is a belief, contrary to Hume, that the relevant economic theory has already been inductively established, using only observable facts with a learning method that is based on a presumably reliable inductive logic. As such, an individual using the same facts inductively to form his or her expectations cannot deviate much from the expectations based on the 'relevant economic theory'.

The only way an individual's expectations can deviate is if not all the available information is used – perhaps because processing all the available information may be too costly for one individual. In this sense, an individual's expectations will not usually be perfect because of the inadequacies of the chosen information set. Thus, Muth added that, 'The [rational expectations] hypothesis . . . [is] that expectations of firms . . . tend to be distributed, for the same information set, about the prediction of the theory . . .' [ibid.]. If we follow Hume and retreat from believing there is a reliable inductive learning method, we will have an additional reason for deviations between those expectations formed by an optimizing individual and those expectations that a model builder would predict that the individual would form, given the relevant economic theory. However, when we give up the belief in reliable inductive learning, there is no reason to suspect that the relevant economic theory would give expectations that are any more accurate than ones which individuals form. Whenever inductive learning is imperfect, there is no reason for expectations to be distributed 'about the predictions of the theory' rather than about some other set of predictions. Thus, it must be concluded that Muth and the advocates of the Rational Expectations Hypothesis definitely believe – contrary to Hume – in the reliability of inductive learning.

As an aside, I need to make a methodological point here. Economists are too often confused about what is meant by induction when it comes to explaining knowledge claims. Induction is not, as some seem to think, just about using observations in the process of building a general model. Induction is more than that as it is really about forming a generalization using *only* observations – that is, without any auxiliary assumptions (including the assumption of maximization). And Hume merely pointed out that if people think their *knowledge* is based *only* on past experience (i.e., past observations), then we can always ask them how they *know* that *that* knowledge is true. To be consistent, they must respond 'by experience', to which, of course, it can be asked how they know that they know that they know, and so on – obviously this leads to an infinite regress, hence one cannot prove that one can learn only by experience (i.e., based on only observations). Hence there is no real induction. Instead, we just have the risky old 'jumping to conclusions', nothing more.[5]

For model builders who rely on the assumption of rational expectations, this is unfortunate, given that there is no reliable inductive learning method. The problem with the Rational Expectations Hypothesis is not that it lacks a theory of learning, but that it relies on a false theory of learning. For the Rational Expectations Hypothesis to provide a means of avoiding the difficult microeconomics questions about learning or expectations formation, facts must not only speak for themselves, but they must say the same thing to every individual. But without a perfectly reliable learning method, we usually find that the method with which one interprets the facts is heavily

[5] As I said, many economic model builders are confused about what inductive learning means. They too often simply think that any argument that includes observational data is inductive. What they really mean is that it is not purely deductive – that is, it is not purely without any observations being used to reach a conclusion.

influenced by one's a priori theories. In other words, expectation formation depends on theories. Facts, if they speak at all, speak only with the help of one's theories – all facts, so to speak, are 'theory laden'. This raises many problems unless there is some reason given for why all individuals believe in the same *a priori* theories [see also Frydman and Phelps, 1983]. Without a reliable inductive logic there is no reason to suspect that any two individuals would believe the same theory nor any reason for why they would react to the same information set in exactly the same way. We see now why some equilibrium model builders see that this implies random behaviour, and thus why they see a necessity of basing macroeconomics or general-equilibrium models on an understanding of stochastic processes [e.g., Hey, 1981].

In effect, the Rational Expectations Hypothesis moves the goalpost. Instead of assuming that in a general equilibrium all decision makers have acquired sufficient knowledge to make correctly maximizing decisions, particularly investment decisions, many general-equilibrium model builders suggest that we should not expect more of decision makers using available observational data than we would of any expert econometrician. Surely, not everyone will see such a suggestion as something realistic. Nevertheless, model builders who do invoke the assumption of rational expectations are satisfied that at least there is a consistency between what the econometric model builders would expect given the available observational data and what the individual decision makers being explained would expect. Surely, it would be said, one cannot realistically expect individual decision makers to have expectations that are any more accurate than the model builder can have using the best econometric techniques. Unsystematic errors on the part of decision makers should obviously be allowed for.

2.8. Equilibrium models in macroeconomics and the alleged need for micro-foundations

> One cannot expect there to be any simple and straightforward mapping from Walras to macroeconomics. Those are ways of looking at economics with different goals in mind, and correspondingly different methods. It would be strange, however, if each did not contain lessons for the other.
>
> Robert M. Solow [2011, p. 101]

For those macroeconomic model builders who accept the critical observations that claim that the unmodified assumption of rational expectations is at best unsupported, one way to get around such criticism would be, of course, to simply explain how individuals form their expectations. And again, could we perhaps get around such criticism by basing our macroeconomic model on Walrasian general-equilibrium analysis? Doubtful, judging by the discussion in Chapter 1. While some might still hope that basing a macroeconomic model on a Walrasian general equilibrium would provide the needed micro-foundations, others such as Robert Solow (as is evident in the quotation at the top of this section) might not see such a model as being even macroeconomic.

Of course, as discussed in Chapter 1, one popular alternative means of providing micro-foundations for macroeconomic models is to employ a representative individual agent for the macro economy. If the economy is being modeled with an equilibrium model, then the representative agent must also be in equilibrium – that is, be maximizing. At minimum, the analysis of the representative agent's equilibrium behaviour should explain how that individual forms his or her expectations. A good start should include explicit analysis of how that individual acquires the needed knowledge to form expectations in a non-inductive manner.

Some of the complaints and criticisms of the use of the representative agent were, of course, discussed in the previous chapter. Obviously, to them we should also add Solow's specific complaint against using a single representative agent [2011, p. 100]:

> In effect the model economy centres on – one could almost say 'consists of' – a single (intertemporally) optimizing household that supplies labour, consumes, saves, and owns the resulting capital.

And on using the representative agent instead of a full-blown Walrasian general equilibrium, he complains [ibid. (emphasis in original)]:

> This approach to macroeconomics strikes me as vastly inferior to the ... Walrasian tradition .... The representative-agent formulation, even in the presence of imperfections, imposes on the model economy – and therefore imputes to the real economy – a coherent purposive character. The economy is *trying* to optimize the utility of the representative agent, subject to whatever frictional or informational limitations there may be. This is a characterization of real macroeconomic behaviour that I would not care to defend.

So, are there circumstances where you can defend the use of the representative agent? As it turns out, Hartley directly addressed the question 18 years ago [1997, p. 66]:

> Whether or not the representative agent assumption is usable in a Walrasian framework depends solely on the answer to this question: Is heterogeneity among people and firms an irrelevant, complicating factor or is it an essential part of the

> real economy? The use of a representative agent in a Walrasian framework is imposing the very powerful assumption that the important features of the economy are unaffected by the fact that real people and firms differ from one another. If this assumption is true, then there is no problem with using the representative agent hypothesis. However, if it is not true, then using a representative agent in a Walrasian model is unjustified. The results from a Walrasian model improperly using the representative agent assumption are valueless.

Apparently, then, the usefulness of the representative agent is limited, at best. And so, as to whether we should think it is useful invoke the representative agent to provide equilibrium-based micro-foundations for any macroeconomic model, Kirman [1992, p. 119] concludes, 'it is clear that the "representative" agent deserves a decent burial, as an approach to economic analysis that is not only primitive, but fundamentally erroneous'.

2.9. Less demanding concepts of equilibrium: self-confirming and stochastic

> Nash equilibrium and its refinements describe a situation in which (i) each player's strategy is a best response to his beliefs about the play of his opponents, and (ii) each player's beliefs about the opponents' play are exactly correct. We propose a new equilibrium concept, self-confirming equilibrium, that weakens condition (ii) by requiring only that players' beliefs are correct along the equilibrium path of play. . . . The concept of self-confirming equilibrium is motivated by the idea that noncooperative equilibria should be interpreted as the outcome of a learning process, in which players revise their beliefs using their observations of previous play.
>
> Drew Fudenberg and David Levine [1993, p. 523]

> Thinking of equilibrium as the result of non-equilibrium learning suggests that players are likely to be better informed about the consequences of actions on the equilibrium path than off the equilibrium path. Indeed, if play converges to equilibrium and players have many observations, then we should expect players to have correct beliefs about the equilibrium outcome. But by definition, off-path actions are never observed in equilibrium, which raises the possibility that incorrect beliefs about off-path play might persist for quite some time.
>
> Drew Fudenberg and David Levine [2009, p. 2355]

> If only good things survive the tests of time and practice, evolution produces intelligent design. . . . Theories of out-of-equilibrium learning tell us not always to expect that. An observational equivalence possibility that emerges from the rational expectations econometrics . . . sets the stage . . . [and thereby] describes how a system of adaptive agents converges to a self-confirming equilibrium in which all agents have correct forecasting distributions for events observed often along an equilibrium path, but possibly incorrect views about events that are rarely observed. This matters because intelligent design of rational expectations

> equilibria hinges on the government's expectations about events that will not be observed. Self-confirming equilibria allow wrong models that match historical data to survive and to influence policy.
>
> Thomas Sargent [2008, p. 6]

In his presidential address to the American Economic Association, Sargent [2008, p. 6] offers the notion of a 'self-confirming' equilibrium as an alternative to assuming an overly demanding Rational Expectations equilibrium. The main problem to be solved with the alternative seems to be that decision makers in the Rational Expectations macro economy are presumed to be using the correct model of the economy, the same one that an expert macro-econometric model builder would arrive at after using all of the available data. Can the individual decision makers within the economy honestly be expected to be able to build the same model to guide their decisions? The consensus seems now to be that they cannot. Instead, as suggested by Drew Fudenberg and David Levine [1993, 2009] in a game-theoretic context, the individual should be seen as learning the model by making decisions, some of which may not be optimal. Presumably, all that is being assumed by the self-confirming equilibrium is that on average the decisions will be in the neighbourhood of the equilibrium. As such, their decisions may temporarily be disequilibrium decisions, but with enough trials, they could converge to the Rational Expectations equilibrium. At least, at minimum, one cannot accuse the model builder of simply assuming either that all decision makers use the same model of the economy as the model builder's model of their macro behaviour or that individual decision makers have had an unrealistic amount of time or number of trials in order to make decisions that will conform to the presumptions of the Rational Expectations model.

One might suspect that critics of Rational Expectations models will see the introduction of the self-confirming equilibrium to be nothing more than moving the goalposts. And one might also expect that defenders of the self-confirming alternative will resort to Friedman's 1953 instrumentalist 'as if' methodology (briefly discussed in Chapter 1; it would be similar to the defense against the criticisms of the realism of the representative agent assumption).

In an earlier paper, Lucas and Sargent [1979] discussed dynamic models, particularly those intended to explain business cycles. There they offered a different alternative to any Rational Expectations equilibrium model that assumed decision makers have perfect knowledge. To do this, they began by discussing what they saw as the failure of Keynesian models of the business cycle. Eventually, they characterized Keynesian economic models as rejections of classical economic theory, particularly rejecting 'its insistence on adherence to the two postulates (a) that markets clear and (b) that agents act in their own self-interest' [p. 7]. They explained that the concept of an equilibrium as it was understood in Keynes' day has since 'changed dramatically'. Instead, they claimed (in 1979) that an economy is now seen as 'following a multivariate stochastic process is now routinely described as being in equilibrium, by which is meant nothing more than that at each point in time, postulates (a) and (b) above are satisfied' [ibid.]. Their way of seeing an equilibrium seems to be just a modified version of the Arrow-Debreu model (the one I have discussed already). As such, one can still expect that any critic will see an equilibrium based on any stochastic process as just another way of moving the goalposts. And as John Hicks [1979, p. 121] cautioned at about the same time

> I am bold enough to conclude ... that the usefulness of 'statistical' or 'stochastic' methods in economics is a good deal less than is now conventionally supposed. We have no business to turn to them automatically; we should always ask ourselves, before we apply them, whether they are appropriate to the problem in hand.

But, of course, there is always Friedman's 'as if' methodology for Lucas and Sargent to use in defense of Hicks's conclusion, too.

2.10. Limits to the usefulness of equilibrium models in general

> Against this background, more and more economists have recently ventured into what Christopher Sims ... characterized as the 'wilderness' of irrational expectations and bounded rationality, aiming partly to create theories of transition dynamics, partly to understand the properties of equilibrium dynamics themselves, and partly to create *new* dynamics of systems that do not settle down. Beyond confirming Sims's characterization of this area as a research 'wilderness', no general theory of transitions or of bounded rationality has yet emerged from this area, but much has been learned, and maybe some of it is relevant to thinking about real transitions. ...
>
> This area is wilderness because the researcher faces so many choices after he decides to forgo the discipline provided by equilibrium theorizing. The commitment to equilibrium theorizing made many choices for him by requiring that people be modelled as optimal decision-makers within a commonly understood environment. When we withdraw the assumption of a commonly understood environment, we have to replace it with *something*, and there are so many plausible possibilities. Ironically, when we economists make the people in our models more 'bounded' in their rationality and more diverse in their understanding of the environment, *we* must be smarter, because our models become larger and more demanding mathematically and econometrically.
>
> Thomas Sargent [1993, pp. 1–2]

Critics of equilibrium model building in economics are fond of telling the story of the drunk who loses his keys in the dark part of the street between street lights but spends his time looking for them under the street light 'because the light is better'. And while some model builders might dismiss the relevance of the story, it fairly captures the state of today's model building methodology, particularly for macroeconomic theory. The reason is simply that, as Sargent suggests, the mathematics of any disequilibrium model are always much more difficult than the mathematics of any general-equilibrium model. In light of such criticism, the main question that should be asked is: Why do economic model builders think an equilibrium model could ever explain the current state of the economy, let alone any future state of the economy?

It is important to keep in mind that today when model builders talk about Walras's general-equilibrium analysis, they are hardly ever referring to something Walras, himself, said. Whether or not Walras said this or that is not important for model builders, although it is for historians of economic thought (for example, see the 1996 book by Donald Walker and Michel De Vroey's 1999 review of it). Walras's name is today being used just to be specific about the type of equilibrium model being referred to. As Solow [2011, p. 99] characterized what he called the 'Walrasian economy', it is for which one *can* define a set of excess demand functions that are continuous, homogeneous of degree zero (i.e., only relative prices matter), and satisfy Walras's Law (aggregate excess demand is always zero since demand equals supply in all markets) – but, beyond that, not much more since that is all that the 'street light' illuminates.

Parenthetically, it should be pointed out that, unlike the typical Walrasian general-equilibrium model, which presumes that every market is in equilibrium by means of participants bidding prices up or down, Francis Edgeworth saw equilibrium in terms of direct exchanges between individuals, and thus his equilibrium model does recognize diversity in that his equilibrium allows for differing tastes and differing endowments or incomes. An Edgeworthian equilibrium is usually characterized in textbooks by using a so-called Edgeworth-Bowley box, which displays two individuals in an exchange equilibrium for the distribution of two goods such that both are maximizing their respective utilities. The Edgeworthian equilibrium is one where neither can gain without the other losing utility. I raise Edgeworth's characterization of equilibrium to point out how, unlike the common view, it can be seen to be nothing more than a characterization of the necessary conditions for a general equilibrium. That is, if there is a state of Walrasian general equilibrium, then it will always be possible to choose any two goods and any two people and be able to show that they are in an Edgeworthian equilibrium. As we will see in the next two chapters, this opens the door to using game-theoretic models. But, what is important to note here is that the use of Walrasian general-equilibrium models is for situations where individuals are presumed to be privately maximizing based only on their private preferences and endowments and the going market prices – that is, based not on the behaviour of other individuals but as price takers, only on the prices being determined in the market.

As discussed in Chapter 1, the assumption of equilibrium in general is secondary to maximization – one might even suggest that it is redundant if we instead assume universal maximization. This is so, of course, only if we do not explain how the equilibrium is achieved and thus why universal maximization is possible. This is the primary limitation of equilibrium-based models used to explain prices and quantities. Unless an equilibrium-based model explains how the prices and quantities come about, it can only use the neighbourhood properties of the equilibrium. We know this from what is taught in most microeconomic principles textbooks, which as I have said are just restatements of what Alfred Marshall talked about in Book V of his 1890 *Principles of Economics*. To use neighbourhood properties, one hypothetically changes a single price or quantity from its equilibrium value to demonstrate how to explain that prices and quantities will change back to the equilibrium value. For example, increasing the price of a good above the equilibrium price would create an excess supply because utility maximizing consumers would demand less and profit maximizing firms would produce more. That is, when the price rises, the result is that firms producing this good now face a price greater than marginal cost, and so they are no longer maximizing profit unless they produce more. And doing so, some (or all) firms will not be able to sell all of what they produce given the fall in demand, and thus at least one firm will bid the price down so as to sell its excess supply. But this heuristic way of illustrating the role of maximization only works as a neighbourhood property. What is missing is any discussion of the institutional structure in which the 'bidding' takes place. Also missing is any recognition of how an individual agent in the economy interacts with the other agents. Moreover, this limitation particularly applies to macroeconomic models that invoke the representative agent to provide the desired micro-foundations since by using the representative agent, one does not recognize other agents and hence one also does not recognize the likely fact that in the real world there is a considerable diversity among the very many agents.

So, if the limitations to using the Walrasian general-equilibrium models to provide the necessary micro-foundations are considered serious, why do we not see a lot of non-Walrasian or disequilibrium models being used to construct macroeconomic models today? Yes, of course, there are many macroeconomic models that now include imperfect competition or even 'sticky' wages, but one obvious reason is, as Kirman points out, 'The informational requirements of adjustment processes seem to be so extreme that only economy specific processes could possibly ensure convergence. This is hardly reassuring for those who argue for the plausibility of the equilibrium notion' [2011, p. 120]. In a limited way, in his 1959 article pleading for a theory of price adjustment, Arrow advocated invoking imperfect competition to supply the needed adjustment theory, but this has two problems. First, consistent with Kirman's view, this would require that the imperfect competitor know everything about the demand curve it faces. But second, even worse, breaking out of such a presumption would mean that the imperfect competitor would be a priori ignorant of the demand curve and would have to make assumptions about it as the firm tries to learn about the demand curve through trial and error. Such a process is problematic if the assumptions made are not realistic. As Robert Clower [1959] demonstrated at the same time as Arrow's article was published, an ignorant monopolist (Clower's focus) who makes false assumptions about the nature of the demand curve it faces will likely reach a price-quantity point at which it thinks profit is maximum and thus acts as if it is in equilibrium, but it is also possible that in fact it is not maximizing in accordance with the real demand curve it faces. From this perspective, it is easy to see why deviating from any general-equilibrium model based on perfect competition is at best problematic and at worse can be grossly misleading.

As Kirman points out, 'in modern macroeconomic models which still claim to be Walrasian, individuals do not interact at all, since they are subsumed into a representative individual' [2011, p. 130]. As some will be quick to point out, this is why many microeconomic model builders have been focusing on building equilibrium models using game theory. Whether or not this is a viable model building option to get around having to rely on a representative-agent-based explanation of the dynamics of reaching an equilibrium will be discussed in the next two chapters.

3

On building theoretical models using game theory

> The last dozen years have seen a reformulation of general equilibrium theory in which 'markets' and 'market behavior' are pushed into the background while the acts of individual exchange are brought into sharper focus. This game-theoretic approach to microeconomics, whose progenitor was Edgeworth not Walras, is likewise important for the light it sheds on the microfoundations of macroeconomics. Although less well-developed than neo-Walrasian analysis, Edgeworthian models too can formulate at the disaggregated level a number of intrinsically macroeconomic concerns. . . .
>
> Consider the concept of equilibrium. . . . In an Edgeworthian framework . . . we are concerned not with markets but with acts of individual exchange. As an equilibrium concept we need some logical rest-point of an exchange mechanism. If it is possible for two individuals to gain from trade, that pre-trade allocation ought not to be termed an equilibrium. Intuitively, equilibrium will occur when no traders can improve their positions by exchange.
>
> E. Roy Weintraub [1979, pp. 128–9]

In his book *Value and Capital*, John Hicks noted [1939/46, p. 20]:

> If an individual is to be in equilibrium with respect to a system of market prices, it is directly evident that his marginal rate of substitution between any two goods must equal the ratio of their prices. Otherwise he would clearly find an advantage in substituting some quantity of one for an equal value (at the market rate) of the other.

In other words, one can easily see the act of individual maximization as a state of personal equilibrium. After all, as in the case of consumer theory, this is the direct consequence of our assuming and using strictly convex-to-the-origin indifference curves when explaining the consumer's choice of a bundle of goods while facing market prices. What consumers will see is that, if along their budget lines they move left or right from the maximizing bundle, they will experience a lower level of utility. Thus, they will move back toward the maximizing bundle. And Hicks's point is simply that this self-correcting behaviour is exactly what constitutes equilibrium behaviour in a market. So, unlike the discussion of equilibrium behaviour of whole markets or even whole macro economies in Chapter 2, Hicks's version gives us a tool to characterize individual behaviour that does not obviously involve the kind of criticism discussed in that chapter, such as that about using a representative agent to provide micro-foundations. Moreover, I think, it is a tool that fits well with the behavioural ideas incorporated in every model based on game theory.

Also beginning in the 1930s, not only were critics of typical microeconomics models and analysis doubtful of the arbitrariness of utility as a measure of anything empirical but they often complained that such models too often rely on calculus to discuss maximization. For example, to calculate marginal cost for the production of a particular good, say can openers or garbage cans, we would need a continuously differentiable total cost function, and this is obviously open to the simple realistic observation that can openers and garbage cans are not infinitely divisible as required for the calculus differentiation underlying the definition of marginal cost – that is, underlying the very definition of a continuous total cost function. Avoiding having to assume that objects of interest are infinitely divisible is, I think, an unappreciated virtue of using game theory.[1]

As Roy Weintraub [1979] observed, the Edgeworthian characterization of equilibrium also addresses a lacuna of using Walrasian general-equilibrium models and provides an alternative micro-foundation if modeled using game theory. This leaves us with three ways that it seems reasonable for turning to game-theoretic models to overcome the problems discussed in Chapter 2: Game-theoretic models allow us to focus on the individuals that make up the economy being modeled by seeing each of them in a personal equilibrium while at the same time interacting with other individuals. And, though not always discussed, game theory is primarily a form of mathematical analysis. As such, game theory provides a way to avoid the problem of assuming infinite divisibility by characterizing choices as being between a finite list of discrete options, as I shall discuss next.

[1] Like linear programming (which in the 1950s and 1960s was a popular way of characterizing optimizing choices), game theory looks at a discrete list of possible equilibria rather than a continuum of differentiable points, most of which would never be chosen. Unfortunately, during that time, the nature of a solution to a non-cooperative zero-sum game was shown to be mathematically equivalent to the simplex method solution to a corresponding linear program [see Vajda 1956]. As a result, model builders lost serious interest in game theory until a couple decades ago. Note, however, that game theory does not have to avoid continuity after all; both Cournot and von Stackelberg characterizations of an oligopoly equilibrium presume continuous action sets.

3.1. Game-theoretic economic models: a brief elementary review

> Game theory studies decisions by several persons in situations with significant interactions. Compared to other theories of multi-person decisions, it has two distinguishing features. One is explicit consideration of each person's available strategies and the outcomes resulting from combinations of their choices; that is, a complete and detailed specification of the 'game'. In noncooperative contexts, the other is a focus on optimal choices by each person separately.
>
> Srihari Govindan and Robert Wilson [2008, p. 1]

Game Theory and Economic Modelling, by the noted game theorist David Kreps, is a commonly used text in beginning graduate classes. Near the beginning of his book he explains the purpose of game-theoretic models [1990, pp. 6–7]:

> Game theory comprises formal mathematical models of 'games' that are examined deductively. Just as in more traditional economic theory, the advantages that are meant to ensue from formal, mathematical models examined deductively are (at least) three: (*a*) It gives us a clear and precise language for communicating insights and notions. In particular, it provides us with general categories of assumptions so that insights and intuitions can be transferred from one context to another and can be cross-checked between different contexts. (*b*) It allows us to subject particular insights and intuitions to the test of logical consistency. (*c*) It helps us to trace back from 'observations' to underlying assumptions; to see what assumptions are really at the heart of particular conclusions.

Before considering how game-theoretic models are used in economics and to avoid possible confusion, let me begin with a brief review in which some basic terminology (dare I say jargon?) can be identified to make sure we are all on the same page. Put in elementary terms, there are just two types of game-theoretic model for representing non-cooperative games: (1) the static, matrix form (also called the normal or strategic form) game, which I illustrate in Figure 3.1(a) and (2) the dynamic, extensive form game, which I illustrate in Figure 3.1(b). To begin building a matrix-form game, one must specify a list of players, such as A and B, a list of strategies or choice options for each player, and for each combination of choice options, a list of payoffs that the players will receive.

Extensive form games would be used to recognize a sequence of moves (such as we might do with chess or checkers), although they can be directly related to the matrix form if one just looks at the end payoffs. In Figure 3.1(b) the arrows indicate the choices that can be made and the dotted line represents a consideration not made in the matrix form – namely, the information available to the player making a choice after a previous player has made his or her choice (again, as in chess or checkers).

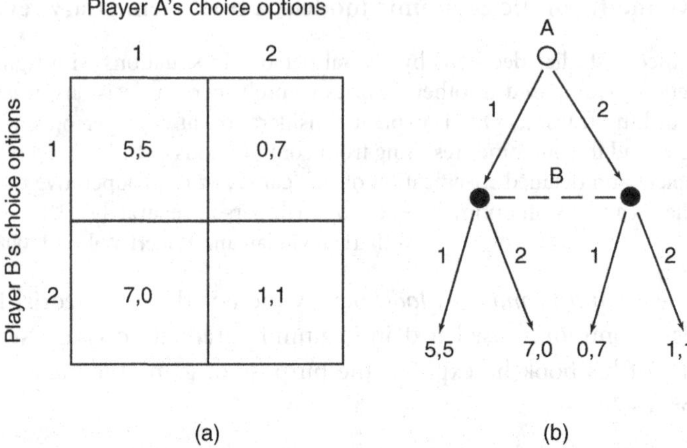

Figure 3.1 Forms of game-theoretic models

About the only intrinsic aspect of either form of model is the presumed motivation for making a choice – for game-theoretic economic model builders, maximizing payoffs in some sense is presumed and they as usual call this being 'rational'.

Since, as I said in the Prologue, my discussion will always be focused on the 'Forest' rather than the 'Trees' (which in this case will apply to game theory), the usual discussion involving many examples will not be ventured here as there are many textbooks for such a 'Tree'-oriented discussion. Instead, the need here is only to consider how game-theoretic models are used in economics today.

3.2. Using game-theoretic economic models

The illustrations of both types of game-theoretic model obviously tell us only the objective or mathematical framework and nothing about the nature or behaviour of the players. Moreover, the extent of either type of model's usefulness depends heavily on identifying an equilibrium for any given posited model that is to be used to explain observed behaviour or to predict an outcome of a situation being represented. As Kenneth Binmore observes [2007, p. 2]:

> With such a wide field of application, game theory would be a universal panacea if it could always predict how people will play the many games of which social life largely consists. But game theory isn't able to solve all of the world's problems, because it only works when people play games *rationally*.

In the language of mathematicians, for a game-theoretic model to be useful in explaining or predicting, it must have a 'solution' that identifies the choice options (or 'strategies', as games theorists would say) that each player makes or will make. A solution should be an equilibrium and as such must be unique and must be, at least, a 'stable' solution. If a solution exists, then it is presumed that so-called 'rational' players will choose the equilibrium options. The point here is simply that once the model builder focuses on what has to be assumed to assure the existence of an equilibrium for the posited model, there is nothing economically new about game-theoretic models being used as instruments for explaining choices made or to be made. However, as I suggested earlier in this chapter, what game-theoretic models do provide is both the ability to avoid the unrealistic complications of using calculus-based characterizations of maximization and the ability to directly address one of the short-comings identified by critics of macro models which is that too often they do not recognize the diversity within any economy.

Continuing this brief review, the first task of the model builder is to identify the eventual outcome of playing the posited game. And as is well known, to do so there are two considerations: dominance and what is called a Nash equilibrium. Dominance is a primary means of eliminating from the list of possible joint options those that have no chance of being chosen – this would be simply because, given the game and the respective payoffs, there is always a better outcome for the players to change to without losing what would be obtained by the dominated joint option. In effect, a dominated pair of options in a two-person game is not Pareto optimal.[2] A Nash equilibrium is an outcome that, if reached, leaves all players seeing no need to change and which defines the minimum necessary conditions for an equilibrium outcome that correspond to the idea of explanation discussed in Chapter 2. If dominance does not eliminate all but one possible outcome, then identifying such a Nash equilibrium is always the next essential step in applying the model to explain or predict. The only problem is that some game-theoretic models have more than one possible Nash equilibrium, which means the model cannot be used to explain or predict, as I discussed in the previous chapter. And, of course, it is conceivable that

[2] 'Pareto optimality' is an indirect and limited criterion of optimality. It simply says that if one person can gain without the other losing, then the state of trade is not optimal. Once a point is reached where one cannot gain without the other losing, then a state of Pareto optimality is reached. It was a puzzle for theoretical model builders in the 1950s, who could easily prove that any competitive long-run or general equilibrium is Pareto optimal but had much difficulty proving the reverse using plausible assumptions.

some games have no Nash equilibrium solution, but even if a Nash equilibrium exists and is unique, as before, we still need to explain why it would be achieved. As Kreps put this issue [1990, p. 31]:

> [O]ne can cook up games with a single Nash equilibrium that is not the self-evident way to play, and one can cook up games in which the majority of play involves strategies that are not part of a Nash equilibrium. ... Unless a given game has a self-evident way to play, self-evident to the participants, the notion of a Nash equilibrium has no particular claim upon our attention. ... Hence when economic analysts invoke the notion of a Nash equilibrium, they are asserting at least implicitly that the situation in question has (or will have) a self-evident way to play.

3.3. The necessary ingredients for game-theoretic economic models

> Some social scientists, particularly those who are committed to individualism, like the strict separation of choice and structure found in game theory because it gives an active edge to choice. Individuals *qua* individuals are plainly doing something on this account, although how much will depend on what can be said about what is likely to happen in such interactions. Game theory promises to tell a great deal on this.
>
> Shaun Hargreaves Heap and Yanis Varoufakis [2004, p. 33]

Clearly, any game to be modeled must have rules that at least specify for the players the choice options and the possible payoffs. And, obviously, as discussed in the previous section, if the game-theoretic model is to be used to *explain* observed behaviour or to explain future behaviour, then at minimum the model must possess an equilibrium solution that not only exists but must also be unique. Beyond this, almost anything goes, except for some obvious questions that need to be addressed. What do the players know about the game and about the other players? What is the motivation of each player? What can the model builder do if the rules of the game allow for multiple Nash equilibria or no Nash equilibria at all? Is there a possibility for more than one play? Is there a possibility of cooperation before or during the play? Are side payments possible? And then there are the questions raised by Kreps after what is quoted at the end of the previous section. How do players have to play in order to reach the equilibrium solution? What if it is not self-evident? Kreps [1990, pp. 128–9] also raised other questions that must be dealt with:

> [T]he 'rules of the game' can matter enormously to the outcomes predicted by game-theoretic analysis. This brings the question, Where do the rules come from?

> And the implicit logic of causation is that changing the rules of the game can change the outcomes; rules are given exogenously, and they then affect the outcomes. But is causation one way only? Can outcomes affect the rules?

Most of the research in game theory is about answers to questions such as these. How model builders go about answering these questions is often not universally accepted. And, there are important questions not often discussed openly. Is all this just a matter of the mathematics of the game-theoretic model building, or is it the more elaborate matter of required institutions that make the play possible? Is it a matter of the behaviour of players or possibly the social culture within which the game is being played?

Over the years, as many textbooks will show, game theorists have come up with many and various *ad hoc* ways to deal with these often difficult questions, but fundamentally, the issue of how we know that the equilibrium of the model is actually reached is no different than what Arrow was advocating when he was asking in 1959 for a theory of price adjustment to make the market theory of prices complete. Identifying a game-theoretic model's possible Nash equilibrium – even if unique – is not always enough. One's model must include reasons for why it will be the chosen outcome. Unfortunately, even though there is almost universal agreement as to the necessary elements of any game-theoretic model, there is seldom universal agreement as to the additional assumptions that some have identified. As with the discussion of Arrow's differential equation about the speed of price adjustment, one can identify such mathematical devices or assumptions which will yield mathematically what is needed to complete the model. But unfortunately, this can be done without a realistic behavioural analysis that assures us that players will actually choose the equilibrium outcome. And so, not much has been accomplished other than identifying what is mathematically necessary. It is difficult to avoid criticizing model builders who are satisfied with just creating a mathematical device or assumption that would overcome some pending model-building puzzle – particularly whenever there is little concern with the apparent and sometimes obvious unrealism of the resulting models. This problematic situation is endemic today in economics, where there continues to be a clash between the innovative culture of mathematics departments, for which realism is always put on the back burner, and the practical concerns of many economic model builders, for whom realism is essential if the models are to be used honestly to explain the real world economy. In the next chapter, I will look at these critical questions and consider what some prominent game theorists have seen as possible limitations of relying on game-theoretic models to deal with the need to address both diversity and interaction between individuals in the micro and macro views of the economy.

3.4. Dealing with questionable equilibrium solutions

There are two problematic equilibrium situations that game theorists have addressed for a couple decades. As discussed earlier in this chapter, they are the case of building a model for which an equilibrium does not exist and the case of there being more than one equilibrium. While there are approaches to building a model that might overcome the absence of a solution for a given game, according to Kreps [1990, pp. 95–9], the way to overcome multiple equilibria is not obvious.

3.4.1. The problem of models without equilibria: equilibrium refinements

Faced with a model with no possible equilibria, the primary approach is to 'refine' – that is, narrow – the definition of an acceptable unique solution.[3] This is done by adding extra assumptions, of course.[4] Again, assumptions acceptable to a mathematician might not be acceptable to anyone who places realism above convenience in model building.[5]

The approach of refining an acceptable solution might be considered problematic. In this regard, Kreps notes that [1990, p. 108]:

> Equilibrium refinements are strengthenings of the requirement that behaviour constitutes a Nash equilibrium . . . strengthenings have been very popular in the application of game theory to economic contexts in the recent past. . . . I wish to make the case that greater scepticism is called for in their application than is normally applied.

As noted already, what economists might see as a choice to be made for a player's move, mathematics-oriented game theorists see as a 'strategy'. The notion of a strategy makes most sense when discussing the extensive form of a game such as the one illustrated as Figure 3.1(b). A strategy is a plan of action which would be expressed to deal with recognized contingencies,

[3] In the case of multiple Nash equilibria, Kreps says that one refinement 'involves the invocation of some stronger notion of equilibrium' [1990, p. 108].

[4] For a recent survey of 'Trees' in the 'Forest' of refinements, see Srihari Govindan and Robert Wilson (2008)

[5] Of course, some model builders will see this as an unavoidable trade-off between predictive power, tractability and realism.

such as if player A chooses option 1, then player B can choose option 1, if A chooses option 2, B chooses option 2. With this in mind, consider any two-player model for which there is no equilibrium pair of strategies (unique or otherwise) – that is, no pair where both players would choose their respective equilibrium strategy.

To be clear, so far we have been discussing what game theorists call a 'pure' strategy, namely, one involving an either-or choice. In contrast, when dealing with a game lacking an equilibrium pair of strategies, some will see a need for a refinement they call a 'mixed' strategy whereby the player might choose any option with a positive probability. From the 'Forest' perspective, in simple terms, a mixed strategy amounts to dealing with the non-existence of equilibria with a 'coin flip' or in general randomizing one's choices or strategies. That is, sometimes choose option 1 and other times choose option 2. Using such an assumption, an equilibrium 'solution' can be constructed. Such a refinement or constructed solution is just the mixed strategy that some see as an alternative to a pure strategy. One can easily think of games for which mixed strategies makes sense, such as poker, since as a player you do not want to be predictable. But this may not be true in other games and certainly not in one-shot games if one is looking for a 'solution'.

3.4.2. Does plausibility matter?

Apart from obvious questions concerning the realism of any added assumptions to narrow the list of possible solutions, even those willing to treat game-theoretic model building as a mathematical quest will raise questions of the plausibility of the behaviour presumed in the extra assumptions. Usually, these questions involve asking how the players could ever be expected to know what they are assumed to know. Dealing with assumptions made about the game players' knowledge seems to be the main subject for equilibrium refinements. The issue of what can or must be assumed about the knowledge of any player in any game-theoretic economic model will be the central concern of the next chapter.

3.5. What do game-theoretic models represent?

Let me go back to the classical interpretation of the game form as a full description of the physical events in the modeled situation. Notice that it is rare that a situation involving a conflict of interests is described clearly and objectively by a set of rules. The exceptions I can think of are 'games' in the colloquial sense.

> Unless the game instructions appear on the box bought at 'toys "Я" us', I cannot see how we can avoid the interpretation of a game form as an abstract summary of the players' actual perceptions of the complicated situations they are in.
>
> Ariel Rubinstein [1991, p. 917]

In his 1991 *Econometrica* article, Ariel Rubinstein identifies many problems or questions about the nature of game theory as it is used in economics. But the main problem, I think, is the one raised in the quotation at the beginning of this section. Usually, when game theory is discussed in textbooks, one gets the impression that the game represents some objective situation that the players are presumed to be placed in. This is most obvious in the situation in which it is assumed that the players know both the rules and the payoffs – as if the game is somehow a feature of the real, physical world, and this is also implicit even in the critical questions about how the players learn the rules or payoffs.

What Rubinstein seems to be suggesting is that the game does not necessarily represent the real world – instead, it represents the individual player's view or theory of the world. All that the widely used assumption of Common Knowledge of Rationality assures is that all players of a game see the game in the same way. That assumption will be discussed in the next chapter. Here the question is only about what an individual player sees as the game being theoretically modeled.

In this regard, let us consider a simple analogy – the textbook explanation of the consumer. Our textbooks, of course, assume that, subject to a limited budget and given (fixed) market prices, the individual consumer makes his or her choice of the bundle of quantities of goods by choosing that bundle that maximizes utility[6] as expressed on an indifference map. All sorts of assumptions are made about the nature of the indifference map. For example, it is assumed that all indifference curves are strictly convex to this origin[7] and that more is always better than less (i.e., non-satiation is assumed or that there does not exist a 'bliss point'). The point here is that the indifference map is an idea imposed on the situation by the economic model builder – it is not nor needs to be a description of psychologically given and known preferences despite what textbooks seem to presume. It need only be what the individual *consumer assumes* to be facing – after all, the consumer

6 Textbooks say if one bundle is preferred to another we can simply say the preferred bundle provides more utility. Utility in this case is just an ordinal measure of relative preference, not a cardinal measure – moreover, this is all that is required to discuss maximization.

7 Which means that if one draws a straight line between any two points on the same indifference curve, all points on the line (not including the two end points) will always be better.

cannot possibly know empirically since that would require tasting all possible bundles and that would take an infinite number of taste tests. In effect, in our characterization of the consumer's choice, we need only assume that this map is what the consumer thinks his or her preferences are, such that, as noted earlier, if as a test the individual were to taste points left and right of the point along the budget line, he or she will perceive that utility goes down [see Boland 2003, pp. 137–9]. If this map is really strictly convex as assumed, then the individual will return to the original choice as it must be the maximum as the model builder's assumed map was intended to indicate.[8]

The analogy here is that the game theoretic model builder makes assumptions analogous to the strict convexity or non-satiation which are not assertions about what the player would actually face in the real world of the game (or the 'physical events', as Rubinstein put it), but only about the player's perception (or theory) of the game, just as the *consumer's presumption* of an indifference map guides the choice of an optimizing bundle and is thus modeled by the consumer theorist. In effect, the consumer and the individual game player are both seen to be black boxes and the consumer theorist and the game theorist are building models of those black boxes. They are not building models of the physical world that the consumer or the individual player will necessarily encounter. So, when discussing the knowledge of the players, we are usually not talking about what philosophers call 'justified true knowledge' (or true 'beliefs', as one game theorist put it [see Binmore 2011, p. 248]) but the player's conjectural knowledge – that is, their assumed knowledge, their theory of what they will encounter in the real world.

8 Another analogy might be, as briefly discussed at the end of Chapter 2, Clower's 'Ignorant Monopolist', who makes assumptions about the market's demand curve that happen to be false and interprets the information provided by the market incorrectly such that the monopolist ends up thinking it is maximizing profit – because at that point the assumed marginal revenue curve equals the known marginal cost curve – but is actually not maximizing profit because the true market's marginal revenue curve is not equal to marginal cost. For more on this, see Clower [1959] and Boland [2003, part VI].

4

On the purpose and limitations of game-theoretic models

> Harsanyi and Selten [1988] embarked on a project to find conditions that would plausibly select a unique noncooperative equilibrium point to be the solution to any matrix game. Central to this approach was the acceptance of ... [John] Nash's [1951] formal concept of a noncooperative equilibrium as the central necessary property of any solution.
>
> The viewpoint espoused here is that the search for a unique noncooperative equilibrium solution to all games poses many interesting philosophical problems in an abstract world inhabited by abstract von Neumann game players with unlimited intelligence and perception and no passions or personality traits. These players act in an institution free world where context is implicitly accounted for in the matrix game or the extensive form of the game. Unfortunately, as a portrayal of human decision-making it fails to appreciate the fundamental limitations in attempting to portray an open evolving system where the dynamics are context dependent and the institutions of any society are the carriers of process.
>
> Martin Shubik [2012, p. 2]

The obstacle facing anyone who wishes to discuss any limitations of using game theory to build economic models or even criticize game theory or game-theoretic models is the bifurcation of the proponents. On the one hand, we have the economists who are building game-theoretic models in the hopes that they can overcome one of the short-comings of both Marshallian partial-equilibrium analysis, which looks only at the behaviour of singular, price-taking individuals who are just minding their own business, and those who complain about Walrasian general-equilibrium models, which do not recognize the diversity in an economy or the interaction between individuals beyond buying and selling in the markets. On the other hand, we have the mathematics-oriented game theorists who lead the way in game-theoretic analysis and who, regardless of realism, are willing to assume anything that helps them construct their proofs or find solutions for their equilibrium models. Most of the critical questions I discussed at the end of

Chapter 3 are the result of these mathematics-oriented assumptions. This chapter will focus on whether the mathematical devices and assumptions that have been invented to answer those questions are as useful as game theorists think or as limited as some critical economic model builders think.

One persistent problem usually ignored by early game-theoretic models concerns where the rules come from or simply the presumption that all players know the rules. As Kreps observes [1990, p. 129 (emphasis in original)]:

> For the most part, game-theoretic analyses take the rules as given and proceed from there. There have been some analyses in which, in early stages of 'game', players choose rules that will be in force in later stages. Analyses of the entry-deterring monopolist in which the monopolist in the first period takes concrete actions that affect the conditions of second period competition can be viewed in this fashion. . . . But despite such analyses, I think it safe to say that *game-theoretic analyses in economics tend to take the rules of the game too much for granted, without asking where the rules come from. And they do not consider very well whether the rules that prevail are influenced by outcomes.*

As an aside, it might be noted that I have been frequently quoting Kreps [1990], even though it has been more than twenty years since his book was first published. His book seemed to arrive at the end of a particularly productive period of work developing game theory for use in economics. Most of the theoretical work for applying game theory to economics today concerns the problems and questions that Kreps presented at the end of his book, some of which were discussed in the previous chapter. It might be said that almost all of what has been done since his 1990 discussion are the *ad hoc* attempts to solve the problems he identified. Rather than address the details of these attempts here, I will be discussing the broad issues such as those raised by Kreps and the others who recognized that there are limitations to how much game theory can assist in economic analysis or who recognize the need to try to overcome these limitations.

4.1. Dealing with the knowledge of game players

> The common knowledge assumption underlies all of game theory and much of economic theory. Whatever be the model under discussion, whether complete or incomplete information, consistent or inconsistent, repeated or one-shot, cooperative or non-cooperative, the model itself must be assumed common knowledge; otherwise the model is insufficiently specified, and the analysis incoherent.
>
> Robert Aumann [1987, p. 473]

> Without intending any disrespect to the authors, I believe that there is little of genuine significance to be learned from any of the literature that applies various formal methods to backward-induction problems – even when the authors find their way to conclusions that I believe to be correct. It seems to me that all the *analytical* issues relating to backward induction lie entirely on the surface. Inventing fancy formalisms serves only to confuse matters. . . .
>
> Formalists will object, saying that an argument is open to serious evaluation only after it has been properly formalized.
>
> Kenneth Binmore [1997, pp. 23–4]

> Knowledge as commitment to a model is impervious to revision within the model in question. It then becomes trivially true that common knowledge of rationality implies backward induction. No history of play can disturb the initial assumption that there is common knowledge of rationality, because knowledge is not subject to revision.
>
> Kenneth Binmore [2011, p. 259]

Kenneth Binmore [1996, 1997] has been criticizing the use of two common assumptions by game-theoretic model builders for almost twenty years. They are the equilibrium refinement assumptions of 'Common Knowledge of Rationality' (henceforth, CKR) and so-called backward induction. In particular he has argued that the use of the latter assumption is denied by the former assumption. His argument is significant given that the Nobel-Prize-winning game theorist Robert Aumann repeatedly argues that, in finite games of perfect information, CKR implies backward induction [Aumann 1995, 1996a, 1996b, 1998]. Both cannot be right.

Although I promised to keep our eye on the Forest and not to be examining Trees, we do need to be careful when discussing issues of knowledge and assumptions involving knowledge. This is because so many problematic philosophical issues get assumed away, and according to the critics this is a major source of difficulty. So, before examining the notions of CKR and backward induction, we need to consider one of the 'Trees' – the finite length centipede game, which commonly uses these assumptions about knowledge and analysis. This is the type of dynamic game for which the extensive form game is appropriate (see Figure 4.1) – with this form, players are considered

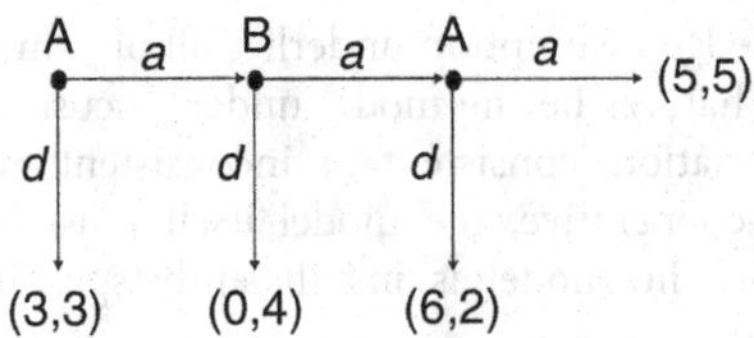

Figure 4.1 A centipede game

to be making moves in turns. At each 'node' of this game, the player must choose between two options, option *a* (across), which continues the game one more turn, and option *d* (down), which promptly ends the game. At each A node, the player A considers what the other player, B, will do if A chooses 'across'. To consider this, the model builder usually would assume that A knows both that B knows the game (namely, its sequence of options and corresponding payoffs) and that B is 'rational', that is, B will always choose the best option available. Such mutual knowledge is assumed when B makes a choice between down or across at a node. This assumption of mutual knowledge about the respective players' knowledge and motivation is what is called CKR.

The common way to determine the equilibrium solution is to use 'backward induction', which has nothing to do with the induction discussed by philosophers or economic methodologists. Instead, it is a variation on what mathematicians call induction. For example, mathematicians might assess the sequence of values determined by a given function for a series 1, 2, 3, 4 . . . N, N+1. *Mathematical induction is an assumption.* It *assumes* that 'if the function gives a true value for 1 and gives a true value for N, then it must give a true value for N+1'. In this way, mathematicians simply assume away what philosophers call the 'Problem of Induction' (which I will discuss in Chapter 11). It is the result of asking whether one can ever prove a purely inductive inference (scientifically or otherwise). As I noted in earlier chapters, this problem was raised in the eighteenth century by Hume, who in effect observed that one cannot use deductive logic to prove a strictly universal statement (e.g., '*all* swans are white') using *only* singular observations (e.g., 'I observed a white swan yesterday in New York and another last week in Chicago'). This problem will come up again when I discuss how philosophers see questions such as this in terms of model building in general. What is important for game-theoretic model builders to understand is that mathematical induction works only by assuming it works. That is, it is not a proof, just an assumption. Backward induction works in a similar way by ignoring matters of realism. In other words, backward induction is just another mathematical tool – one that seems to have been invented or at least introduced for use in economics by John von Neumann and Oskar Morgenstern [1953, p. 116] in their famous book, *Theory of Games and Economic Behavior*.

In a finite length centipede game, backward induction begins by considering what either player would do at the next-to-last node – for now, let us say it is player B as in Figure 4.1. Given the assumption of CKR, game theorists simply ignore the philosopher's Problem of Induction and say that

B knows that A will choose the best available option at the last A node (which in Figure 4.1 is down since 6 is better than 5). As I will discuss, there is never any explanation as to how such knowledge is acquired – instead, for example, Aumann [1998] specifies 'perfect information' hence presumably as there is no need to explain. If at the last A node, A does choose down, B would get only 2, but at the immediately prior node, if B instead plays down, B gets 4. Being 'rational', as CKR presumes, B will choose down at the B node. With this in mind, A at the first node considers what B would do at the next B node – and as just noted, B would choose down. If B chooses down then A would get 0, but if A at the first node chooses down, A gets 3. So, by this backward method of analysis, it follows that A would end the game at the first opportunity – namely, at the first node. In other words, a finite length extensive centipede game unravels once the next to last move is considered.

Binmore's challenge was rather simple. To even consider the next to last move, at least one prior move must have been contrary to the presumption of CKR. If both players are 'rational', the first player would play down so there is no point to ever consider subsequent moves as they will never happen – as they are precluded by player A's first move. So, according to Binmore, CKR cannot be used to *justify* backward induction analysis for determining the solution to the finite length centipede game.

Contrary to Binmore's challenge, Aumann [1998] argues that CKR is consistent with backward induction in the centipede games with perfect information, and he thus sees no need to abandon the assumption of common knowledge when determining the solution by using the assumption of backward induction. Binmore and Aumann have gone back and forth with this and neither seemed willing to budge. So, Binmore [2011] suggests that maybe they do not mean the same thing when talking about knowledge. Perhaps, given Aumann's definition of what constitutes knowledge, Aumann does not need to abandon his claim that CKR assures the backward induction result (viz, the game ends at first node). Binmore suggests that Aumann's concept of knowing is not what economists or most philosophers would usually presume. Specifically, Binmore claims that Aumann's concept is that knowledge means a commitment to the axioms of a model, whereas Binmore thinks economists see knowledge as beliefs subject to reconsideration.[1] This is an important distinction

[1] Most philosophers go even further to claim that knowledge is 'justified' belief – that is, tentatively proven but open to revision should events contradict the proof.

whenever facing a counter-factual move that implies 'irrationality', such as would be the case in the centipede game if the first player chose across.

This, nevertheless, does raise the question for those who might still agree with Aumann: why would the second player not abandon CKR following the first player's 'irrational' across move? The classic *ad hoc* response since Reinhard Selten [1975] is to invoke an 'off-model' story to explain away the erroneous choice as being the result of a 'trembling hand', and thus there is no need to abandon CKR – that is, no need to abandon the commitment to the axioms of game theory. But those who might still agree with either Binmore or Kreps and say that if trembling hands are going to be part of the game, then the rules of the game need to be reconsidered. Perhaps, instead, the players' knowledge should be considered subjective probability-based as would be the case with so-called 'Bayesian rationality' such that rather than maximizing utilities (i.e., payoffs), the players maximize their expected utilities in accordance with the axioms suggested by Leonard Savage [1954]. But going this probability-based route to avoid the contradiction that Binmore identifies does seem to abandon the commitment to axioms that he claims Aumann has assumed when recognizing the knowledge of the players.

4.1.1. Concepts of knowledge used in economic model building

> Overall, game theory accomplishes only two tasks: It builds models based on intuition and uses deductive arguments based on mathematical knowledge. Deductive arguments cannot by themselves be used to discover truths about the world. Missing are data describing the processes of reasoning adopted by the players when they analyze a game. Thus, if a game in the formal sense has any coherent interpretation, it has to be understood to include explicit data on the player's reasoning processes. Alternatively, we should add more detail to the description of these reasoning procedures.
>
> Ariel Rubinstein [1991, p. 923]

> A lesson for which there will be few takers is that mathematics is often best left on the shelf until the philosophy of a problem has been properly sorted out.
>
> Kenneth Binmore [2011, p. 259]

Clearly, the problem of how to incorporate knowledge explicitly in game-theoretic models is a problem that Binmore thinks we should properly sort out before jumping in to create mathematical devices to refine the search for the needed equilibrium. And I agree with Binmore, so let us try now to sort out the question of what we should mean whenever we wish to recognize knowledge explicitly in game-theoretic models. Binmore [2011] is a good place to start. So, again, in contrast to 'knowledge as commitment to a model or set of axioms' [p. 248], which Binmore attributes to Aumann's view of CKR, Binmore thinks we should also consider 'knowledge as belief', which he says 'seems to be the default theoretical position both in economics and philosophy' [ibid.]. While Binmore compares this alternative view of knowledge to Socrates, the interpretation he recreates is more like what philosophers of the 1930s advocated, not Socrates. All that it has in common with Socrates is that, for Socrates, knowledge is always open to reconsideration and hence not a commitment that puts the realism of the axioms of game theory beyond question.

While most philosophers connect knowledge with beliefs, I think such a connection is misplaced. A belief involves an attitude toward criticism or counter-factuals. A belief as opposed to a conjecture is knowledge that an individual puts beyond question at least from anyone else's challenge. What is important for Binmore is the contrast between knowledge-as-commitment (to axioms or prior assumptions) with what I will call knowledge-as-conjecture (which is thus always open to criticism) to stress that the latter allows for reconsideration and possible acceptance of counter-examples but the former does not. And again, this is important for the centipede game in order to deal with what would be the first player's unexpected choice of across instead of down.

While the Socratic view of knowledge (specifically, the view Plato illustrates in the early Socratic dialogues) is clearly contrary to the knowledge-as-commitment view that Binmore attributes to Aumann, the Socratic view does not endorse the philosophers' view that Binmore discusses – the view of 'knowledge traditionally being defined as justified true belief' [ibid.]. Too often philosophers think one's knowledge cannot be considered true unless it is 'justified' – that is, unless one can give sufficient reasons to claim one's knowledge is true.[2] Philosophers aside, I think Binmore just wants us to recognize that the reasons offered for any justification are always open to question so that the justification is always tentative rather than axiomatic.

Until Alfred Einstein succeeded in removing the common belief that Newton's physics was true because it was inductively proven, scientific method had been always considered to be an application of scientific induction. But Newton's physics is not true (e.g., his theory of mechanics is incapable of

2 To the contrary, it is easy for one's knowledge to be true (empirically, of course) even if one cannot prove it. The classic example is the claim that 'all ravens are black' can be true even though, as a matter of quantificational logic, one could never prove that it is true empirically (i.e., by observing ravens). This will be discussed again in Chapter 9.

explaining simple things like the movement of a compass needle [see Einstein and Infeld 1938/61]!). Recognizing this thus challenges the reliability of an induction-based scientific method. Unfortunately, rather than give up on the idea that the inductive scientific method is reliable, philosophers in the 1930s moved the goal posts and accepted probabilities as an acceptable measure of the truth of ideas or beliefs.

Before going on, I need to return to the matter of what *economists* too often mean by 'induction', which I explained in Chapter 2[3] – specifically, it is not what philosophers mean, that is, not what Binmore calls 'scientific induction'. Today, when economic model builders talk about induction, they usually are merely trying to distinguish an empirical argument from a purely deductive one.[4] That is, they only mean that some empirical observations are being used in the argument. They do not mean a justification of a belief using only observations, as was once thought to be the basis of Isaac Newton's physics. So, I want to be clear that when I am discussing induction here, I am always talking about induction in the sense of a method of proving or justifying a knowledge claim[5] and never just that empirical data is recognized (since, of course, using data is also possible in any deductive argument). And before going on even further, while it is important to recognize the two views of knowledge that Binmore [2011] discusses, it is also important to point out Socrates' third view that claims of knowledge must always be actively challenged by looking for counter-examples – this is a main message of the *Apology*, Plato's report of Socrates's defense at his trial for 'impiety'. For the Socrates of Plato's early dialogues, the pursuit of knowledge was never looking for justifications but for testing one's knowledge by looking for counter-examples (for Socrates, it was to find a man who was wiser than Socrates and thereby refute the knowledge of the Delphi who claimed Socrates was the wisest of men). In Socratic terms, one learns only from criticism – or more specifically, one learns by discovering errors in one's knowledge.

The importance of Socrates's view of knowledge for Binmore [2011] is that it opens the door to recognizing uncertain knowledge (contrary to knowledge-as-commitment) and thus the need to deal with uncertainty – particularly, the

3 See note 5 in that chapter.

4 Pure deduction comes in two forms: either a tautology (which is true regardless of the meaning of the non-logical words) or an analytically true statement (which is true only by virtue of the definition of the non-logical words) – for more on the economists' use of induction, see Boland [2008a].

5 That is, I am definitely not suggesting that true knowledge can be induced from empirical observations beyond the specific (non-general) knowledge of the observations themselves.

uncertainty caused by the event of a counter-factual. Among economic model builders, there are ways to recognize the uncertainty of a decision maker's knowledge. The simplest way is to place a probability on one's knowledge claim, such as one would do for placing a bet. A more sophisticated version is expected utility analysis, as was used by von Neumann and Morgenstern. Others today are more interested in what Binmore calls Bayesian rationality, which I briefly review next.

4.1.2. Bayesian rationality and uncertain CKR

As some readers will know, Bayes's theorem is an equation that simply says the probability of a general event *B* given the particular event *A* equals the probability of event *A* given the event *B* multiplied by the probability of *B* and divided by the probability of event *A*. Naive proponents of Bayesian rationality claim that Bayes's theorem says that one can always calculate the probability of event *B* given the event *A* from the probability of event *A* given the event *B* in this manner.[6] And, although Binmore does not mention this, since Bayesian rationality involves going from particulars to generals, this is sometimes even claimed to be a solution to the Humean Problem of Induction [e.g., Lindley 1987, p. 207]. But it is not.

If it were necessarily true that all uncertainty must be expressed as a probability, as many 1930s philosophers decided, and if one denies the possibility of the probability of the truth status of one's knowledge being 1.00, then one could accept the conditional probability provided by Bayes's theorem as the best we can do. However, to do so is, at best, merely to accept the view that substitutes probabilities for the truth status of a knowledge claim. At worst, it is to accept a vacuous, uninformative theory of learning [see Albert 2001]. As I explain in Boland [2003, chapter 12], one would have to be willing to abandon the benefits of ordinary logic whenever one accepts the probability substitute for the proven or justified truth status that induction is erroneously believed to provide.[7] To avoid confusing uncertainty with probabilities, one needs merely to recognize that uncertainty means the

[6] Or formally, where P(·) stands for 'probability of' and | stands for 'given',

$$P(B|A) = P(A|B) \cdot P(B)/P(A)$$

[7] Specifically, to use ordinary logic to prove a statement, one relies on the three axioms of logic, and in particular any proof must use only premises that are either true or false, as would be allowed particularly by the axiom of the excluded middle. Specifically, the truth status of any statement forming a premise of a logically valid proof cannot be a probability between 0 and 1 and thus probabilities are precluded (see Kneale and Kneale [1962]). Note, this does not preclude statements about probabilities; it just refers to the statements themselves.

lack of knowledge – or perhaps, just not knowing whether one's conjectural knowledge is strictly true – whereas probabilities are for assessing risk, such as the probability of rolling dice and obtaining a pair of sixes where the probability of such an event is known for fair dice. Unfortunately, many economic model builders are stuck in the 1930s and feeling the philosophers' need to restore the belief in science and inductive scientific method for justifying any claims to knowledge.

Binmore is careful about this as he is only interested in presenting a view of knowledge that is contrary to what mathematicians are willing to conveniently assume for the purposes of the mathematics of game theory rather than the purposes of conforming to common understanding of such things as knowledge and any learning from observable evidence such as counterfactuals. It is most important to recognize that Socratic learning is not a view to which one can apply Bayes's theorem. About using Bayes's theorem as a way to use observations to update the probability of player B's knowledge claim about player A after observing an 'irrational' move by A, Binmore says [2011, p. 258]:

> Replacing knowledge-as-belief by knowledge-as-commitment allows the problem of scientific induction to be freed from the (naive) claim that it can be reduced to the kind of Bayesian updating that follows from honoring Savage's consistency axioms .... Scientific revolutions arise when scientists find that the tensions involved in explaining away anomalies in the data with off-model stories become too great to allow them to maintain their commitment to a particular model. They then throw away their old model and adopt a new model – freely admitting as they do so that they are being inconsistent. Bayesian updating has no place in such a revolution. It needs to be seen instead merely as a humdrum updating of [player B's] beliefs about the parameters of a model to whose structure he is currently committed.

Clearly then, Bayesian updating would not be easily used to explain the replacement of Newtonian physics by that of Einstein. It may also be a

For readers unfamiliar with the so-called axioms or canons of logic, note that a proof is a conjunction of explicit premises, and it can be valid only if the statements forming the premises of the proof satisfy all three axioms of logic: the axiom of 'identity' (which says that, for example, the X in one equation of a model must refer to the same thing whenever that X appears in any other equation of that model), the axiom of 'non-contradiction' (which says any statement or premise of a logically valid argument cannot be both true and false), and the axiom of the 'excluded middle' (which says that every statement or premise must be true or false, and which, together with the axiom of non-contradiction, says every premise of a logically valid proof is true or false but not both). To see the importance of the axiom of the excluded middle, for example, it can be noted that without this axiom, one could never provide an indirect proof.

drawback for relying on Bayesian rationality to seemingly operationalize knowledge-as-belief. But for Binmore's purposes, recognizing that Aumann and likely most game-theoretic model builders consider CKR axiomatic (i.e., beyond revision by the game players) makes it is easy to see why one might think backward induction and CKR are not inconsistent. Of course, many critics think using mathematics to build economic models – particularly, game-theoretic models – should still employ a realistic view of knowledge; otherwise, such critics will continue to see the inconsistency. Perhaps the critics would be happy if the model builders just specify how the players learn what they need to know just to play the game whenever the model depends on the achievement of an equilibrium.[8]

There has been little discussion of how the players learn what they need to know, particularly when it comes to explaining why CKR becomes so common. There have been some recent efforts to suggest that there is a role for social norms and institutions, but if they matter, surely it would require a modification of the structure of a non-cooperative game theory. Learning remains a problem for game-theoretic model builders, particularly with extensive form games. Some model builders allow players to count on the other player remembering that player's past moves. They call this 'forward induction'. This is not 'induction' in the usual philosophical or mathematical sense, but induction in the sense of *inducing* behaviour in the other player. For example, in a centipede game, where the first player does not drop out, as backward induction might predict, instead chooses to continue because there is a later move that the second player can make where both would be better off. One, however, can still think of this as expecting the second player to learn inductively from the first player's moves.

Even if game-theoretic model builders are ignoring the philosophers' Problem of Induction involved in how one player is assumed to know what the other player's next move will be based on past moves, few seem even to be concerned with how the players learn the rules of the game before it is played or how they know the other player's payoffs.[9] At best, the assumption of CKR can be seen to simply assume away the Problem of Induction. And those game-theoretic model builders more interested in the convenience of mathematical devices will simply follow Aumann by invoking some version of his view of scientific methodology such as this [1985, pp. 36 and 42]:

8 Interestingly, Friedrich Hayek [1937] made a plea for this as a necessity for any equilibrium-based explanation.

9 Although it could be pointed out that there are recent efforts to deal with these problems with players' knowledge by building 'level-k' and cognitive hierarchy models – see Crawford and Iriberri [2007] and Crawford et al. [forthcoming].

> [W]e cannot expect game and economic theory to be descriptive in the same sense that physics or astronomy are. Rationality is only one of several factors affecting human behavior; no theory based on this one factor alone can be expected to yield reliable predictions. . . .
>
> We strive to make statements that, while perhaps not falsifiable, do have some universality, do express some insight of a general nature; we discipline our minds through the medium of the mathematical model; and at their best, our disciplines do have beauty, simplicity, force and relevance.

4.1.3. Bounded rationality and imperfect CKR

In the last chapter of Kreps's 1990 book, he suggests [pp. 150–1]:

> We must come to grips with the behaviour of individual agents who are boundedly rational and who learn from the past . . . if we are to provide answers to questions like: When is equilibrium analysis appropriate? How do players select among equilibria?

Bounded rationality is usually attributed to Herbert Simon's 1950s alternative to assuming decision makers successfully maximize, as microeconomic theorists of his day uncritically assumed. Simon's main complaint about maximization was that it requires more knowledge and cognitive ability than is humanly possible [Simon 1947]. Instead of maximizing, Simon said we should assume decision makers are 'satisficers' whereby the individual, rather than seeking the absolute maximum profit or utility, decides on what would be a minimum acceptable level of profit or utility which is, of course, acceptably less than the absolute maximum. Thus, rather than an individual's choice being predictably unique, all that we could expect is that the choice is bounded between the largest and smallest satisfactory choice options. Simon originally called this 'approximate' rationality [1955, p. 114].[10]

If game-theoretic model builders assume satisficing behaviour and thereby bounded rationality, they give up the possibility of uniqueness and thereby limit the usefulness of universality in the process of explaining the behaviour of the decision makers that populate economic models. Given the original pursuit of selecting equilibria in game-theoretic models, it is not clear what

[10] Since Simon's day, there is at least one other alternative, usually attributed to Sargent [see Sent 1997]. This version is based on the recognition that even if a decision maker could lay out all of the reasons for making a choice so as to form an argument to justify the choice, given that one cannot be sure the reasons are 100% true, the justification is more probabilistic than exact. Boundedness in this case is seen as an allegedly maximizing choice that is reasonably and acceptably bounded by, say, a standard deviation of the true maximum.

such a bounded explanation accomplishes. Moreover, how would we know that such an explanation is false or when to say some choice amounts to a counter-example? Unless we know what the player's minimally acceptable payoff is, we have no idea when a choice is out of bounds. That is, what constitutes a counter-example such that we would be able to conclude that the explanation is false? What part of the explanation is false? Is the player doing something other than satisficing? Perhaps the player has a lower standard of a satisfactory level of payoff. Unless the model is explicit in what is assumed to be the minimum level of satisfactory payoff, it is not clear what is being assumed with bounded rationality. Simon [1955] suggests one obstacle to maximization is the cost of collecting the information necessary to assure that the choice is rational. But I think invoking cost here to justify less than exact maximization is inconsistent. How does the player know the cost of information has been minimized? Of course, the player could be merely satisficing when accepting that the cost does not exceed a maximum satisfactory level of costs. So, again, we can ask, how do we know when this explanation of cost minimization is false? And again, how does the player decide what is the satisfactory level of information costs? It is not clear to me that the assumption of bounded rationality actually solves the problem as intended, although it may be mathematically convenient, however unfalsifiable.

4.1.4. Expected payoffs and uncertain knowledge

As I mentioned earlier in this chapter, moving the goal post in the 1930s to accommodate the recognition that induction is unreliable,[11] philosophers and economists accepted the notion that one should be able to place a probability assessment on the truth status of a statement or theory. Again, according to this moved goal post, theories are not to be considered true or false, but only better or worse – such that the better one is the one with the highest probability assessment.

One might wonder, where did economists get such an idea that probabilities could be substituted for a 'true' or 'false' truth status? Apparently, this was the result of a clever move by the young mathematician and economic theorist Frank Ramsey in the late 1920s. Ramsey [1926/31] showed that choices expressed as being between gambles can be made to yield measures of one's preferences (subjective utilities) and one's 'beliefs'

[11] As shown by the failure of Newton's physics to explain simple things like a compass needle.

(subjective probabilities). Using gambles to measure subjective assessments of probabilities was employed by von Neumann and Morgenstern [1953] and is the major source for arguments of this type among game-theoretic model builders. Savage [1954] also employed Ramsey's demonstration to make it part of his view of decision making under uncertainty.

Interestingly, Savage wished to avoid making assumptions about desires and beliefs (both deemed to be psychological attributes) and instead, like Paul Samuelson did with his 'revealed preference' theory, Savage posited a set of conditions which, if met, allow the utility-maximization to be the basis for explaining a decision maker's choices and yet to be 'bleached of all psychological content' [Hollis and Sugden 1993, p. 7]. Rather than assuming a conscious maximizing decision process, for the purpose of model building, Savage only requires that the choices made be consistent with his posited conditions – one of which is that whenever the decision maker considers one event subjectively more probable than a second event, the decision maker prefers to bet on it rather than the second. Placing such a bet reveals the decision maker's preference, much as Ramsey suggested.

The result of Savage's analysis is that, by considering choice to be a matter of ranking options and then choosing the best, knowing the decision maker's psychologically given preferences is unnecessary. For game-theoretic model builders, by using Savage's approach to dealing with uncertainty, rationality *appears* to be only a matter of logical consistency – at least for the model builder but doubtfully for any real decision maker. And like the continuing problem, there is no attempt to explain how decision makers make such choices.[12]

Amazingly, the notion that expected utility can be a basis for explaining decision making begs to be critically examined. With few exceptions [see Davidson 1991 and Lawson 1988], hardly anyone seems to recognize a problem here. Specifically, why do economic theorists in general, and game-theoretic model builders in particular, see no reason to question the assumption that all decision makers treat a choice as a gamble when facing uncertainty and thereby presume uncertainty always requires probabilities to be used.[13] The basic problem is simply that economic model builders confuse uncertainty with risk despite the cautioning of both Frank Knight [1921] and John Maynard Keynes [1937]. Simply put, probabilities are not for uncertainty; probabilities are for gambling, which involves known risk.

[12] Dissatisfaction with the limits of Savage's approach has led some to try to get away from expected utility theory [e.g., La Mura 2009].

[13] For more about the methodology behind all of this, see Boland [2003, chapter 8].

4.2. Are game-theoretic models as limited as critics claim?

> The ambitious claim that game theory will provide a unified foundation for all social science seems misplaced to us. There is a variety of problems with such a claim. . . . Some are associated with the assumptions of the theory . . . some come from the inferences which are often drawn from these assumptions . . . and yet others come from the failure . . . to generate determinate predictions of what 'rational' agents would, or should, do in important social interactions.
>
> At root we suspect that the major problem is . . . that people appear to be more complexly motivated than game theory's instrumental model allows and that a part of that greater complexity comes from their social location.
>
> Shaun Hargreaves Heap and Yanis Varoufakis [1995, p. 260]

> The ambitious claim that game theory will provide a unified foundation for all social science seemed misplaced to us ten years ago. . . It still does.
>
> Hargreaves Heap and Varoufakis [2004, p. 302]

> The development of increasingly stronger refinements by imposing *ad hoc* criteria incrementally was a preliminary to more systematic development. Eventually, one wants to identify decision-theoretic criteria that suffice as axioms to characterize refinements. [There are] two groups of refinements . . . [that] approach this problem differently. Those that consider perturbations . . . [that] are mathematical artifacts used to identify refinements with desirable properties, but they are not intrinsic to a fundamental theory of rational decision making in multi-person situations. Those in the other group directly impose decision-theoretic criteria. . . Their ultimate aim is to characterize refinements axiomatically. But so far none has obtained an ideal refinement of the Nash equilibria.
>
> Srihari Govindan and Robert Wilson [2008, p. 12]

Most dedicated game-theoretic model builders are unlikely to follow the advice from the various critics to give up forward induction, backward induction, Bayesian rationality, bounded rationality or CKR. Instead, they will see whatever problems noted as just mathematical puzzles to be solved. It can easily be argued that the primary reason for this is that game theory is nothing more than a mathematical tool of analysis. With the possible exceptions of Aumann's [1985] musings about the purpose for game theory and Cristina Bicchieri's [1993] concerns about what she calls the 'paradoxes of rationality' and now Binmore's [2011] attempt to understand Aumann's attachment to backward induction, few serious attempts have been made by game theorists to address the methodological problems of explanation. When game theory is put to test as a mode of either explanation or description of observed behaviour, few critical game theorists have been satisfied with the results.

4.2.1. Game theory and methodological individualism

Non-cooperative games have been the major focus of my discussion here, so what about cooperative games? At a basic level, what separates games into these two types is determined by whether prior commitments (including promises, agreements, threats and side payments) are enforceable. In a non-cooperative game, all players have to make their decisions based solely on their knowledge of the game. There is either no communication with the other player or no way to enforce any prior agreements. In this sense, non-cooperative games are fully compatible with the methodological individualism that most economic theorists take for granted. Methodological individualism is about what constitutes an adequate explanation in social life.[14] Specifically, as I noted in Chapter 1, methodological individualism is a methodological commitment of the model builder that says *things do not decide, only individuals decide*. In textbooks about market economics, decision makers make their decisions autonomously, knowing only the going prices and the Nature-given constraints (including Nature-given productive and learning abilities, resource availabilities, etc.). For game-theoretic models, this means that only those aspects of a game that are Nature-given do not need to be explained. In non-cooperative games, any Nature-given aspects are built into the structure of the game. Still, anything involving non-natural (i.e., social) aspects has to be explained. But as Martin Hollis and Robert Sugden have observed [1993, p. 32],

> The attempt to view social life as strategic interaction is proving immensely fertile yet disturbingly prone to paradox. Game theory provides an elegant, universal logic of practical reason, offering much to anyone whose notion of rationality is instrumental and whose view of the social world is individualist. Yet paradoxes beset its account even of coordination, trust and the keeping of promises.

4.2.2. Game theory rules versus social commitments

> Although matrix games (using the classic work of Luce and Raiffa [1957]), and the study of choice behavior in such games, provided an elegant means of demonstrating equilibrium concepts and elements of conflict and cooperation in markets, I never viewed these austere environments as constituting the corpus of experimental economics. To reduce market competition, under the many institutional forms in which trade occurs, to a two-person (or larger) matrix of interdependent profit payoffs does much violence to the economics of exchange. It is a wise firm indeed that can identify its own cost, demand, and profit function,

14 I have explained the methodological role and nature of methodological individualism in chapter 2 of Boland [2003].

> let alone reduce these, and the actions of a competitor to a bimatrix game of payoffs (see Shubik [1959, p. 17]). Also the normal form game matrix trivializes the concept of an institution and the language of the market by reducing the distinctive effects of the environment and the institution to their net combined effect on payoffs.
>
> Vernon Smith [1992, p. 275]

Cooperative games present an interesting dilemma for game-theoretic model builders. Whenever commitments are enforceable, they should be treated as a fixed part of the game's structure and its rules. Alternatively, since commitments involve conscious involvement of the players, should they be explained as something chosen by the players – that is, something for which each player is maximizing in a methodological-individualist manner? Simply put, socially created commitments, enforcement rules, or rules of the game are not Nature-given. Yet, there does not seem to be much effort on the part of the game-theoretic model builders to explain where the rules and commitments come from. As I have been stressing, the main reason for this is simply that almost all game theorists are interested only in the mathematics and mathematical devices of the game. Plausibility or realism of any mathematical device is, as Aumann says, only of secondary interest. More and more the issue of plausibility is a growing concern among critics and even among dedicated game-theoretic model builders. Failure to deal with questions of realism or at least of plausibility will remain the primary limitation for game-theoretic models.

PART II

EMPIRICAL MODELS

5

Microeconomic versus macroeconomic empirical model building

[T]here are several aspects of the quantitative approach to economics, and no single one of these aspects, taken by itself, should be confounded with econometrics. Thus, econometrics is by no means the same as economic statistics. Nor is it identical with what we call general economic theory, although a considerable portion of this theory has a definitely quantitative character. Nor should econometrics be taken as synonymous with the application of mathematics to economics. Experience has shown that each of these three view-points, that of statistics, economic theory, and mathematics, is a necessary, but not by itself a sufficient, condition for a real understanding of the quantitative relations in modern economic life. It is the *unification* of all three that is powerful. And it is this unification that constitutes econometrics.

Ragnar Frisch [1933b, p. 2]

Some of the most fundamental economic facts ... already present themselves to our observation as quantities made numerical by life itself. They carry meaning only by virtue of their numerical character. There would be movement even if we were unable to turn it into measurable quantity, but there cannot be prices independent of the numerical expression of every one of them, and of definite numerical relations among all of them.

Econometrics is nothing but the explicit recognition of this rather obvious fact, and the attempt to face the consequences of it. We might even go so far as to say that by virtue of it every economist is an econometrician whether he wants to be or not, provided he deals with this sector of our science and not, for example, with the history of organization of enterprise, the cultural aspects of economic life, economic motive, the philosophy of private property, and so on. It is easy to understand why explicit recognition of this fact should have been so difficult, and why it has taken so long to come about.

Joseph Schumpeter [1933, pp. 5–6]

In order to draw inferences from data as described by econometric texts, it is necessary to make whimsical assumptions. The professional audience consequently and properly withholds belief until an inference is shown to be adequately insensitive to the choice of assumptions. The haphazard way we

> individually and collectively study the fragility of inferences leaves most of us unconvinced that any inference is believable.
>
> Edward Leamer [1983, pp. 43]

> Can we economists agree that it is extremely hard work to squeeze truths from our data sets and what we genuinely understand will remain uncomfortably limited? We need words in our methodological vocabulary to express the limits. We need sensitivity analyses to make those limits transparent. Those who think otherwise should be required to wear a scarlet-letter O around their necks, for 'overconfidence'.
>
> Edward Leamer [2010, pp. 22 and 39]

In Chapter 1, the discussion was about the differences between micro and macro *theoretical* models. Here the discussion will be about *empirical* models. The first question to consider is whether empirical models differ when they are about microeconomics rather than macroeconomics. Historically, there have been differences, of course. For fifty years or more, macroeconomics came in many different flavours which changed frequently until the 1990s. Before that, choosing a macroeconomic textbook to use in one's class was always a challenge. During those days, microeconomists found this situation humorous, given that microeconomics was a single viewpoint and had not changed during those fifty years. But while the view of macroeconomics in disarray may no longer be true, the view of a united microeconomics could also be based on an outdated view of empirical microeconomics. That is, today it is tempting to say that things may be reversed, as there are many varieties of microeconomics, yet when it comes to macro-econometric models, things are much more limited.

5.1. Empirical microeconomic model building

> In applied micro fields such as development, education, environmental economics, health, labor, and public finance, researchers seek real experiments where feasible, and useful natural experiments if real experiments seem (at least for a time) infeasible. In either case, a hallmark of contemporary applied microeconometrics is a focus on a conceptual framework that highlights specific sources of variation.
>
> Joshua Angrist and Jorn-Steffen Pischke [2010, p. 12]

Prior to the 1990s, the distinction between empirical macro and micro models was always considered fairly straightforward. Specifically, empirical models can usually be distinguished either by the differences in the empirical data being described or represented or by the differences in the questions addressed with the models. While some microeconomic theorists today may see clear distinctions between micro and macro, macroeconomic theorists often do not. I will return to macroeconomics later, for now let us look at what is considered 'empirical microeconomics'.

In one sense, for decades empirical or 'applied' microeconomics was distinguished by the data used. Empirical labour economics models were about explaining available data about the labour markets; empirical public finance models were are about explaining usually available governmental data; empirical family or household economic models were about explaining available survey or panel data; and so on. Apart from employing standard microeconomic theory to build the models, little else was common among the various sub-disciplines of microeconomics except possibly the use of econometrics, which, of course, was the common empirical way to address the data. Seemingly for decades, we would rarely see anyone referring to empirical microeconomics as a distinct field as it now is. So, given the history of both applied and theoretical microeconomics with its once separate sub-disciplines, one might wonder why so many academic economists now list 'empirical microeconomics' as their main research field.

To answer such a question we need to first consider the intended purpose for building microeconomic models in any of the diverse sub-fields. Is it just to explain observed data? If yes, would simple regressions be enough, or more importantly, would such regressions be reliable if such results are to be used to advise economic policy? Is it something that empirical macroeconomic models cannot do? As Joshua Angrist and Jörn-Steffen Pischke [2010] argue, unlike large macro models, empirical microeconomic models are intended to address questions of causality – the 'sources of variation' [p. 12]. But can empirical models based on the assumptions needed to build econometrics-based models do this? If any econometrics-based model depends on 'fragile' or 'whimsical' assumptions made for the convenience of econometrics, then, as Edward Leamer [1983] noted, if we are honest, the results are not usually reliable or convincing. If the purpose of building empirical microeconomic models is just for the sake of building a model to econometrically explain (i.e., 'fit') observed data, then perhaps anything goes. But if it is to identify the 'sources of variation' (i.e., causes), as Angrist and Pischke suggest, then there are issues of the logic embodied in one's model that limit what one can claim with one's model. They characterize this as a matter of research design. And research design depends heavily on the purpose for any model building exercise, and it is the research design that is usually the basis for the credibility of the results of the research.

If one chooses the scientific purpose for building an empirical model, one would think the research design would somehow involve experimentation – unless one is building a model for astronomy, of course. For most economists, it is difficult to imagine how one would ever conduct an experiment on an entire macro economy. Passive macro observations, even if deliberately obtained, produce data that is difficult to distinguish from the type of data one would use to build models of astronomy. But if one is building a model to understand the workings of a small sector of an economy or one particular market, it is conceivable that one could conduct an experiment. As Leamer recognized, what is needed is some sort of randomization. Angrist and Pischke [2010] talk about various examples of using randomized experiments to identify the causes in empirical microeconomic studies. The examples they discussed involved such things as the effect of smaller class sizes and the effectiveness of banning capital punishment. The point of their examples is that such research studies, if properly designed, can be not only reliable but also creditable and hence convincing. Whether this is the future of empirical microeconomic model building as a primary means of consolidating empirical microeconomic model building remains to be seen, but without such model building in microeconomics, criticism of data analysis cannot be ignored – such as David Hendry's [1980] accusation that empirical modeling seems more like astrology than science or Leamer's indictment of poorly applied econometrics. For now, I will postpone further discussion of experimental research in economics until Chapter 8, where the empirical microeconomics of behavioural and evolutionary game theory as well as experimental macroeconomics will also be considered.

5.2. Empirical macroeconomic model building

> Over the last three decades, macroeconomic theory and the practice of macroeconomics by economists have changed significantly – for the better. Macroeconomics is now firmly grounded in the principles of economic theory. These advances have not been restricted to the ivory tower. Over the last several decades, the United States and other countries have undertaken a variety of policy changes that are precisely what macroeconomic theory of the last 30 years suggests.
>
> V. V. Chari and Patrick J. Kehoe [2006, p. 3]

> While the early macroeconomists were engineers trying to solve practical problems, the macroeconomists of the past several decades have been more interested in developing analytic tools and establishing theoretical principles. These tools and principles, however, have been slow to find their way into applications. As the field of macroeconomics has evolved, one recurrent theme is the interaction – sometimes productive and sometimes not – between the scientists and the engineers. The substantial disconnect between the science and engineering of macroeconomics should be a humbling fact for all of us working in the field.
>
> N. Gregory Mankiw [2006, p. 30]

As his description of the history of modern macroeconomics indicates, N. Gregory Mankiw [2006] says there have been two different purposes for building models. Specifically, is one's purpose that of a social engineer, 'to solve practical problems'? Or is it that of a scientist, 'to understand how the world works'? While Mankiw may have been talking just about the history of macroeconomics, the choice faces every economic model builder, particularly those building empirical models.

As noted, for a long time there was a unity among the various empirical sub-fields of microeconomics. This is a status that many empirical macroeconomic model builders might once have thought to be a unique situation that was limited to the empirical microeconomic models, but today this is no longer the case. The simple reason is that model building in empirical macroeconomics is also now a consolidated field, as will be discussed in the next chapter. However, apart from model building, before macroeconomics was ever taught as an identifiably separate course in universities, its contents existed as the separate theoretical sub-fields of business cycles, growth, monetary theory, banking, and so on. But today, macroeconomics is characterized more by its model building methods than by its sources of data.

As far as non-experimental empirical macroeconomic model building goes, there are fans such as V.V. Chari and Patrick Kehoe [2006] who, as seen in the quotation at the top of this section, see a very successful research program. There are critics, of course, not only Leamer and Hendry but also more recent critics including Mankiw [2006] and Solow [2008]. As Solow sees it [p. 243]:

> When Chari and Kehoe speak of macroeconomics as being firmly grounded in economic theory, we know what they mean. They are not being idiosyncratic; they are speaking as able representatives of a school of macroeconomic thought that dominates many of the leading university departments and some of the best journals, not to mention the Federal Reserve Bank of Minneapolis. They mean a macroeconomics that is deduced from a model in which a single immortal consumer-worker-owner maximizes a perfectly conventional time-additive utility function over an infinite horizon, under perfect foresight or rational expectations, and in an institutional and technological environment that favors universal price-taking behavior. In effect, the industrial side of the economy carries out the representative consumer-worker-owner's wishes. It has been possible to incorporate some frictions and price rigidities with the usual consequences – and this is surely a good thing – but basically this is the Ramsey [1927] model transformed from a normative account of socially optimal growth into a positive story that is supposed to describe day-to-day behavior in a modern industrial capitalist economy. It is taken as an advantage that the same model applies in the short run, the long run, and every run with no awkward shifting of gears. And the whole thing is given the honorific label of 'dynamic stochastic general equilibrium'.

As Solow notes and as will be discussed more extensively in the next chapter, empirical macroeconomic model building today is no longer separated from microeconomic theory. On the one hand, as I explained in Chapter 2, Walrasian general-equilibrium modeling plays a significant role since, as some have claimed, every Walrasian general-equilibrium model is talking about the same macro economy. On the other hand, questions of the micro-foundations for any macroeconomic policy prescriptions have led to a widespread use of representative agents which are quite amenable to microeconomic analysis – such that many macroeconomic models are mostly about applications of microeconomic theory. However, when it comes to the common dependence on econometric methodology to build empirical macroeconomic models, it is not clear that the criticisms of Leamer and Hendry are being avoided.

Mankiw [2006] provides a concise history of modern macroeconomic model building. He stresses that while there have been two schools of thought, the most important thing to keep in mind is that it has not always been a choice between competing ideologies or theoretical perspectives; rather, as I mentioned earlier in this chapter, it has been between the methodological perspective of engineers versus that of scientists. There nevertheless has been an ideological struggle between builders of the once popular Keynesian model and the 'counter-revolutionaries' who promoted what became known as New Classical models. The New Classicals came in three waves, beginning with Milton Friedman's monetarism, followed by a rational expectations perspective that deliberately challenged any long-term effectiveness of government monetary policies, and culminating in so-called real business cycle theories that omitted any role for monetary policies and focused instead on the role of random shocks to the real economy such as those shocks due to changes in technology. The models based on real business cycle theories were heavily dependent on the assumptions more commonly used in microeconomics – particularly the presumption of quickly clearing perfect markets. And as such, they were more directed at a pursuit of the scientific purpose for model building than the more practical engineering purpose.

In the middle of all of this, some began to pursue a more microeconomics-oriented modification of the old Keynesian approach, and this too, according to Mankiw, came in three waves. The first wave of New Keynesian models began by relaxing the perfect market assumption, followed by the use of rational expectations without quickly clearing markets, and culminated in New Keynesian attempts at realistic models in which assumptions more commonly associated with imperfect competition playing a bigger role.

Mankiw [p. 37] seems to conclude that this New Keynesian approach was more directed toward promoting the engineering approach to model building, recognizing that few of the New Classicals ever played a role in government but many of the New Keynesians had. Nevertheless, as Mankiw said, noting the published views of Laurence Meyer, a former governor of the Federal Reserve [p. 40],

> The book [Meyer 2004] leaves the reader with one clear impression: recent developments in business cycle theory, promulgated by both new classicals and new Keynesians, have had close to zero impact on practical policymaking. Meyer's analysis of economic fluctuations and monetary policy is intelligent and nuanced, but it shows no traces of modern macroeconomic theory. It would seem almost completely familiar to someone who was schooled in the neoclassical-Keynesian synthesis that prevailed around 1970 and has ignored the scholarly literature ever since. Meyer's worldview would be easy to dismiss as outdated if it were idiosyncratic, but it's not. It is typical of economists who have held top positions in the world's central banks.

Actually, this common realization of how little effect sophisticated scientific economic model building has had on the business of forming governmental economic policies is not new. In 1977, William Allen conducted a survey of economists working in government and concluded [pp. 86–7]:

> In speaking with economists who are or have been in government, one obtains a picture and gains an impression which are sobering. The government economist typically is not a highly independent researcher and analyst, free first to pick many of his subjects and entirely free then to broadcast generally the results of his labors. He is a member of an organization, commonly devoting the bulk of his time to topics specified from on high . . . conscious of a prevailing orientation and purpose on the part of those administrative superiors who constitute his main audience; conscious, also, that the decision makers he is more or less directly advising are themselves subject to constraints of worldly realism and political feasibility – along with innocence in the area of economic analysis; bringing to his task an accumulated intellectual capital which, even if impressive at the outset of his government work, may not thereafter be greatly enlarged or even well maintained; having more or less available a corpus of theory and an arsenal of techniques which, for all their elegance, refinement, and academic glamour, are often too time-consuming for purposes of shooting from the hip and too esoteric for the data, the colleagues, and the audience. . .

Needless to say, the credibility of empirical macroeconomic model building has also been put into serious question as a result of the 'Great Recession' of 2007–2009. While Angrist and Pischke do not bring up this challenge brought by the Great Recession to the credibility of econometric model building, it surely would prompt any such advocates to suggest the need to continue developing experimental-based empirical microeconomic methodology. Advocates of the kind of empirical macroeconomic model building methodology that Chari and Kehoe celebrate will most likely say that more sophisticated models will cure the problem. Perhaps they are right, but the credibility of any ad hoc new sophisticated assumptions may still be open to the criticism we have seen about empirical macroeconomic models before the Great Recession. Above all, in this light, who is the audience for empirical macroeconomic model building? As Christopher Sims [2010, p. 60] warns,

> The audience for applied work includes people whose interests or ideologies are affected by the outcome, but who have little technical training. There is therefore a payoff to making the methods and messages of applied work simple and easily understood, even when this involves otherwise unnecessary simplification or distortion. On the other hand, there is a danger that procedures not understood by much of the audience for a paper may lend unjustified weight to the paper's conclusions.

6

On building macro-econometric models

Macroeconomics no longer claims that the study of aggregate phenomena requires a distinct methodology; instead, modern macroeconomic models are intertemporal general equilibrium models, derived from the same foundations of optimizing behavior on the part of households and firms as are employed in other branches of economics.

Michael Woodford [1999, p. 31]

Despite its obvious potential, econometrics has not had an easy time from many who have made major contributions to the development of economics, beginning from Keynes' famous review in 1939 of Tinbergen's book, *Statistical Testing of Business-Cycle Theories*. . . . Forty years after Keynes wrote, his review should still be compulsory reading for all who seek to apply statistical methods to economic observations.

David Hendry [1980, pp. 389, 396]

We cannot appeal to the same econometrics that lets a rational expectations econometrician learn an equilibrium because an econometrician is *outside* the model and his learning is a sideshow that does not affect the data generating mechanism. It is different when people learning about an equilibrium are inside the model. Their learning affects decisions and alters the distribution of endogenous variables over time, making them aim at moving targets.

Thomas Sargent [2008, pp. 13–14]

As noted in the Prologue, economists have been building macro-econometric models for well over seven decades. Today, in academic departments, there is a certain homogeneity in macro-econometric model building, although there are differences depending on where the department is located. In North America, the dominant approach to macro-econometric models (briefly mentioned in Chapters 1 and 5) is Dynamic Stochastic General Equilibrium models, usually referred to as DSGE models. The other approach, promoted mostly in a few universities in Europe, is usually called the Cointegrated Vector Autoregression approach, often referred to as the CVAR approach.

The differences also extend to the related methodological approaches concerning which comes first, model construction or analysis of the statistical adequacy of the available data. This chapter will be about these two approaches. It will again discuss the use of the representative agent in the development of empirical macro-econometric models particularly in the context of the alleged need for micro-foundations for any complete macro model.

Before discussing these approaches to academic model building, it should be noted here that by talking about macro-econometric models, I will not be talking about the large commercial models that I briefly discussed in the Prologue – namely, the econometric models some governments and large corporations buy for the purposes of assessing their future policies. Instead, I will be discussing the models produced in academic economics departments today. However, there is one thing in common between today's macro-econometric models and the commercial models used by governments and corporations – namely, they all are concerned, of course, with empirical data. And, of course, econometric model building is the primary means of addressing economic data today, although one can still find macro model builders talking about calibrating instead of estimating econometric models.

Since I will continue metaphorically focusing on the 'Forest' rather than the 'Trees', this is not the place to discuss either the history of empirical macroeconomic model building or the technical mechanics of building econometric models – fortunately, there are many articles published that do discuss their history or their mechanics (or both in some cases) [e.g., Blanchard 2000, Woodford 1999, Hoover 2003].

6.1. The first two forks in the road for building macro-econometric models

> A model economy consists of a collection of agents arranged in a particular way over time and space; a description of agents' endowments of and preferences for goods; a technology for converting goods into one another, possibly at different points in time and space; and a mechanism for arranging agents into coalitions or institutions, and for coordinating decisions both within and across coalitions. This conception of an economy is so broad that it leaves open whether the coordination mechanism is a Walrasian one, or an alternative one that, when compared with a Walrasian mechanism, seems to constitute a 'disequilibrium'.
>
> Thomas Sargent [1984, p. 409]

Every empirical model builder faces an obvious question of how one uses data in building an empirical macro model. Does one collect macro data and then construct a model that explains that data or does one use available theoretical micro and macro models to produce an explanation of such variables and then test the resulting macro model to see if it fits the available data? This fork in the road will be discussed more as we go along in this chapter and also later in Chapters 10 and 12. The other fork in the road involves the primary problem facing anyone who wishes to explain observable macroeconomic data. It is the problem of overcoming the complexity inherent in any large economy.

Everyone agrees that simplification is necessary but not on how to go about doing it. In the development of economics there are two ways of going about dealing with the complexity. First, there is Alfred Marshall's simplification for the explanation of a complex economy in his famous 1890 *Principles of Economics*. His approach involved two simplifications. One simplification was to focus on the behaviour of individual decision makers in a state of market equilibrium (as whenever the economy is in a state of equilibrium, so are all individuals in a state of personal equilibrium – or otherwise, one or more of the individuals would have a reason to change their behaviour and hence reveal the market not to be in equilibrium). His other simplification was in his explanation of individuals' behaviour; he chose to simplify their decisions by breaking down the set of interrelated variables that individuals choose by recognizing time and change – his device was the ubiquitous long-run versus short-run characterization we learn in introductory economics classes whereby the economist first explains those variables that can be changed fastest. Of course, this is done by employing the often criticized *ceteris paribus* assumption to handle the other variables for the period of time under consideration. His procedure[1] was to recognize that to explain all the other, slower variables, the time period for explanation would need to be expanded to allow for the extra time needed to change the slower variables.

Marshall's strategy for explanation stands in contrast to the other approach proposed at about the same time – namely, that of Walras, who chose to recognize that any large economy is made up of many individuals all seeking to maximize while at the same time interacting in the same market economy. Although it is easy to dispute the nature of Walras's intentions in building his general-equilibrium models of the economy (some have claimed he was looking for a tool to help market socialism), it is convenient and common to characterize his intentions as just a matter of mathematical modeling. In this regard, Walras's approach is concerned only with the extent to which it can be used to *explain* an observed set

[1] For a discussion of Marshall's methodology of explanation, see chapter 2 of Boland [1992].

(or, as we would now say, an observed vector) of *all* market prices. And, as explained in Chapter 2, being able to do so would require that there exist a unique set of prices that would clear all markets (thereby allowing a general equilibrium in which all participants are maximizing). If such a unique set existed, then such a model could be used to explain the observed prices. One might think that solving a Walrasian general-equilibrium model for a set of prices is merely a matter of counting and assuring the equality of the number of equations and unknowns, but, as I have noted, that does not really work.[2] In the usual construction of the Walrasian general-equilibrium model, simplifications usually include: (1) assuming everyone has sufficient knowledge of all constraints so that they know when they are maximizing, (2) assuming that the only interaction between individuals that comprise the economy is through buying and selling in markets and (3) assuming that the amount of money in the economy can only affect the overall price level with no effect on relative prices. Implicitly, time and social institutions are presumed not to matter.

6.2. General-equilibrium models as micro-foundations

> The microfoundations of macroeconomics was a problem long before the new classical revolution and long before the term 'micro-foundations' was current. . . . The advocates of representative-agent microfoundations face the same barrier to complete disaggregation that Klein and advocates of the aggregation program faced. The difference is that Klein took the data as the binding constraint: disaggregate as far as the data permit, looking for a general consistency with microeconomic theory. In contrast, Lucas and the representative agent program take theory as the binding constraint: work out the theory in a tractable special case and disaggregate as far as the technical advance of microeconomic theory permits, looking for a general, nearly impressionistic, consistency with the available data.
>
> Kevin Hoover [2012, pp. 21 and 51]

As was mentioned at the end of Chapter 1, the distinction between micro and macro in economics has always been problematic once it is recognized that a Walrasian general-equilibrium model is also about the whole macro economy. And as noted, Walrasian general-equilibrium models are still part of microeconomics since they are based on a presumed explanation of every individual in the economy such that Marshall's type of individual

2 As shown in the quotation at the top of section 4 of Chapter 2, Wald [1936/51; p. 370] gives the examples of a two-equation and two-variable model which has no solution for x and y; and a three-equation and three-variable model which has an infinite number of solutions for x, y and z. For more about this, see chapter 4 of Boland [1992].

maximizer is simply presumed in Walrasian models – and so it might be said, we have a distinction without a difference.

In his 1936 *General Theory*, John Maynard Keynes, of course, proposed an entirely different way of explaining the macro economy than that of Walras.[3] Keynes proposed that the economy's supply and demand be aggregated for the whole economy and then explain the behaviour of those aggregate variables. Some critics of Keynes's aggregative macroeconomics question whether his approach could actually provide a complete explanation in the microeconomic sense, and other critics simply observe that if one is going to use a macro model to explain the effect on the whole economy of a government policy change then surely the macro variables will change only if individuals change their behaviour. That is, microeconomics always intends to provide reasons for why individuals choose the micro quantities that are being aggregated to form the macro variables in a macro model. Thus such critics claim every macro explanation requires micro-foundations to ensure a complete explanation for any change in a macro variable.

In the 1950s heyday of Keynesian model building, we find attempts such as Don Patinkin's [1956] to rectify the situation by characterizing macroeconomics as a version of general-equilibrium analysis. As Patinkin [1987] put it on page 27 of his *New Palgrave* entry on Keynes: 'a basic contribution of the *General Theory* is that it is in effect the first practical application of the Walrasian theory of general equilibrium: "practical", not in the sense of empirical ... but in the sense of reducing Walras's formal model of n simultaneous equations in n unknowns to a manageable model from which implications for the real world could be drawn'. Today, as I explained in Chapters 1 and 2, the theoretical paradigm of general-equilibrium analysis is the Arrow and Debreu [1954] axiomatic analysis of general-equilibrium models, which set out to prove the existence of a set of prices that would clear *all* markets – both today's markets and all foreseeable future markets. In other words, since the Arrow-Debreu model involves many periods of time,[4] basing a macro model on their analysis will produce what many today usually consider a dynamic general-equilibrium model. Surely, one might go on to say, there cannot be anything more in a Keynesian model than what can be found in the Arrow-Debreu model. Whether this is a fair characterization of

[3] As I said in the last note in Chapter 1, one can argue even that Keynes advocated that microeconomics needs macro-foundations [see further Boland 1982, p. 83; 1986, pp. 166–7; 2003, p. 143].

[4] Which, as I explained in Chapter 2, is problematic since their use of a time index is indistinguishable from how one would use a space index.

macroeconomics is not an important issue here. What is important is to recognize that if Patinkin is correct, such an interpretation of the economics of Keynes means there are ready-made micro-foundations for every attempt to model Keynes's *General Theory* – at least to the extent of making the macro consistent with the micro.

Critics of such an interpretation will readily point out that such a model leaves out many important elements of Keynes's *General Theory*, such as expectations, involuntary unemployment, liquidity preference or the uncertainty of the knowledge needed for explaining investment decisions. The critics of the Patinkin-type Walrasian interpretation of Keynes's economics will also point out a fundamental problem: such an interpretation allows only the building of equilibrium models rather than facing the decision problems that must be recognized when explaining micro investment decisions.

6.3. Dynamic Stochastic General Equilibrium (DSGE) models

> With a given mechanism, the economy can be viewed as the solution of a dynamic game. In a dynamic game, the strategy of each agent depends on the strategies chosen by 'nature' and the other agents in the system. Such strategic interdependence is the reason that when an equation in a vector autoregression[5] describing one agent's strategy is hypothetically altered, other equations should also be expected to change. The 'rational expectations revolution' in macroeconomics consists of a broad collection of research united mainly by an aim to respect the principle of strategic interdependent.
>
> Thomas Sargent [1984, pp. 409–10]

Before discussing DSGE models, I need to at least mention the situation in macroeconomics just prior to their modern development. And in this context, it is difficult to avoid recognizing simmering ideological controversies. Specifically, on the one hand, once Keynes suggested that the government might have a significant role in bringing economies out of deep recessions or even depressions, those politicians and economists of his day who regularly presumed the market can solve all problems were offended. This was particularly so for those who were later associated with the so-called Chicago school (such as Milton Friedman and his followers, but not necessarily including all those teaching today at the University of Chicago). As it turns out, many of them were also offended by the Patinkin-type general-equilibrium-based interpretations of Keynes's

5 Autoregression simply refers to a time series analysis in which today's value of a variable depends on its value in prior periods. More will be said about this later.

General Theory, even though by being equilibrium-based, the market is not being rejected as a means of solving social and economic problems. Obviously, it would seem that, in the minds of believers in the market, the mere presence of a role for government in any model makes the model 'Keynesian' even if, by being equilibrium-based, the model was intended to undo one of the key elements of Keynes's economics, such as involuntary unemployment or investment-decision uncertainty, both of which undermine the notion of an economy truly in equilibrium. But on the other hand, followers of Keynes will always reject any equilibrium-based interpretations of the *General Theory* such as the Patinkin-type general-equilibrium-based models. The presence of two such views will always be manifested in an ideologically tense atmosphere.

I raise all of this ideology infused perspective not to bring up its history but to explain the problem that proponents of today's DSGE approach think it solves.[6] I think one can always understand any new innovation by seeing how it solves a burning problem. So, what problem do the proponents think the DSGE approach solves? Well the believers in the power of the market's ability to solve all problems – and thus their rejection of any role for the government in the economy – were always unhappy with the espousal of 'Keynesian economics' in the 1960s and waited for it fail. So, when the American economy suffered the shock of the OPEC's cutting the oil supply in the mid-1970s that resulted in major inflation and an increase in unemployment, the cry went up that Keynesian models could not explain this 'stagflation' situation and thus it was time to reject 'Keynesian' economics. As followers of Keynes can point out, the problem was not the economics of Keynes but the equilibrium basis of Patinkin-type 'Keynesian' economics.[7] But, as Robert Lucas would counter, this just shows the need for including microeconomics to explain how the economy responds to such shocks in any macro model.

The ideological problem, I think, is simply that the Patinkin-type Keynesian models, or as they were eventually called, the neo-Keynesian models, included a role for government rather than relying just on the market equilibrium to stabilize the macro economy. Moreover, some neo-Keynesian models also purported to recognize institutional price rigidities

[6] For more about the history of recent macroeconomics and DSGE models, see Pedro Duarte [2011].

[7] Stagflation is difficult to explain only if you insist on starting with a long-run equilibrium and comparative-statics type analysis expecting to produce stagflation by changing *just one* variable such as the price of oil. If you begin with a model of a long-run *non*-equilibrium, explanation is possible.

and imperfect information of decision makers which might make it difficult to reach an equilibrium even in the long-run as usually presumed by equilibrium models.

6.3.1. The immediate predecessors to DSGE modeling

Long before DSGE modeling, there was the pre-1980s view of macro-econometric modeling which was the product of the Cowles Commission.[8] Today, it is known as the simultaneous-equation structural-models-based research program, whereby data is used to estimate the values of the model's posited parameters. Examples of such models are the previously discussed very large macroeconomic models. As James Heckman [2000] notes in his review of twentieth century econometrics, many worried about the reliability and credibility of such models. He notes [p. 78]:

> In application, structural econometricians often impose onto the data many assumptions not intrinsic to the economics of the problem for the sake of computational convenience.

One alternative was the early 1970s development of vector autoregression (VAR)[9] methodology, which is still used. But, as Heckman argues [p. 49]:

> [T]he VAR program . . . sticks more closely to the data and in that sense is more empirically successful than structuralist[10] approaches. At the same time, its critics argue that it is difficult to interpret the estimates obtained from application of this program within the context of well-specified economic models and that the Cowles vision of using economics to evaluate economic policy and interpret phenomena has been abandoned by adherents of this research program.

[8] This is the well-known research program set up in the 1930s to promote the mathematical development of economic theorizing. Its program is a major source of the pre-1980s view of economic models as being representations of economic theories. For a discussion of the role of the Cowles Commission in the development of empirical macroeconomic modeling, see Mary Morgan [1990].

[9] See Christopher Sims [1980]. An autoregression model is merely one that looks at the dynamics of a variable as being related to its lagged value – that is, where $x_t = \alpha x_{t-1} + \varepsilon_t$. To go beyond such a single equation model, one can expand this to be a vector of x's such that the α is then a matrix that incorporates all of the parameters or coefficients. This expansion is what is called vector autoregression. As Heckman [2000] says, Sims was objecting 'to the "incredible" nature of the identifying assumptions used in the Cowles Commission models and advocated application of more loosely specified economic models based on developments in the multivariate time series literature. . . . Its use of economic theory was less explicit' [p. 48].

[10] Structuralist approaches just refers to building models consisting of a sets of simultaneous equations.

Much of the discussion involving the Cowles structuralist approach to economic modeling and the VAR approach to dealing with non-experimental data was primarily about research methodology rather than ideology – although, I suspect, if one dug deep enough it would be there.

For those who believed in the power of the market to solve all problems, a key alternative was what is called the Real Business Cycle (RBC) approach. To avoid the empirically questionable presumption of the monetary sector being the basis for business cycles, monetary neutrality was usually presumed, much as one can find in the original Walrasian general-equilibrium models. The primary presumption of the RBC models is that the only reason for business cycles is that changes in real variables can be explained by changes in other real variables, such as changes in productivity or production technology, and never by changes in government monetary policy. Monetary policy aside, this is contrary to the view of many Keynesians, who saw business cycles as the result of market failures, in turn resulting from various rigidities and false expectations. As Lucas had done earlier, expectations in RBC models employ Muth's [1961] assumption of Rational Expectations whereby individual decision makers, who, as I noted in Chapter 2, would be presumed in effect to be expert and rational econometricians (again, see Benjamin Friedman [1979]) and thus individual agents in any model would form the same expectations as the model builder. Any data available to a model builder is also available to every individual. Since the RBC model builders were still believers in the market, equilibrium is always assured within the stochastic limit of econometric estimation and random errors.

Were the ideological tensions of the 1970s and 1980s the motivating problem that led to the development of DSGE models? The problems seem to be merely the need for micro-foundations for any macro model and the recognition, thanks to the presumption of Rational Expectations, that uncertainties need to be dealt with if one is going to be building dynamic empirical macro models. Apparently, applying RBC models to available data ran into problems when it came to identifying a real shock or even the effect of monetary shocks. And so it was not clear that an RBC model was very useful in the explanation of business cycle dynamics [see Hartley et. al. 1997].

Many credit Kydland and Prescott [1991] with moving beyond RBC models into the previously mentioned DSGE models. After discussing some of the earlier attempts to apply econometrics to general-equilibrium models, they noted [p. 169] that the existing

> approach is ill-suited for the general equilibrium modeling of business fluctuations because dynamics and uncertainty are crucial to any model that attempts to study business cycles. To apply general equilibrium methods to the quantitative study of business cycle fluctuations, we need methods to compute the equilibrium processes of dynamic stochastic economies, and specific methods for the stochastic growth model economy. Recursive competitive theory and the use of linear-quadratic economies are methods that have proven particularly useful. These tools make it possible to compute the equilibrium stochastic processes of a rich class of model economies.

And as for econometrics itself, they go on to say [ibid.]:

> The econometric problem arises in the selection of the model economies to be studied. Without some restrictions, virtually any linear stochastic process on the variables can be rationalized as the equilibrium behavior of some model economy in this class. The key econometric problem is to use statistical observations to select the parameters for an experimental economy. Once these parameters have been selected, the central part of the econometrics of the general equilibrium approach to business cycles is the computational experiment. This is the vehicle by which theory is made quantitative. The experiments should be carried out within a sensible or appropriate model economy that is capable of addressing the question whose answer is being sought. The main steps in econometric analyses are as follows: defining the question; setting up the model; calibrating the model; and reporting the finding.

Rather than using data to econometrically estimate the model, we see that they would have us set up their 'model economy' [p. 170], with which they would have us 'calibrate' the model using various sources of data on individuals or households, such as estimates of demand elasticities. Then going on, they would have us use this model economy to conduct 'computational experiments' to answer specific questions about the economy modeled [p. 171]:

> If all the parameters can be calibrated with a great deal of accuracy, then only a few experiments are needed. In practice, however, a number of experiments are typically required in order to provide a sense of the degree of confidence in the answer to the question.

It would seem that we have a third fork in the road. Do we build our macro model then calibrate it with available data in order to conduct computational experiments, or do we just apply it to available data by econometrically estimating its parameters as usual? One can find practitioners of both branches of DSGE modeling.

Today, since we see DSGE models moving on by including things such as imperfect competition, wage and price rigidities and imperfect information, some see the DSGE modeling approach as a synthesis of Keynesian and anti-Keynesian elements.[11] This has probably helped the DSGE to become dominant (although there may be other aspects involving the sociology of academic economics, as will be discussed in Chapter 12). To the extent that it is such a synthesis, the ideological tensions have been significantly reduced. One hopes so, but, at what cost? So far, nobody seems concerned.

6.3.2. The nature of DSGE modeling

The obvious ingredients in a DSGE model include the Arrow-Debreu-type general equilibrium, which means that, unlike the static Walrasian general equilibrium from the 1930s and 1940s, a DSGE model recognizes dynamics at least in terms of multi-period optimization. At any point in time, decision makers are assumed to face 'state variables', which represent the result of all past decisions and thus form part of the constraints facing decision makers. Today, because a multi-period optimization is assumed, unlike in the old Walrasian models, decision makers are not being presumed to possess full information, and thus instead decisions must also be based on expectation-states of the economy. Since there is no reason for all decision makers' expectations to be perfect, achieving the general equilibrium will be a stochastic matter such that the general equilibrium is unlikely in the short-run and likely if at all only in the long-run. This is mostly because, unlike the old versions of general-equilibrium-based macro models, these DSGE models do not usually assume instantaneous price adjustments. Thus, any DSGE model builder must specify how the model deals with each of these ingredients.

Within this framework, DSGE model builders will need to specify the situation facing the individuals making up the micro-foundations. The all-too-common way to do this has necessarily been, as discussed in Chapter 2, to represent all individuals with one representative agent and then to analyze this individual agent's choice behaviour to explain how the macro

[11] Mankiw [2006, p. 39] explained this as the creation of a new neoclassical synthesis whereby,

> From the new classical models, it takes the tools of dynamic stochastic general equilibrium theory. Preferences, constraints, and optimization are the starting point, and the analysis builds up from these microeconomic foundations. From the new Keynesian models, it takes nominal rigidities and uses them to explain why monetary policy has real effects in the short run. The most common approach is to assume monopolistically competitive firms that change prices only intermittently.... The heart of the synthesis is the view that the economy is a dynamic general equilibrium system that deviates from a Pareto optimum because of sticky prices (and perhaps a variety of other market imperfections).

economy changes in response to any shock or policy change. This involves specifying the constraints and objective functions of the household or the firm as well as the technology facing the firm. In most cases, how the represented individuals interact must be specified, and this may require some specification of the prevailing institutional structure.

While there may be hope that the old ideological differences could be put aside, the differences can coexist, and so now, apparently, we can have it both ways. Depending on how one deals with the ingredients such as the speed of adjustment and accuracy of expectations, DSGE models can be constructed that conform to either the RBC or the Keynesian preconceptions. Of course, the tensions may still exist but they are nevertheless reduced given that both are at least accepting DSGE models as their common framework for research and analysis of real world data.

6.4. Limits and criticism of the DSGE approach to empirical modeling

> It should be clear by now that the assumption of a representative individual is far from innocent; it is the fiction by which macroeconomists can justify equilibrium analysis and provide pseudo-microfoundations. . . . [W]hen the conclusions of such a model are tested with empirical data (not a particularly frequent occurrence) and should they, by chance, be rejected, this may simply reflect the fact that the assumption that the economy could be represented by a single individual was erroneous.
>
> Alan Kirman [1992, p. 125]

The main methodological criticism of the DSGE approach to modeling is its common use of the representative agent [e.g., Kirman 1992] to provide the needed micro-foundations in order to deal with the reasons for why change might occur in response to monetary or real changes. Implicitly, as discussed in Chapter 2, critics charge, using the representative agent unwarrantedly presumes that the diversity of individuals in an economy does not matter. In principle, the representative agent assumption is not necessary for the building of DSGE models; it is just considered convenient. What is problematic is the question of how data is used to build and apply an empirical DSGE model to data.

As noted earlier concerning the first fork in the road, one can choose to build one's DSGE model and then apply it to available data econometrically, or, instead, one can work at collecting and assessing data first to see if it is statistically adequate for the purposes of econometric estimation of such a model. When this second path is taken, much more time is devoted to assuring that the subsequent model's assumptions are not inconsistent with the statistical nature of the available data. I will talk more about this in Chapter 10, but here we need to be aware of the issues involved.

6.5. The CVAR alternative to the DSGE approach to empirical modeling

> The art of model specification in the LSE framework is to seek out models that are valid parsimonious restrictions of the completely general model, and that are not redundant in the sense of having ... even more parsimonious models nested within them that are also valid restrictions of the completely general model.
>
> Kevin Hoover and Stephen Perez [1999, p. 168]

Econometric theory was developed to deal with how economic models are not directly amenable to classical statistics [Kennedy 2008, chapters 1 and 3]. Part of the problem is that classical statistics was developed to deal with controlled experimental data. But, of course, very little if any macroeconomic data is experimental or controlled (although some think this need not be the case, as will be shown in Chapter 8). For this and other reasons, DSGE models are often criticized by those associated with the LSE (London School of Economics) approach to econometrics, which promotes the alternative modeling method whereby models are preceded by data analysis. As Kevin Hoover and Stephen Perez characterized the alternative LSE perspective: 'A model is tentatively admissible on the LSE view if it is congruent with the data in the sense of being: (i) consistent with the measuring system (e.g., not permitting negative fitted values in cases in which the data are intrinsically positive), (ii) coherent with the data in that its errors are innovations that are white noise as well as a martingale difference sequence relative to the data considered,[12] and (iii) stable' [1999, p. 169]. These are all issues that precede building an empirical model.

In a 1991 article [p. 129], Lawrence Summers began an excoriation of the state of empirical macroeconomics with:

> Many macroeconomists and most econometricians believe and teach their students that (i) empirical work in macroeconomics should concentrate on identifying 'deep structural parameters' characterizing preferences and technology; (ii) the best empirical work in macroeconomics formally tests substantive hypotheses rigorously derived from economic theory; (iii) sophisticated statistical technique can play an important role in sorting out causation in systems with

[12] The white noise and the Martingale difference sequence are technical conditions needed for conventional statistical inference procedures. More detail can be found in econometrics textbooks [e.g., Greene 2008, p. 912–16].

> many interdependent variables. These beliefs constitute the core of what I regard as the scientific illusion in empirical macroeconomics.

His article goes on to argue [pp. 129–30]

> that formal empirical work which . . . tries to 'take models seriously econometrically' has had almost no influence on serious thinking about substantive as opposed to methodological questions. Instead, the only empirical research that has influenced thinking about substantive questions has been based on methodological principles directly opposed to those that have become fashionable in recent years.

Katarina Juselius [2011] notes that the DSGE approach to modeling macroeconomics is 'One of the key developments after Summers's critique' [p. 405]. About these types of macro model she goes on to say:

> These models combine the assumptions of a representative agent and the 'Rational Expectations Hypothesis' . . . together with a dynamic stochastic structure à la Sims's VAR. The added dynamics and stochasticity render the models more flexible than earlier representative agent models. Nonetheless, in the way they are practiced, one may say that the DSGE approach gives the primary role to the theory model and a subordinate role to the VAR. In this sense the DSGE model embodies a pre-eminence of theory over empirics or what I call the 'theory-first' approach. . . . At the beginning of the new century the popularity of the DSGE models in graduate programs and among editors of top economics journals and researchers at central banks suggested that economics as a science has finally converged to a state of unanimity regarding both theory and how to apply it to data.

Summers concluded his critique with the observation that [1991, p. 146]:

> Good empirical evidence tells its story regardless of the precise way in which it is analyzed. In large part, it is its simplicity that makes it persuasive. Physicists do not compete to find more and more elaborate ways to observe falling apples. Instead they have made so much progress because theory has sought inspiration from a wide range of empirical phenomena.
>
> Macroeconomics could progress in the same way. But progress is unlikely as long as macroeconomists require the armor of a stochastic pseudo-world before doing battle with evidence from the real one.

Juselius takes up Summers' challenge and argues that the Cointegrated Vector Autoregression (CVAR)[13] approach 'is likely to meet Summers's 1991 critique . . . on many points' [p. 405]. Since DSGE models are supposedly about economies moving through time, proponents of CVAR, such as

[13] As Kennedy [2008, p. 504] explains, 'if a linear combination of non stationary variables is stationary [mean, variance, etc. do not change over time], the coefficients of this linear combination form what is called the cointegrating vector' – see also Hoover et al. [2008].

Juselius, think more work needs to be done to address the nature of the data being explained. Some think this means being an archeologist when examining available data; she sees it more as being Sherlock Holmes [p. 419]:

> More than a quarter of a century ago, when Søren Johansen and I started working on the CVAR approach, I was taken by the beauty of this model, its rich structures and its potential for addressing highly relevant questions within a stringent statistical framework. What I did not expect was that the data consistently refused to tell the stories they were supposed to. After many frustrating attempts, it seemed that I had the choice of either forcing data to tell a theoretically acceptable story or approaching the complex reality without the guide of a reliable theory. I chose the latter and started using the cointegrated VAR model in the spirit of Sherlock Holmes, an experience that best can be described as a long series of 'why's.

And about how the great detective leads to CVAR, she says [p. 420]:

> Though economic puzzles are probably harder to solve than crimes, I believe it is in the Sherlock Holmesian spirit that a well-structured empirical CVAR analysis can inspire new economic thinking. It is based on the following important principles: (1) data are allowed to speak as freely as possible against a background of not just one but several theories; (2) falsification is considered more important than verification; and (3) results that go against conventional wisdom are considered more interesting than confirmatory results.

Clearly, going the alternative road of CVAR analysis is not just a minor improvement in DSGE modeling. But if the CVAR is as good as Juselius and others seem to think, one might wonder why it has not taken much of a hold on empirical macroeconomic modeling in North America. Offering an answer to this will be postponed until Chapter 12. It might be enough here to merely observe that CVAR requires a lot more time spent on the data before even beginning building one's macro-econometric model. In Chapter 10, the question of how to go about assessing statistical adequacy of data before empirical model building, as the LSE approach requires, will be further considered in the specific context of testing.

6.6. Beyond DSGE models

> The only justification of the hyper-rational, self-interested agent typically used in standard macro models was that it was consistent with the characterization used in micro theorizing. And even that justification is now disappearing with the rise of behavioral economics.
>
> David Colander, Peter Howitt, Alan Kirman, Axel Leijonhufvud and Perry Mehrling [2008, p. 236]

Many observers of how macro-econometric models have been developing over the last two decades are now calling for model builders to go beyond DSGE modeling [e.g., Colander 2006]. Several avenues for advancement have been suggested. Advocacy of using the CVAR approach is not really moving on but more a plea for going back and starting over. And those advocating moving forward, beyond DSGE models, argue that since DSGE models incorporate some form of micro-foundations, one avenue would be to recognize that microeconomics itself has begun to examine the behavioural aspects of the basic micro assumptions.[14] Other critics of DSGE, such as Paul Borrill and Leigh Tesfatsion [2011], advocate what is called an 'agent-based model' (ABM) approach. This alternative offers what is claimed to be a different form of mathematics. As Borrill and Tesfatsion say [pp. 229–30],

> Social systems consist of heterogeneous communicating entities in an evolving network of relationships. One branch of mathematics that deals with networks of relationships is graph theory, and significant new perspectives and results are emerging from that field . . . Another is category theory, which specifies relationships (morphisms) among collections of objects as first-class citizens along with the objects themselves . . . Category theory is being promoted as the intellectual successor to set theory, which for generations has been considered the foundation of mathematics.
>
> Graph theory and category theory are powerful tools supporting deductive reasoning in many sciences, including the social sciences. Indeed, . . . certain classes of ABMs representable as finite dynamical system 'objects' with appropriately defined types of morphisms can be shown to constitute a category.

Whether many if any macroeconomic model builders will jump on this ABM wagon remains to be seen. Of course, there are those who would go beyond DSGE modeling by going back. This in particular includes the many critics of the specific practice of building macro-econometric models using the DSGE approach who have eagerly noted that the use of such models did not help predict the 2007–2009 crisis involving the real estate bubble and the subsequent 'Great Recession'. For example, as Randle Wray [2011, p. 467] puts it (referring to model builders such as those that stay with the equilibrium-based DSGE approach):

> The current crisis has shown this approach to be irrelevant for analysis of the economy in which we live. By contrast, the Keynesian revolution that began with the [*General Theory*] offered an alternative that does allow us to understand the world around us. Keynes's different methodological approach

[14] This latter aspect of going beyond micro-foundations and DSGE models will be postponed to Chapter 8.

allowed him to develop a theory that was at the same time 'general' but also 'specific' in the sense that it incorporated those features of the capitalist (entrepreneurial) economy that cause it to move toward crisis. Economists working in that tradition did see 'it' coming, and they have offered policy advice that would help to get the economy back on track and to reform it not only so that it would be more stable, but also so that it would operate in the interest of most of the population.

Alan Kirman, the critic of using the representative agent to characterize any needed micro-foundations, wrote the foreword to David Colander's 2006 book of articles by advocates of macroeconomic modeling moving beyond DSGE. In it, Kirman took the opportunity to make specific suggestions as to what ingredients should be required of any alternative for going beyond DSGE. Specifically, Kirman [2006, p. xiv, emphasis in original] suggested:

First, we would like to model the economy as a system in which there is a *direct interaction* among individuals. We would like to specify agents who, in a sense, have local as opposed to global knowledge. It may well be the case that they have a limited, even wrong, view of the world. Second, we should require that agents behave in a 'reasonable' but not 'optimal' way; for example, they may use simple rules and they should not act against their own interests. Moreover, these reasonable agents should evolve in the sense that they learn from previous experience. Third, the system should function over time but without necessarily converging to any particular state. It would be good to have a different notion of equilibrium from the standard one, a notion that corresponds to an economy that is in continual movement. Finally, whatever model we develop should have some testable conclusions; we should be able to imagine some empirical evidence that would lead us to refute our model.

Heckman [2000] seems to think another way of going beyond DSGE is needed: we should instead go backwards to before the Cowles Commission structuralist approach based on estimating parameters, and to what is called 'nonparametric' econometrics. About this he says [p. 50] it is a research program involving

econometrics and the earlier 'sensitivity analysis' research in statistics that views the functional forms and distributional assumptions maintained in conventional structural (and nonstructural) approaches as a major source of their lack of credibility and seeks to identify the parameters of economic models nonparametrically or to examine the sensitivity of estimates to different identifying assumptions. The nonparametric identification analyses conducted within this research program clarify the role of functional forms and distributional assumptions in identifying causal parameters. Using hypothetical infinite samples, it separates out what can in principle be identified without functional form and distributional assumptions from what cannot. Many question the practical

> empirical relevance of nonparametric theory in the limited sample sizes available to most economists. Others question the novelty of the approach.

He goes on [p. 78] to complain about the many applications of the structuralist method and of VAR methods:

> [T]here is an appeal to formal statistical methods that have 'black-box' features, and the numbers produced using them are often not perceived to be transparent or easily replicable. The quest for transparency underlies all of the recent research programs in econometrics, although there is no agreement over what constitutes transparency.
>
> Methods developed in nonparametric econometrics and sensitivity analysis in statistics in principle reduce some of this arbitrariness.

Clearly, one way or the other, there is much work to do.

7

Modeling and forecasting

> We should not indulge in high hopes of producing rapidly results of immediate use to economic policy or business practice. Our aims are first and last scientific. . . . The only way to a position in which our science might give positive advice on a large scale to politicians and business men, leads through quantitative work. For as long as we are unable to put our arguments into figures, the voice of our science, although occasionally it may help to dispel gross errors, will never be heard by practical men.
>
> Joseph Schumpeter [1933, p. 12]

> The . . . fundamental point is that it will be necessary to distinguish between 'forecasting' and 'prediction'. Forecasting will be limited to the extrapolations based on empirical models or data exploration, whereas a prediction will be formed from a theoretical model.
>
> Clive Granger [2012, p. 312]

> It's tough to make predictions, especially about the future.
>
> Yogi Berra

Economists have been building econometric models for several decades. Econometric models by design attempt to capture or represent simultaneously the data of interest and the ideas about how the modeled economy functions as reflected in that data. The primary task is one of identifying a set of parameters or constants that can be seen to characterize the economy being modeled. Such models are thought to represent a cause and effect relationship between two types of observable quantities. The effects are the endogenous variables being explained and the causes are the exogenous variables whose values are determined either by nature or by public policy autonomously but not necessarily independently of the model. Truly exogenous variables are variables determined by events beyond anyone's control or by prior artificial constructs that by design are completely within the control of governmental policy makers (e.g., tax rates, subsidies, etc.).[1] It is the posited fixed parameters that ultimately determine the effects of any changes in the causes. The hope has always been that econometric model builders could succeed in developing a model that would simulate accurately the workings of the economy, and with such a model, if the values of all its fixed parameters could be measured, we would then have an excellent and reliable tool for forming predictions and forecasts of the future state of the economy or of the effects of changes in government policies. For this to be the case, however, the parameters of the model must represent not only the past state of the economy but its future as well. Presuming that this is even possible may be open to question.

Forecasting researchers have for the most part been disappointed with the performance of econometrics-based forecasting models. The reason for the unsatisfactory performance of econometrics-based forecasts has always been considered a puzzle to be solved. Few critics have ever thought that the puzzle might be unsolvable. Nevertheless, as long as econometrics is to be the basis for building forecasting models, it is very unlikely that the puzzle will be solved.

The obstacle that stands in the way of solving this puzzle is to be found at the very foundation of econometric methodology. It is the fundamental view that sees the task of econometric theory to be one of developing techniques to measure the values of *fixed* parameters. But, as Hicks [1979, p. 39] has explained:

> One aspect of the difference between the sciences and economics has yet to be noted. The sciences are full of measurements which, over a wide field of application, can be regarded as constants – the absolute zero of temperature is –273° centigrade, the number of chromosomes in the human zygote is forty-six, and so on – but there are no such constants in economics. There are indeed some price-ratios which for long periods have been fixed by law . . . but to the economist these are 'artificial' and clearly exceptional. Again, there have been some apparent constants, or near-constants, such as the nine- or ten-year length of the Trade Cycle, which for roundabout half a century, between 1820 and 1870, appeared to have become established (so established, indeed, that [Stanley] Jevons dared to associate it with the sunspot cycle, thus reducing it into strictly physical terms); but *regular* fluctuation, on this pattern, has not persisted. The economic world, it has in our day become increasingly obvious, is inherently in a state of flux.

[1] Unfortunately, too often textbooks erroneously call 'independent' variables exogenous simply because they are presumed constant by way of the usual *ceteris paribus* assumption. The source of this problem is the textbook's Marshallian partial-equilibrium analysis, which holds some variables constant in the short-run but treats them as endogenous in the long-run.

So, while physics may be based on the notion that Nature provides fixed parameters such as the gravitational constant or the speed of light, it is questionable whether society can truly be seen to be governed by a set of Nature-given fixed parameters. To think that fixed parameters can be the basis for an explanation of all of society ultimately leads to the view that all individuals' actions are predetermined by the Nature-given fixed parameters.

This obstacle leads forecasters to a forced choice. On the one hand, if one recognizes that parameters can be fixed (if at all) only for short periods of time then only short-term forecasts are warranted and only when based on recently collected data. On the other hand, if one builds only short-term forecasting models, then the forecasts will be plagued by the noise inherent in short-term data such as daily records of market prices. The noise is often the result of unexpected unusual events that can temporarily distort prices and other data from their usual seasonal or trend related values. Many forecasting researchers seem to be resigned to the following dilemma. Either we reject the possibility of making model-based forecasts or we accept the necessary level of inaccuracy that is inherent in econometrics-based forecasting. Since the beginning of the 2007–09 'Great Recession', overcoming this dilemma has become more urgent. Some [e.g., Levin 2010] think it is merely a matter of developing 'non-linear' models that are capable of dealing with such dramatic changes – which raises the question of whether this avoids the dilemma or buries it at a lower level. And, as will be discussed later, others today are suggesting all this needs is an injection of human intuition – which seems to concede the point of the critics of econometric forecasting models.

Despite the overly optimistic views of Ragnar Frisch and Joseph Schumpeter in the first issue of *Econometrica*, the overriding idea to keep in mind is that (business or governmental) policy making is virtually the only reason for building forecasting models. And few economists, if any, would ever be engaged in building forecasting models for the fun of it. So, the only question of interest here is whether economists and econometricians can build models that are useful rather than whether they are mathematically elegant.

7.1. The elements of model building in general

[T]he logic of economic knowledge and of its uses ... is the same whether or not mathematical symbols are used. However, mathematical presentation is of great help in testing whether a set of structural relations proposed by a theorist is internally consistent and whether it can be determined numerically from observations. Mathematical presentation is hardly avoidable when appropriate statistical methods are to be applied to observations in order to estimate the structure or (if no structural change is envisaged) to estimate its reduced form.

Jacob Marschak [1953, pp. 25–6]

The theoretical economy is often assumed to be deterministic as results are usually easier to obtain under this assumption.

Clive Granger [2012, p. 312]

As I noted in the Prologue, today theoretical economics is synonymous with economic model building. There are many indications that theoretical business disciplines and the other social sciences have also moved in the direction of model building. While many models used by business analysts today are simple single-equation models representing time-series data, most methodological problems involving model building arise from building complex models, particularly, those consisting of multiple equations discussed in previous chapters. Before going much further in the consideration of forecasting models, we need to recognize a fundamental problem that *must* be dealt with in any construction of a complex model. It is a formal problem, related to the important philosophical idea that there cannot be a theory or model which explains everything, there must always be some 'givens' or some exogenous variables. This problem is taken for granted today, but it is still important both because it is logically prior to any attempt to use a model for statistical purposes and because it places constraints on the explanatory significance of a model. There is also the pervasive problem of the stochastic nature of models that are designed to deal with less than perfectly accurate data since all observations of such variables are subject to observational errors.[2]

The word 'stochastic' is based on the idea of a target[3] and in particular on the pattern of hits around a target (in the sense that the greater the distance a given unit of target area is from the center of the target, the less frequent or dense will be the hits on that area). In effect, an econometric model is a shot at the 'real world' target. There are many reasons why a model might miss the target, but they fall into two broad categories: (1) it was a 'bad' shot – that is, the model was logically invalid or empirically false – or (2) the target moved – that is, there was random *unexplained* variation in the objects the model is designed to explain (or to be used in an explanation). A stochastic

[2] There is also the problem that decision makers may not always be as perfect as textbooks usually assume, but, if so, this requires a different model that includes assumptions that explain such behaviour rather than seeing this as a source of observational errors.

[3] Actually, it is based on the Greek word Στόχος, which refers to aim or target.

model is one which allows for the movements of the target. In particular, stochastic models follow from a methodological decision *not* to attempt to explain anything *completely*. Every *non*-stochastic model claims to offer a complete explanation, and, for this reason, the logic of the underlying explanation is non-stochastic. That is, most explanatory theories are inherently non-stochastic (the obvious exceptions are those theories dealing with problems involving known risk). Fundamentally, it is the non-stochastic logic of the model that determines the usefulness of the model.[4]

7.1.1. Dealing with truly stochastic models[5]

For the purposes of discussion, and to keep everything clear, I want to back up from the more complicated discussions of the various approaches to building empirical models of Chapter 6 and return to the simple world of beginning economics students, which is a much better place to start a discussion of forecasting models. For this purpose, let us begin by reviewing elementary econometrics by considering a very simple, *non-stochastic* theoretical model of the equilibrium market price (P) and quantity (Q) for some particular good, where we allow for two observable exogenous variables, such as annual rainfall (R) and the size of the population (S):

$$\alpha - \beta P - Q + \mu S = 0 \tag{1}$$

$$\gamma + \lambda P - Q + \omega R = 0 \tag{2}$$

To a beginning economics student, equation (2) might look like equation (1); both say that P and Q are *linearly* related and are not affected by any other consideration than the two exogenous variables (which in a theoretical model are usually considered, *ceteris paribus*, constants). The usual interpretation of the model of a market is to say the P and Q in the two equations are equilibrium values, that is, the price and quantity at which the market clears. To determine the values of these two endogenous variables, obviously one can treat the two equations as a set of simultaneous equations since they are claimed to be true simultaneously.

4 To keep things simple here, I am ignoring the models that consider decision makers dealing with uncertainty, which might also introduce a stochastic element. Such a stochastic element is not relevant to this discussion of elementary aspects of model building in econometrics and forecasting.

5 Any reader who feels that they understand the fundamentals of elementary econometrics-based model building may wish to skip this section and move on to Section 7.2.

It is very important to keep in mind that since, by assumption and design, the values of the parameters (i.e., the value for each of α, β, γ, λ, μ and ω) are fixed constants,[6] which means that, no matter when the observations are made, the observed values of the P and Q will never change if R and S are naturally constant.[7] That is, without a change in either of the exogenous variables of this non-stochastic model, P and Q cannot change unless the value of at least one of the parameters changes, and this is exactly what has been ruled out by design. However, if we build a stochastic version by adding an error term to each question, the observed values of P and Q can change even though the parameters and the exogenous variables do not change.

Seventy years ago, Trygve Haavelmo [1944, section 13] examined the methodology of building stochastic models and pointed to the fact that statistically measuring parameters (say, in the case of estimating future prices) can easily yield questionable results. The primary difficulty is that, if one were merely to substitute the econometrically measured values of the parameters into the non-stochastic equations representing the demand and supply curves (as, say, in the above theoretical model of demand and supply), one could not legitimately treat the price P and the quantity Q as algebraic solutions to a set of simultaneous equations. The reason is that the logic and rules of algebraic manipulation of any equation are based on the variables having exact values. But, given the unavoidable observation errors, statistics would provide only averages with a probability of observational error over specified ranges. Said another way, consider the textbook assumption that aggregate consumption is linearly related to the level of aggregate income, that is, $C = \alpha + \beta Y$. Statistics might indicate that there is a 90 percent probability that the value of the marginal propensity to consume, β, is 0.74 plus or minus, say, 0.04. And if the estimated value of the constant α is similarly accurate only with a 90 percent probability, then the accuracy of the calculated level of aggregate consumption, C, may be off by a significant percentage. In models with many more variables and parameters, the calculations could be off by very wide margins.

There are other more obvious problems with the process of making statistical estimates of the values of parameters. Despite all of the advances

6 For the benefit of beginning economics students, it should be pointed out that μ and ω are merely a means to translate units of measurement so that every term in an equation is measured in the same units. In the case of equations (1) and (2), every term is measured in the same units as Q.

7 Obviously, population size is not a natural given, but to keep things simple, let us pretend that it is over a significant period of time.

in the mathematics of statistical estimation techniques, I suspect that most estimation of parameters today – particularly in applied economics or business models – may still be based on classical least-squares analysis, whereby the estimates of the values of the parameters are those values which would minimize the errors between the calculated values and the observed values.[8] All of the rules of classical statistical inference using least-squares analysis are based on certain assumptions about the nature of the variables being observed. Many econometric theorists are careful to observe that these assumptions were developed to deal with data generated in controlled experiments. Usually, that is, the presumption is that any endogenous or dependent variable is a linear function of a specified list of so-called independent variables, plus some supposedly random variable used to capture errors (for which the mean of these errors is zero). There are a few other characteristics of the independent variables that presume that the independent variables (those usually on the right-hand side) are independent in some particular way – namely, in a way characteristic of what one would expect from data collected from controlled experiments. In controlled situations, by experimental design one can assume that the independent variables are independent of each other. However, the entire point of building econometric models (particularly the models with many equations) is that they allow us to recognize the *interdependence* of variables. As noted in Chapter 6, one could go as far to say that the study of econometric theory has been devoted to finding ways of overcoming deviations from the requirements of classical statistical inference.

Modern econometric modeling addresses these and other elementary methodological problems by explicitly recognizing that the equations representing relationships between observable variables may be inaccurate. To compensate for the inaccuracy, each equation of a model is simply adjusted by including an error variable that accounts for the inaccuracy (thus the deviation from it being an equality). For example (and continuing to keep things simple as possible), consider the above simple non-stochastic two-equation model of a market's demand and supply. Let us rearrange the equations to put the dependent variable, Q, on the left with the independent variables, P (here we are presuming the demanders and suppliers are

8 There are other methods which can be claimed to be improvements, including Instrumental Variables, Generalized Method of Moments, and non-parametric methods – see further, Spanos [2012, p. 336]. And, let us leave aside the alternative of using Bayesian types of econometric inference [e.g., Lancaster 2004] to continue keeping things simple.

price-takers), S and R, on the right (R and S are merely the exogenous variables required to assure the equations are statistically identifiable[9]):

$$Q = \alpha - \beta P + \mu S \tag{1}$$

$$Q = \gamma + \lambda P + \omega R \tag{2}$$

The stochastic version of this model would thus simply be the following:

$$Q = \alpha - \beta P + \mu S + \varepsilon_1 \tag{1'}$$

$$Q = \gamma + \lambda P + \omega R + \varepsilon_2 \tag{2'}$$

where the two ε's correct for the inaccuracy; that is, they render what without the ε's could be an observable inequality into an equality with the ε's.

If we make observations at many points in time, the average error is zero by assumption.[10] But there remain many problems that must be dealt with when estimating the values of the parameters with such a model, not the least of which is when the error variables are correlated either with each other or over time.[11]

One obvious justification for the inclusion of error variables is the recognition that observations suffer from human errors, such as mistakes in observation reports, but of course, there can be the more serious errors that would be due to the construction of the model (e.g., perhaps it is missing a variable). Thus, even if the underlying non-stochastic model accurately represented the real world relationships (e.g., no missing variables), the model would not likely represent an exact fit using the inaccurately observed values of the variables. The assumption of a zero average error would be appropriate when the only reason for the inexactness is the common occurrence of random observational errors. But there are other reasons for errors. The obvious one would be that, contrary to the beginning assumption, the

9 Statistical identifiability refers to the classic identification problem, which in turn refers to a logical requirement of econometric models consisting of more than one equation. Historically, it was the problem raised whenever using market data consisting only of the transacted price and quantity (i.e., no exogenous variables) – whenever those observed variables change, was it due to a movement in demand or supply or both? In other words, such data is insufficient for modeling any changes in a market. One needs a way to be able to distinguish movements of the demand curve from those of the supply curve, and to do so, one needs a different exogenous variable for each – such as changes in annual rainfall for supply and changes in the population for demand.

10 Or by construction if one includes a constant term which can be assumed to absorb any deviation from zero average error.

11 On the other hand, some might see this as an opportunity if the equations are estimated separately, but the estimates may not be accurate.

relationships are not always linear; another is that the assumed relationship might fail either to recognize all relevant variables as noted or include a variable that is not truly related. For example, the true supply relationship might be as follows:

$$Q = \gamma + \lambda_1 P + \omega_1 R + \lambda_2 P^2 + \omega_2 R^2 + \xi PR \qquad (2'')$$

which means that, unless $\lambda_2 P^2 + \omega_2 R^2 + \xi PR = 0$, the ε_2 in equation (2′) exists partially to compensate for this so-called structural error. Similarly, it might be the case that the true supply relationship is instead:

$$Q = \gamma + \lambda P + \omega R + \xi W \qquad (2''')$$

where W might represent the going average wage rate. In (2‴), there is what was once called an errors-in-variables case (but today we would usually call a case of omitted variables); that is, the error variable must compensate for the term ξW missing in (2′). Obviously, in this case there would not seem to be a good reason for assuming a zero average error. In other words, the inclusion of error variables may not be enough to avoid inaccurate estimates and calculations.

7.1.2. Using econometric models to test theories

As will be discussed in Chapter 10, to the extent that an econometric model attempts to represent a specific theory of how all the observable variables (such as national income, aggregate investment, interest rates, etc.) interrelate, such a model can be seen to be a useful tool to test that theory. Testing theories by building models of the theories is unavoidably a matter of judgment. The usual question posed is whether a particular model in some statistical sense does or does not 'fit' the available data.

There are two views of testing depending on the purpose. The positive view says that a successful test is obtained when the model of an explanatory theory 'fits' the data according to acceptable statistical criteria. In short, a successful test is a confirmation. The other view is critically oriented and says that a successful test is obtained when, by acceptable statistical criteria, the model fails to be confirmed. That is, the model is deemed to not 'fit' the data. Needless to say, whether a particular model is deemed to 'fit' or not depends on how strong or weak the criteria are – hence, the question is one of judgment.

Whether or not a model can be the basis for a test of an explanatory theory of the economy is a matter of logic. Specifically, since every model involves decisions on the part of the model builder (e.g., is the relationship between consumption and income a linear relationship or a non-linear relationship?), any model which is deemed to be a 'bad fit' does not *force* us to give up our economic theory or any of its behavioural assumptions represented in the model. Perhaps a different set of modeling decisions will lead to a model that does not yield a 'bad fit'.

Similarly, there are logical problems with any claim that our model represents a confirmation of our economic theory. Not only is there a judgmental question of the strength of our statistical criteria, there is always an open question of whether a model of some other explanatory theory might also be confirmed with the available data. There is also a question of whether the inclusion of future data will still yield a confirming test. For now, let us leave this for the discussion of using models for testing in Part III.

7.1.3. Elementary models that promote understanding: measuring parameters

From the beginning of the formal development of econometrics in the 1930s, the hope has been that econometrics would make it possible to marry economic theory with both mathematics and statistics. As previously noted in this chapter, for some this has been considered a question of measuring the constants that characterize an economy, much like parts of physics can be characterized by such things as the well-known gravitational constant or the speed of light or the more obscure Boltzmann's constant or Plank's constant, and the hope has long been that this can be done in economics. For example, in the days of active Keynesian macroeconomic model building, it was often assumed that during any twelve-month period aggregate expenditure on consumer goods (C) is simply a linear function of the aggregate national income (Y) for that period. Specifically, it was often the textbook assumption mentioned earlier that $C = \alpha + \beta Y$. The presumption is that β represents a psychologically given 'marginal propensity to consume', that is, a Nature-given constant.[12] In some versions of this theory's models of aggregate consumption, the coefficient α may be considered a constant which reflects the minimum necessary expenditure for survival. One published calculation of β concluded that the marginal propensity to consume had the value 0.74, discussed in a previous section. There are other such constants even in elementary economics, such as the

[12] This 'propensity' is the presumed natural constant whereby whenever given an extra dollar of income, the consumer will always spend the same proportion β of the dollar.

'elasticity of demand'[13] for specific goods. And it is often felt that over a significant period of time the elasticities for some goods are relatively stable, and thus there have been many efforts to measure such elasticities [see Stigler 1954].

The data available to model builders, of course, is rarely exact. Data has to be collected[14] by people, and people can make mistakes. That is, model builders must always contend with observation errors, and this is even more problematic when using data collected by someone else under unknown circumstances. Without observation errors, building complex models would be mostly an exercise in applied algebra, that is, solving a set of simultaneous equations given accurately observed values for the variables involved (e.g., the values of national income, the interest rate, etc.). For example, in business if you think that the sales level for your product is in fixed proportion to the level of the national income, you could try to calculate that proportion by observing both the national income level and the sales level at one point in time. Of course, if there are no observation errors, you could also test any theory that says the proportion is fixed by making observations at different points in time. But when you recognize that observations can be inaccurate, you must then also recognize that if the second observation implies a different proportion, you cannot validly conclude that the true relationship between sales and national income is not a fixed proportion. That is, any apparent deviation from a fixed proportion may be due entirely observation errors. Although it has been known for some time [e.g., Marschak 1953; Lucas 1986; Davidson 1991], observational errors may not be enough; what must be recognized is that the basic parametric structure of the model may have dramatically changed. And this means that the textbook notion of effective government policies is more complicated than was probably thought in the early days of building econometric models of the macro economy.

7.2. Using models to make predictions

We are usually interested in predicting the values of economic variables, not only for a single point or interval of time, but for a whole succession of such points or intervals. We are interested in the path of the variable through time. As often pointed out by economists, the properties of the path (for example, the intensity of the oscillations of, or the rate of growth in, income) are of direct concern to the individual or the nation.

13 As every economics student learns, this is merely the percentage change in the quantity demanded per percentage change in the price.

14 Or today, at least entered by someone directly or indirectly into a digital database.

> Suppose that the exogenous variables and/or the structure will undergo specified changes during the future period in question, and disregard for a moment any disturbances and errors. Then the value of each endogenous variable, being at any time exactly determined by exogenous variables, will change throughout the period in the manner prescribed by the relevant equation of the reduced form.[15]
>
> Jacob Marschak [1953, p. 17]

> For many routine decisions, assuming the uniformity and consistency of nature over time (that is, assuming ergodicity) may be a useful simplification for handling the problem at hand. For problems involving investment and liquidity decisions where large unforeseeable changes over long periods of calendar time cannot be ruled out, the Post Keynesian uncertainty model is more applicable. . . . [T]he postulate that economists must throw over is that individuals must use objective or subjective probability distributions to make economic decisions in the face of true uncertainty. The result is a more general theory, encompassing cases of both ergodic probability and non-ergodic uncertainty.
>
> Paul Davidson [1991, pp. 142–3]

Let us for the moment assume that, using the available data, we have a well confirmed econometric model that represents an explanatory theory dealing with many interrelated variables of the economy. How can such a model be used to make predictions about the future state of the economy?

Since predictions about the future must somehow involve time, whether a model can be used for prediction depends on whether the explanatory theory represented actually includes at least one time-based relationship and how such a relationship has been represented in the model. From a theoretical point of view, there are many ways time can be recognized in a model. For example, even if we do nothing, trees of course can grow, so a model might include an equation describing how the rate of growth varies with the size and age of a tree. Similarly, even though it may be true that aggregate consumption is a static relationship,[16] it is possible that over time there is variation in the distribution of that consumption between various goods. In this case, the model would have to disaggregate consumption so as to recognize changes in the distribution. If one is modeling the market for softwood lumber, not only must one recognize (and model) the dynamic aspects of growing the source of the lumber, one must also recognize changes in the demand for lumber, such as that caused by changes in the interest rate (or mortgage rate). If there are reasons to think that the interest rate will fall

[15] 'Reduced form' simply refers to the equation that would be obtained for an endogenous variable once the system consisting of two or more simultaneous equations has been solved for that variable as a function of exogenous variables alone.

[16] Such as the linear relationship discussed in Section 7.1.1.

next year, a model might be used to predict the price of softwood lumber next year depending on one's conjecture as to the fall in the interest rate.

Whether a model can be used to make predictions or forecasts depends heavily on the extent to which that model adequately incorporates time-based relationships. Obviously time-based relationships must be involved when dealing with investment decisions. A decision today to invest depends heavily on what one thinks will happen at some date in the future. It may also depend on what has happened in the recent past.

There are two basic techniques for incorporating time in forecasting models. One technique is to recognize the recent past as 'time-lagged' variables. For example, it is easy to see that some decisions today depend on what happened yesterday.[17] We could see that a relationship between aggregate investment and the level of aggregate income might be seen to be that today's investment is a linear function of both today's income and last year's investment – should we be dealing with less-aggregated variables, we would be building a form of the so-called VAR model discussed in Chapter 6. The other technique yields very complex models. Rather than simply recognizing two observed values for one variable or vector of concern – such as this year's and last year's – all variables involved could be dated, as in the case of the Arrow-Debreu model's 'dynamics' discussed in Chapters 1 and 2. Recall, by dating the variables it is possible to treat the demand and supply for softwood lumber in the year 2024 as if it were for an entirely different product from softwood lumber in the year 2014. That is, rather than modeling the same good at different points in time, for every point in time we would recognize a different product in a different market. While this view of time is commonplace in commodity markets as a basis for building models, it leads to very large and very complex models; if for no other reason, it increases the number of variables that have to be modeled. While such large models might be appropriate for modeling an explanatory theory, given their complexity, they are rather useless for making predictions for policy purposes. Thus, until recently, most models used to make predictions use the time-lagged variables approach.

Many decades ago, the hope was that we could model the business cycle. If we had such a model and it was confirmed, then we would have a basis to make predictions about where we are in such a cycle. Forecasting with such a model would be rather mechanical. There is, however, one obvious difficulty with such a hopeful state of affairs. As noted already, all model

[17] Recall, in Chapter 6 this time-based relationship was what was involved in so-called autoregressions.

building presumes that the parameters of our models are fixed or constant (the technical term for this presumption about parameters is that they are 'ergodic'). In a Platonic sense, one cannot deal with change unless one first recognizes something that is fixed – in short, change is apparent only relative to some fixed background. So, in other words, only after we have successfully estimated those fixed parameters can we have a basis to predict or understand how the variables we wish to predict are affected by the other variables that have autonomous or endogenous dynamics of their own. But as Hicks noted already, fixed parameters may make sense in physics, but they remain questionable in economics except possibly in very short periods of predictions and forecasts.

7.3. Models as the basis for business forecasts

> Occasionally economic theorists who are used to making a perfect foresight assumption will criticize an economic forecaster for producing imperfect forecasts.
>
> Clive Granger [2012, p. 319]

Forecasting plays an essential role in almost every business enterprise. Forecasts range from simple short-term estimates of the delivery time of a firm's product to complex long-term estimates of future prices needed for investment decisions. There does not yet seem to be a reliable, all-purpose economic forecasting technique, and as a result different techniques have been developed for short and long-term forecasting. While short-term techniques most frequently involve single-equation time-series extrapolations from available information and data, long-term techniques seem to require more elaborate multi-equation econometric modeling.

The easy availability of personal computers has long made forecasting an exercise almost all managers can do from their desktop computers or their laptops. But there are limitations – the primary limitation on forecasting is on the informational basis that can be used. All quantitative forecasting is based on mountains of quantitative data. For example, one might need to collect figures for every month and every product over the last ten years for sales, production, output levels, inventories, material costs, wages paid, etc. The quality of such diverse information can have a profound impact on the quality of the forecast. And, of course, it may also be very costly to collect the needed data.

The primary means of organizing the data is to build a model. Again, a model can be as simple as a linear equation, perhaps one which, as suggested before, states that the sales volume will be proportional to the level of the national income. A model can also be much more complex, involving many more variables and many more equations. The development and maintenance of a complex model can be very expensive, and so only large firms are able to afford the development of such large forecasting models. If all that is needed is a forecast of the macroeconomic variables for the whole economy, as noted in the Prologue, there are numerous commercially available macroeconomic forecasts. Smaller companies may find such services more cost effective than developing their own model.

Effective use of forecasting models requires an appreciation of their limitations. The primary limitation of model-based forecasting is that the models and modeling techniques used are derived from the studies of econometric models. Econometric modeling techniques are, by design, suited for building and evaluating economic explanations rather than deriving economic predictions. For this reason, simpler models usually perform as well or better than the more costly complex econometric models.

In the remainder of this chapter I will explore model-based forecasting and examine whether there are ways to improve model-building methodology such that some or all of the limitations of econometric modeling can be overcome.

7.4. The requirements for structural dynamic forecasting models

The difficulty facing all model-based forecasting involves a fundamental trade-off. The fundamental methodological problem facing every econometric model builder is that such models are based on the prior collection of data (e.g., weekly prices for softwood lumber for the years 1954, 1955, ... 2013) and using this data to estimate the values of all Nature-given parameters (in the spirit of physics). But, as noted already, there is no good reason why these parameters would remain constant over time. Specifically, if one's model is dealing with observations made over several years, it is highly unlikely that the parameters would be constant. One could try to overcome this problem of non-constant parameters by reducing the span of time over which the data is to be collected. There are two ways to do this, but both have insurmountable problems. One could simply reduce the time span to one for which it is more likely that the parameters would remain constant. For example, rather than collecting monthly average prices for the years 1954 to 2013, one could reduce the span and instead collect yearly average data for the prices over the years 2003 to 2013. The difficulty is that, depending on the size of the model, there may not be enough observations to perform the estimation, that is, to estimate the values of the parameters. The alternative is to collect weekly or daily data so that the reduced time span will still permit the assumption of constant parameters to be accepted without compromising the need for enough data. The difficulty with this alternative approach, as I already noted, is that the short-term data can be 'noisy'. That is, while monthly average prices can remain stable over an entire year, market prices can vary widely day to day and week to week. Variability of daily or weekly prices is not *per se* a problem. What is a problem is when the variation is spurious. Perhaps during one week there was a power-outage that limited supply and thus led to a higher than normal price. Perhaps in another week there was an equally unusual drop in demand, say, because of a holiday or hurricane leading to a fall in the price. By using data averaged out over longer periods of time, many of the spurious variations will cancel out. A related difficulty with short-period data is that it is difficult to sort out whether or not the data are being affected by long-term trends or seasonal deviations.

With the above obvious and elementary methodological considerations in mind, one can easily see why even short-term forecasting is not very accurate. The reason, again, is that the large data requirements needed to ensure that the model is identified[18] and thus that more frequent data must be collected. Clearly, yearly data will not do since even ten years of average price data may not be enough for a forecast of next year's demand, and worse, to ensure enough data would require such a long period of time that it would call into question any presumption of a stable set of fixed parameters. Unless the values of the parameters do remain constant, the usual econometric methods used to measure those parameters will be profoundly called into question. And without unquestioned values for the parameters, theoretical model-based forecasts are virtually impossible. Thus we can see why, in the minds of many critics of model-based forecasting, the trade-off between long-term and short-term forecasting is hopeless. Either way, as we will see, the forecasts have not been accurate.

[18] Being identified here refers to the property of a specific model which assures that, if the model is posited as being the hypothetical 'generator' of the observed data, a *unique* structure can be deduced (or identified) from the observed data. By hypothetical generator I mean that if one is given the true values of the parameters, then whenever the observed values of the exogenous variables are plugged into the model, the resulting values for the endogenous variables are said to be generated by the structure of the model. The usual mathematical means of avoiding the problem of identification for any given model, as discussed in note 9, is to ensure that there are at least as many exogenous variables as there are endogenous variables.

Can these problems be overcome? There is little optimism expressed in the various survey articles about econometric model building technology that would indicate that these problems can be overcome. While some adventurous econometric theorists decades ago proposed ways to deal with endogenously non-constant parameters [see Swamy 1970], little of this work has been noticed by forecasting researchers. The reason remains the same. Specifically, forecast model builders must face the trade-off between avoidance of the questionable stability of a model's parameters when the time period for collecting data is expanded and the noise caused by increasing the number of observations in the reduced time period to accommodate the needs of identification. Of course, one can always ignore the trade-off and learn to accept and accommodate inherently inaccurate forecasting models. In what follows I will discuss how forecasting model builders now think these problems can be dealt with.

The classic identification problem[19] has always been seen as an obstacle when dealing with large dynamic models. Most dynamic studies today seem to be based on autoregression models and much of the econometric forecasting is done with vector autoregression (VAR) models rather than with elaborate theory-based structural models[20] that we have been discussing so far. Nevertheless, the same problems of non-constant parameters still apply whenever the data spans large periods of time.

7.5. The rocky history of econometrics-based forecasting

> The problem with the standard textbook approach to economic forecasting is that for the most part it only deals in the 'known uncertainties', that is, in the quantifiable variability that can be derived analytically (or approximated by simulation). These sources derive from model estimation and future shocks. Standard approaches calculate prediction intervals around forecasts, accounting for only these 'knowable sources' ... But ... when there are unanticipated intermittent location shifts, such interval forecasts will understate the likely range of outcomes, and forecasts will be systematically biased. The well-known problem is that we don't know what we don't know ... so it is difficult to account for 'unknown uncertainty'.
>
> Michael Clements and David Hendry [2008. p. 11]

Early econometric studies were limited to correlation theory in the mold of classical statistical theory. The modern era of econometrics began in the

[19] See the previous note.
[20] That is, multi-equation structural models.

early 1940s with the recognition that errors must be recognized within the models. And today it is safe to say that econometric theory has become a special branch of mathematical statistics with its primary focus being statistical analysis of non-experimental data.

The 1950s represented a consolidation of various approaches to econometric model building. In the 1960s econometric modeling began taking center stage in the economics profession.[21] One obvious factor was the expansion of government interventions in Western economies. Almost all of the government-sponsored econometric modeling in the 1960s was based on Keynesian macroeconomics. Many government policy makers were convinced that they could use large econometric models to 'fine-tune' the economy. The 1970s saw a steady growth of econometric model building fostered mostly by the development and availability of large mainframe computers. An additional factor was the growth of available data banks. The 1980s continued the development with evermore sophisticated statistical estimation techniques and tools. By the end of the 1990s, anyone with a desktop computer could engage in sophisticated econometric model building with readily available and inexpensive computer software.

Until the end of the 1960s, most forecasting was limited to simple single-equation time-series estimations except for those forecasters trying to use the few large scale simultaneous-equations models that began to be developed in the 1940s and that eventually led to models in the 1950s such as the Klein-Goldberger model discussed in the Prologue. For those using the single-equation models, the only question ever at issue was whether one could identify trends or seasonality in the observed time-series. Forecasting in the 1970s benefited from the introduction of so-called Box-Jenkins methodology,[22] which provided a systematic approach to time-series analysis [see Kennedy 2008, chapter 19]. But the Box-Jenkins methodology was severely limited both by the need to assume that the time-series in question was sufficiently stable and by the need to have very large amounts of data available to be sure that the model of the time-series could be identified.

In the 1970s, multi-equation, structural econometric models, much like those earlier 1940s and 1950s models, began to be widely used to make

[21] One reason for its domination might be the worldwide popularity of Richard Lipsey's 1963 economics textbook *Positive Economics* – at least, outside of American economics departments. In the American departments, Samuelson's *Economics* was dominant and it did not give a major role to any empirical analysis, such as econometric analysis.

[22] This methodology for forecasting just focuses on the past behaviour of variables being forecasted rather than explanatory econometric models. As Kennedy [2008, p. 297] says, 'in essence, it is a sophisticated method of extrapolation'.

economic forecasts, and the motivation seems to have been a presumption that human judgment is inherently faulty. Somehow computer-based forecasting was thought to be unbiased and able to handle data more efficiently than a human forecaster. The 1970s also saw a growth of literature devoted to evaluating the performance of econometrics-based forecasts and, in particular, to comparisons with the performance of less complex time-series analysis. While econometric models could deal with many variables at the same time as well as deal with complex interrelationships, such an ability came at the cost of requiring much more detailed data. Collecting such data is a costly process, and so the question has always been whether the additional cost relative to simpler time-series analysis is warranted. Where the question of cost is involved, there is always an opportunity for someone to set up a business to provide the data and even provide ready-made models and forecasts. Thus, as already noted, several commercial econometric models became available for forecasts.

Several studies [e.g., Zarnowitz 1967, Klein 1971, Miller 1978; see Dawes et. al. 1994] showed that econometrics-based forecasting failed to live up to expectations. Most in the field of econometric model building [e.g., Zellner 1978] thought econometric forecasts should do well in the short-run since the parameters could safely be assumed to be constant. Others [e.g., Armstrong 1978] thought econometric forecasts might do well in the long-run since econometric models were able to incorporate more variables and thus better capture the effects of long-term trends. Neither of these expectations has been upheld by documented performance. Some critics [see Makridakis 1986] have even argued that minimizing errors during model fitting is not necessarily the best way to assure accurate forecasts.

Given the growing dissatisfaction in the 1970s with econometrics-based forecasting, the time was obviously ripe to actually try to figure out why econometrics-based forecasts were failing. Perhaps new techniques could be developed to overcome apparent shortcomings. Were some types of econometric models or estimation methods better than others? So, by the end of that decade, an explicit effort was made to identify specific problems. Spyros Makridakis and Michele Hibon [1979] set out to do just this.

Makridakis and Hibon set up a comparison of 'a large number of major time series methods across multiple series. Altogether 111 time series were selected from a cross section of available data, covering a wide range of real-life situations (business firms, industry and macro data)' [Makridakis and Hibon 2000, p. 452]. Their major conclusion was that 'simple methods, such as exponential smoothing, outperformed sophisticated ones' [ibid.]. Since this was contrary to the view of many statisticians, Makridakis launched a competition to empirically compare time series using forecasting models and methods [Makridakis, et al., 1982].

This became known as the M-Competition. For this first competition, the number of series was 1001 and involved 24 methods or variations of methods. The results of this M-Competition were similar to those of the earlier Makridakis and Hibon study, and they summarized them as follows [2000, p. 452]:

(a) Statistically sophisticated or complex methods do not necessarily provide more accurate forecasts than simpler ones.
(b) The relative ranking of the performance of the various methods varies according to the accuracy measure being used.
(c) The accuracy when various methods are being combined outperforms, on average, the individual methods being combined and does very well in comparison to other methods.
(d) The accuracy of the various methods depends upon the length of the forecasting horizon involved.

Many subsequent studies by other researchers seemed to replicate these conclusions [ibid.]. Makridakis and Hibon note that despite the frequent replications of the conclusions, there were still 'emotional objections to empirical accuracy studies' [p. 453].

A second competition (the M2-Competition) was subsequently set up to study the accuracy of forecasting models and methods [Makridakis, et al., 1993]. Again the hope was to understand what affects the accuracy of econometrics-based forecasting. This second competition was 'organized in collaboration with four companies and included six macro-economic series [and] was designed and run on a *real-time* basis' involving data and experts provided by these companies [Makridakis and Hibon 2000, p. 453]. This competition 'was run for two years and the participating experts had to forecast for the next 15 months [and a] year later the actual values for the last 15 months were given to the participating experts so that they could check the accuracy of the forecasts they had made a year earlier' [ibid]. And the conclusion was [2000, p. 453]:

> The results of the M2-Competition were practically identical to those of the M-Competition. Statistically sophisticated or complex methods did not provide more accurate forecasts than simpler ones. The relative ranking of the performance of the various methods varied according to the accuracy measure being used. The accuracy of combining various methods outperformed, on average, the individual methods used. And, the accuracy of the different methods depended upon the length of the forecasting horizon involved.

Makridakis and Hibon again note that despite what is thought to be 'strong empirical evidence', theoretical statisticians continue to think all that is needed is more sophisticated models or methods to perform more accurate forecasts. So, Makridakis and Hibon devised an M3-Competition, which included more methods, more data series and more researchers. This time, there were 3003 time series. In Makridakis and Hibon [2000], they report on the results of the M3-Competition.

An obvious question might be raised about the accuracy of these tests: how is the accuracy to be measured? In the M3-Competition, there were five accuracy measures employed: Median absolute percentage error, average ranking, median symmetric absolute percentage error, percentage better and median relative absolute error.

Makridakis and Hibon [2000] concluded that this third competition confirmed the original conclusions of the previous M-Competitions – even though, as they note, this competition involved a newer and much larger set of data. Moreover, they say that 'it demonstrated, once more, that simple methods developed by practicing forecasters ... do as well, or in many cases better, than statistically sophisticated ones like ARIMA and ARARMA models' [p. 460].[23] They also concluded that three new methods (not employed in the previous competitions) did well, one was excellent though simple, and all three outperformed the other methods.

7.6. Is it possible to overcome the methodological obstacles?

> Macroeconomic forecasts are frequently produced, widely published, intensively discussed and comprehensively used. ... In practice, however, most macroeconomic forecasts, such as those from the IMF, World Bank, OECD, Federal Reserve Board, Federal Open Market Committee (FOMC) and the ECB, are typically based on econometric model forecasts jointly with human intuition. This seemingly inevitable combination renders most of these forecasts biased and, as such, their evaluation becomes non-standard.
>
> Philip Hans Franses, Michael McAleer and Rianne Legerstee [2012, p. 2]

Today, many econometric forecasting model builders have resorted to employing 'intuition' [see McAleer 2011] or what some call 'expert systems'. Obviously, one can perhaps produce a more accurate forecast this way, but

[23] ARIMA is short for autoregressive integrated moving average, and ARARMA is a non-stationary autoregressive followed by an autoregressive moving average. See Kennedy [2008, p. 297] or Maddala [2001, p. 524] for a definition of ARIMA and an explanation of the need for integration.

is it reliable? Most critics of the use of expert systems say it is not. Benito Flores and Stephen Pearce [2000] examined the use of an expert system as part of the M3-Competition and found that 'In general, the intervention did not improve the accuracy and the effort required to do it was substantial' [p. 485]. But sometimes consulting an expert can improve accuracy. I am reminded of a story told by a colleague about his work at the Bank of Canada, which at the time was using a large econometric model. One day, the expert econometricians were having difficulty producing a forecast of GDP that was positive. So, they trudged downstairs to the basement where the old, gray-haired statistician still worked, and they asked for his expert help. After he answered, they rushed upstairs to fix the model so that it would produce the old expert's prediction – which was much more accurate, of course. But again, the issue is reliability and expert systems still are not considered reliable.

Needless to say, all this calls for a theory of economic forecasting that can address the various reasons for the differences in the accuracy of the various forecasting models and methods. One issue relevant to the M-Competitions is how a forecasting model deals with errors and tries to correct for them in real time. Some error correction procedures just move the intercept to compensate for the observed error, but the issue is always one of whether the error is due to a temporary or permanent change in the underlying structure. Was the error due to a structural change in one of the model's key parameters or exogenous variables or was it due to a change in a variable not recognized in the model which would leave us not able to know what caused the change?

As the econometrics theorist, Hendry, puts it[24], the fundamental problem facing any theory of economic forecasting is that:

> The key issue is unknown unknowns, specifically unanticipated shifts in the underlying processes that were not pre-modelled.

He goes on to say:

> The current generation [of econometric model builders] seriously misunderstand the roles of theory and evidence, and do not grasp the lessons from forecast failure for economics generally.

Econometrics theorists such as Hendry [1980] have argued for many years, a primary problem with econometric models is that their builders too often

[24] Personal correspondence dated 7 June 2011.

make assumptions that are inconsistent with the probabilistic structure of the available data. As Aris Spanos puts it,[25]

> The problem of statistical misspecification is ignored at the detriment of forecasting capacity. For optimal forecasting one should use econometric models whose statistical adequacy has been established first, and any theory induced restrictions have been tested and accepted by the data before imposed.

Until potential business or government users of econometric forecasts are convinced that they can be more reliable and are less likely to fail – perhaps as a result of following suggestions such as those offered by Hendry, Spanos and other economics forecasting theorists – it is still doubtful that many business users will be turning to the econometric model builders any time soon.

[25] Personal correspondence dated 10 May 2011.

PART III

TESTING AND MODELS

8

On the role and limitations of experimental and behavioural economics

Ignorance is a formidable foe, and to have hope of even modest victories, we economists need to use every resource and every weapon we can muster, including thought experiments (theory), and the analysis of data from nonexperiments, accidental experiments, and designed experiments. We should be celebrating the small genuine victories of the economists who use their tools most effectively, and we should dial back our adoration of those who can carry the biggest and brightest and least-understood weapons. We would benefit from some serious humility, and from burning our 'Mission Accomplished' banners. It's never gonna happen.

Edward Leamer [2010, p. 44]

Behavioural studies by and large do not necessarily assume that people always behave by the dictates of standard theory, and especially in the early days repeatedly showed deviations etc., but increasingly are concerned with looking at the source of the departures and with their implications, etc.

Jack Knetsch[1]

[I]t would be useful for theory to identify behavior for which the theory cannot account, in the sense that the observations would force the theorist to reconsider. This would ensure that the theory is not performing well by 'theorizing to the test' . . .

Similarly, it would be helpful to have the experimental design indicate which outcomes would be regarded as a failure as well as which would be considered a success. This question appears to be trivial in many cases, with success and failure riding on the statistical significance of an estimated parameter. However, one of the advantages of experimental work is the ability to control the environment and design the tests. This allows us to direct attention away from issues of statistical significance and toward issues of economic importance. The strength of the experiment will often be reflected in the content of this 'failure' category. . . .

[I]t is important that both theoretical models and interpretations of experimental results be precise enough to apply beyond the experimental

1 Personal correspondence dated 13 April 2013.

> situation from which they emerge. This allows links to be made that multiply the power of single studies.
>
> Larry Samuelson [2005, pp. 100–1]

In the decades before 1980, as I explained in the Preface and Prologue, model building was directed at giving mathematical expression and rigor to theoretical ideas and behavioural hypotheses. In this sense, theories and models were separate things. As illustrated throughout Parts I and II, model building is the main activity today in academic economics, and as such today one usually does not distinguish between theories and models but between two different types of model, theoretical and empirical. In what I have called the pre-1980 view, building a model was often thought to be a means of either simulating or testing someone's theory or theoretical proposition against observable data. And, of course, econometrics was the primary tool for such testing.

Today, testing economics is considered also to be the domain of experimental and behavioural economics.[2] Ironically, as will be subsequently explained in this chapter, the perspective of experimental and behavioural economics is a reversion to the pre-1980s view of theories and models. But first, let us look at experimental economics and its purposes as well as the major problems recognized by many of its proponents.

8.1. Experimental economic model building

> Laboratory micro-economies are real live economic systems, which are certainly richer, behaviorally, than the systems parameterized in our theories. Consequently, it is important to economic science for theorists to be less own-literature oriented, to take seriously the data and disciplinary function of laboratory experiments, and even to take seriously their own theories as potential generators of testable hypotheses. . . . [I]t is equally important that experimentalists take seriously the collective professional task of integrating theory, experimental design, and observation.
>
> Vernon Smith [1982, pp. 923–4]

> [I]n an economics experiment, participants are asked to solve fairly simple decision-problems, generally in conditions of anonymity, and are paid on the basis of their performance. Besides defining a salient reward structure capable of inducing economic motives in experimental subjects, economists carefully create fairly neutral and abstract problem-situations to avoid the interference of individuals' subjective perceptions of the context of interaction, and thereby prevent

2 For a discussion and analysis of the philosophy and history of experimental economics, see Francesco Guala [2012].

> subjects from acting in conformity (or defiance) of whatever they think is the goal of the experiment . . .
>
> Ana C. Santos [2011, p. 46]

The primary task for an experimental economist is to produce an experimental design that at minimum can isolate a central behavioural hypothesis of interest. An experimental design is a model – a model of an application of a specific behavioural theory or theoretical proposition. In the early days of experimental economics, the purpose for experimental design was to test mainstream microeconomic theories. A major proponent of experimental testing of economics is, of course, Vernon Smith, who in the 1950s and later with his colleagues at Purdue University in the 1960s set about testing basic theoretical propositions. One of his colleagues was the late Cliff Lloyd, who was subsequently my colleague at Simon Fraser University. In a 1965 *Metroeconomica* article Lloyd explained the logic of how to refute 'traditional demand theory'. Before his untimely death in 1977, he had made elaborate arrangements to test traditional demand theory by installing his agent in a Hudson's Bay Company general store in Labrador, Canada. His agent would have adjusted prices and thereby have tested the standard demand theory [Lloyd 1980]. But unlike Lloyd's field experiment, Smith [1962] set out to test traditional microeconomic theory in a laboratory setting where intervening factors can be controlled and where any falsification can be logically defended. Yet, as David K. Levine and Jie Zheng observe [2010],

> The idea that experimental economics has somehow overturned years of theoretical research is ludicrous. A good way to wrap up, perhaps, is with the famous prisoner's dilemma game. No game has been so much studied either theoretically or in the laboratory. One might summarize the widespread view as: people cooperate in the laboratory when the theory says they should not. *Caveat emptor*. . . . What experimental economics has done very effectively is to highlight where the theory is weak, and there has been an important feedback loop between improving the theory . . . and improving the explanation of experimental facts.

Nevertheless, in more recent years experimental economists have followed Smith's lead and turned to using the laboratory to generate observable and repeatable evidence or patterns of behaviour. As Robert Sugden [2008] explains, today we can find experimental designs that are models which, rather than being designed for finding falsifying evidence for a theoretical proposition of interest, are instead often being designed to look for support for and giving credibility to that proposition. Specifically, he says [pp. 621, 624 and 627]:

> Experimental economics began to move beyond theory testing as a result of the accumulation of what I have called *exhibits* – replicable experimental designs that

> reliably produce interesting results – and through exhibits becoming objects of interest in their own right ... 'Exhibits' ... are taking over some of the functions formerly performed by theoretical models. ... Experimental designs are substituting for theoretical models as vehicles for firming up hunches and appraising their credibility.

Whether one wishes to conduct laboratory experiments to falsify aspects of traditional economic theories and behavioural propositions or one wishes to build replicable experimental designs to accumulate credible 'exhibits', most experimental model builders today recognize some unavoidable criticisms and the inherent logical problems of model building, whether the model is just an experimental design or one based on the pre-1980s notion of testing a theory by building a model of it and seeing whether or not it is consistent with available data. There are two main criticisms – questionable 'external validity' of the test or of exhibits produced by an experimental design and the inherent ambiguity of the results that one produces whenever the results depend on the additional assumptions or conditions needed to conduct the experiments. These two criticisms are just two aspects of what today's experimental economists know as the Duhem-Quine problem (or the Duhem-Quine thesis) that was briefly discussed in the Prologue.

As Smith explains the Duhem-Quine problem, 'experimental results always present a joint test of the theory (however well articulated, formally) that motivated the test, and all the things you had to do to implement the test' [2002, p. 98]. In Chapter 9, I will be examining the use of models of any type (viz, experimental designs or passive empirical or field tests) to assess the 'validity' of any claimed falsification or claimed credibility of experimentally-derived exhibits. The Duhem-Quine problem is a matter of logic. This is because any model consisting of more than one assumption is a compound statement – that is, it is a conjunction of multiple statements, perhaps in the form of equations or conditions – and it is true only if *all* of the constituent statements are true.[3] Moreover, one uses the logically valid model to claim some prediction or logical deduction is true *because* the compound statement

[3] This is at the root of the logic of any *explanation*. For those unfamiliar with formal logic, let me explain. An argument is a set of assumptions or reasons for which each is claimed to be literally true. If it is a *logically valid* argument, then whenever *all* of its constituent statements are literally true, to be logically valid it must be the case that *any* statement that can be logically deduced from that argument must also be literally true. From the point of view of logic, an explanation of why some given statement is true (perhaps a statement or proposition about some particular economic event) is the conjunction of the statements that make up one's logically valid argument. Using an argument in this positive mode (that is, explaining the truth of a statement) is called *modus ponendo ponens* [see Kneale and Kneale 1962, p. 98] (but usually without the *ponendo*). Now, if one can deduce from one's

is true – after all, this is how we use theories and models to explain observable events. Should a prediction or logically deduced statement turn out to be false, then we know that at least one of the constituent statements of the logically valid model must be false. The problem simply is that we do not know which of the constituent statements is false – that is, whether the deduced statement's false status is due to the theoretical behavioural assumptions we were trying test themselves or one of the additional assumptions we made to construct the model. In the case of seeking credible exhibits, we cannot know for sure whether the apparent behavioural regularity we observe in the application of a particular experimental design was due to those additional assumptions we needed to add to make the experiment practical. This logically ambiguous situation is the Duhem-Quine problem that Smith was explaining.

8.2. The logical problems facing experimentalist model building

> In a computational experiment, the researcher starts by posing a well-defined quantitative question. Then the researcher uses both theory and measurement to construct a model economy that is a computer representation of a national economy. A model economy consists of households, firms and often a government. The people in the model economy make economic decisions that correspond to those of their counterparts in the real world. Households, for example, make consumption and savings decisions, and they decide how much to work in the market. The researcher then calibrates the model economy so that it mimics the world along a carefully specified set of dimensions. Finally, the computer is used to run experiments that answer the question.
>
> Finn E. Kydland and Edward C. Prescott [1996, p. 69]

What Kydland and Prescott call computational experiments are computations, not experiments. In economics, unlike experimental sciences, we cannot create

logically valid argument a statement that is literally false (i.e., not true – leave aside for now how we would know whether a statement is or is not literally true) then one would have proof that *at least one* of the constituent assumptions of one's logically valid argument must be false. This is because, if all the statements were true *and* the argument is logically valid then any such logically deduced statement *must* be true, and thus given that it is false, it cannot be the case that *all* of the assumptions are true. Most important, if there are two or more constituent statements in one's argument, logically one does not know which statement is responsible for the false deduced statement. This means that, from a perspective not involving statistics, testing an argument such as an explanatory model is exactly a matter of deducing a statement and determining whether it is false – that is, deducing a statement for which, if it is false, it would contradict the assumed truth of *all* of the constituent assumptions. Using the logicality of an argument in this negative mode is called *modus tollendo tollens* [ibid.] (again, usually without *tollendo*).

> observations designed to resolve our uncertainties about theories; no amount of computation can change that.
>
> Christopher Sims [1996, p. 113]

In addition to the logical problem of ambiguity in test results recognized by the Duhem-Quine problem, there is the problem recognized by David Hume more than 200 years ago – the so-called Problem of Induction [see chapter 1 of Boland 1982 and 2003]. Some experimental economists may think that, instead of designing an experiment to test a behavioural theory or proposition, they can use an experimental design to produce exhibits and thereby 'induce' the truth status of behavioural propositions or hypotheses – however, doing so they will face an unavoidable problem. As Smith simply puts it in a Proposition based on the work of Imre Lakatos, 'Particular hypotheses derived from any testable theory imply certain observational outcomes; the converse is false' [2002, p. 94]. The reason why the converse is false is that it is impossible to prove (by pure induction) the truth status of an empirical general statement by listing a *finite* set of singular observations whose truth status is implied by that empirical general statement.[4] What one must prove instead is that there do not exist any conceivable 'observational outcomes' that would be logically denied if that empirical general statement is actually true (or as some would say, it requires 'proving the negative').

As Smith said [2002, pp. 92–4] when discussing deriving testable hypotheses from game-theoretic models,

> The wellspring of testable hypotheses in economic (game) theory are to be found in the marginal conditions defining equilibrium points or strategy functions that constitute theoretical equilibrium. . . . Behavioral point observations conforming to an equilibrium theory cannot be used to deduce or infer either the equations defining the equilibrium, or the logic and assumptions of the theory used to derive the equilibrium conditions. Hence, the importance of guarding against the belief that the theory has got to be true, given corroborating evidence. . . . Thus, in general, we cannot backward induct from empirical equilibrium conditions, even when we have a large number of experimental observations, to arrive at the original model. The purpose of theory is precisely one of imposing much more structure on the problem than can be inferred from the data.

8.3. Avoiding the Duhem-Quine logical problem

Almost all experimental economists seem to consider the Duhem-Quine problem to be an insurmountable problem. So, rather than making any claims

[4] Technically, by 'empirical general statement' one means a universal statement (such as '*all* decision makers are maximizers' and not '*some* decision makers are maximizers').

about the truth status of falsifying tests or positive exhibits, experimental economists have for the most part given up and turned to looking to experiments to provide 'positive evidence of a particular regularity in behaviour' [Sugden 2008, p. 625]. In this regard, as Smith says [2002, p. 103], much of laboratory work is being devoted to improving the techniques involved in obtaining

> new experimental knowledge of how results are influenced, or not, by changes in procedures, context, instructions and control protocols. The new knowledge may include new techniques that have application to areas other than the initiating circumstance. This process is driven by the [Duhem-Quine] problem, but practitioners need have no knowledge of the philosophy of science literature to take the right next local steps in the laboratory. Myopia here is not a handicap.

Myopia may not be a handicap, but it does not avoid the Duhem-Quine problem that confronts the challenge of establishing external validity. However, what the results of laboratory experiments can do is present puzzles that theorists and theoretical model builders need to address. After all, economic theory is supposed to apply to real economic situations and even the limited nature of laboratory experiments still may involve the choice behaviour purportedly explainable with traditional microeconomic theory and models. And if an experimental design presents exhibits that appear to be anomalies, it can indicate that there is some work to be done – perhaps to fix some aspect of traditional theory.

One of the obstacles for establishing external validity is obviously that no observation can be 100 percent accurate. Any claim for the truth status of any empirical claim – whether it is about anomalies or about support for theoretical and behavioural propositions being examined in the laboratory – the claim must be qualified, as any stochastic claim needs to be. Economic students usually learn about the various conventional statistical criteria to use in assessing the limited claim for the truth status of empirical propositions. That is, a proposition or even a claimed falsification is never claimed to be proven with observable evidence beyond being consistent with acceptable stochastic criteria (e.g., an acceptable R^2). In the next chapter I will present a method by which the so-called Duhem-Quine problem can be overcome, at least when it comes to testing economic hypotheses.

8.4. Using experimental models

> As Marc Isaac [1983] points out, one great virtue of laboratory work is that it forces [scientists] to *operationalise* theoretical models, and in doing so the

> scientist is led to reflect on several aspects of the model and the experiment that wouldn't otherwise have been considered problematic.
>
> Francesco Guala [2012, p. 608]

Ana Santos [2011, pp. 50–5] identifies what she calls an 'epistemic distinction between two kinds of economics experiments' [p. 51] or, I would say, two ways to use experiments: (1) *technological* – which may involve mechanism designing; and (2) *behavioural* – which includes decision making experiments and game-theory experiments and which may involve searching for behavioural regularities and patterns or just tries to generate anomalies and puzzles, as I suggested in the previous section. Santos says [ibid.] that the distinction is about 'the content of the knowledge claims that can be derived from' the two kinds of experiments. Let us consider these two ways to use the knowledge derived from experiments.

8.4.1. 'Technological' experimental models

> [E]xperimentalists can claim credit for developing some new and distinct approaches to tackling economic problems. One such approach would be the use of experiments as test-beds for institutional design ... This genre of experiment provides a social science analogue of the wind-tunnel: in this case the 'models' being tested are typically new institutional forms, such as proposed regulatory mechanisms. The purpose is to investigate the behaviour of these proposed institutional designs as a prelude to potential application in the field.
>
> Chris Starmer [1999, p. 24]

Double auctions were the subject of one of Smith's [1962] early experiments that was designed to test traditional price theory. Experiments such as this have eventually been concerned with the institutional aspects of specific markets. This, of course, includes rules that provide incentives and disincentives such that the outcomes of the market meet some desired results. The test aspect of the early experiments was whether traditional theory was sufficiently specified to produce the outcomes presumed by the traditional theory of market behaviour.

Since these experiments are conducted in the laboratory, there remains the persistent problem of external validity. Often, applying what seems to have been learned in the laboratory using ordinary people breaks down when what was learned is applied to a real world situation. A classical example is the use by the Federal Communications Commission (FCC) of a mechanism design for auctioning off some of the broadcast spectrum. When the FCC conducted an auction for licenses for personal communications systems, they supposedly benefited from experimental methods of economics [Plott 1997, Guala 2001]. Unlike a similar British spectrum auction, which was based on game-theoretic models and was deemed a great success, the FCC spectrum auction has not been so deemed [see Nik-Khan 2008]. The problem might be that in the FCC's auction, the players hired game theorists [Smith 2002, p. 101, Banks et al 2003].[5] As Edward Nik-Khan put it [p. 76],

> [R]ather than capturing enormous revenues for the treasury, it is closer to the truth to credit game theorists with delivering licenses to these telecoms at bargain prices. Contrary to widespread belief, auction theory failed to promote public policy.

Experimental economists will, of course, point out that the experimentalists' advice might not have been correctly followed.[6] Nevertheless, clearly, technical experimental models may have limits as social engineering tools. As Santos [2011, p. 52] says, 'It is clear from the various accounts of the applications of technological experiments that the success of mechanism design depends on the possibility of controlling the actions of market participants'. She adds, 'While experimenters can achieve a high level of control in the lab, this control is very difficult to obtain outside of the laboratory' [ibid.]. The problem of external validity will not go away easily, it seems.

8.4.2. 'Behavioural' experimental models

> Control is the essence of experimental methodology, and in experimental exchange studies it is important that one be able to state that, as between two experiments, individual values (e.g., demand or supply) either do or do not differ in a specified way. Such control can be achieved by using a reward structure to induce prescribed monetary value on actions. The concept of induced valuation ... depends upon the postulate of *non-satiation*. ... This postulate applies to experiments designed to test price theory propositions conditional upon known valuations. Separate experiments can be designed to test propositions in preference theory.
>
> Vernon Smith [1976, p. 275]

We must keep in mind that the perfectly controlled experiment is an idealisation, and in reality there are always going to be uncontrolled background factors,

5 It might have also been that, while in lab experiments the bidders' privacy would be maintained, in the FCC version, the FCC actually made public who submitted each bid. If so, some form of collusion would also be possible [see Smith 2008, p. 121].

6 Specifically, on using a 'combinatorial' auction [see Ledyard, Porter and Rangel 1997] rather than the 'simultaneous ascending' auction that was used.

> errors of measurement, and so forth. In order [to] neutralise these imperfections, experimenters use various techniques, like for example *randomization*. In a randomized experiment subjects are assigned by a chance device to the various experimental conditions, so that in the long run the potential errors and deviations are evenly distributed across them. This introduces an important element in the inference from data, i.e. *probabilities*.
>
> Francesco Guala [2012, p. 615]

Obviously, the idea of behavioural experimental economics has been around for some time. Today it is a thriving business in academic economics. And unlike 'technological' experiments designed to create markets in the real world based on what has been learned from experiments in the laboratory, behavioural experimental designs might be claimed to not need to assure external validity. Again, the basic idea is that, since economic theory and models are claimed to be relevant for explanations of economic behaviour in the real world, it must be the case that they are also relevant for explanations of behaviour in the laboratory. Thus, if carefully designed, any test of an economic theory or model applied to explain the behaviour in the laboratory would be a test of that theory or model should it be used in the external world.

Many such laboratory tests have yielded modestly claimed 'anomalies' that are really situations in which the predictions of the traditional theory of economic behaviour – for example, of utility maximization – fail to be confirmed. Various 'exhibits' or regularities of behaviour in the laboratory are claimed to be contrary to what is assumed in traditional theory and models. Early well-known examples of this are 'preference reversals' [see Lichtenstein and Slovic 1971] and an exhibit of how choices can vary depending on how the choice question is framed [see Kahneman and Tversky 1979]. Preference reversals were the observed behaviour resulting from testing revealed preference theory, and the observed framing issue was the result of testing expected utility theory.

Whether an observed experimental result constitutes an anomaly that must be dealt with may be only a matter of interpretation. When deciding what to do with an anomalous result, Daniel Friedman [1998, p. 942] thinks:

> [E]conomists should focus their energies on two sorts of questions. First, which learning environments encourage or discourage specific kinds of anomalies? Second, which institutions are sensitive to anomalous choice behavior? Anomalies can be ignored when the economic situation of interest (for example, a simple competitive market) involves an institution insensitive to anomalous behavior or when the institution allows effective learning. Otherwise, economists should take anomalies seriously, not by relaxing axioms of choice theory, but rather by modelling the specific institutional sensitivity and/or the incomplete learning.

Keeping in mind that an experimental design is a model of economic behaviour that supposedly can be explained by ordinary microeconomic theory, it is significant, I think, to note that while it is one thing to claim observed anomalies constitute refutations of such theoretical explanations of economic choice behaviour, it is quite another thing to claim a resulting observed regularity in the laboratory has external validity. But worse, even the claim that the observed anomalous behaviour constitutes a refutation of traditional theory is not out of the woods since such a claim cannot avoid the Duhem-Quine problem that concerns Smith [2002] that was discussed earlier in this chapter.

As Smith explains, ongoing research in experimental economics strives to learn and refine the experimental methods used to test economic behavioural theories and models. It's an ongoing and evolutionary process. Even those experiments that might be dismissed by virtue of the Duhem-Quine problem might lead to modified experimental designs. After all, this is true of the evolution of science in general. Nevertheless, it is questionable, or at least an open question, whether refinements in experimental design methods can ever overcome the challenge of external validity when performing experiments with sentient beings rather than inanimate objects such as atoms.

8.5. Laboratory-based experimental macroeconomic models

> Economists can do very little experimentation to produce crucial data. ... Astronomers can't do experiments, but they have more data than we do. Cosmology is short of relevant data and has contending theories, but is not pressed into service on policy decisions. Epidemiology is policy relevant and has limits on experimentation, but some kinds of experimentation are open to it – particularly use of animal models. Atmospheric science has limited experimental capacity, but in weather forecasting has more data than we do and less demand to predict the effects of policy. In modeling the effects of pollution and global warming, though, atmospheric science begins to be close to economics, with competing models that give different policy-relevant answers.
>
> Christopher A. Sims [1996, pp. 107–8]

> [C]ontrary to the claim of Sims [1996] ... 'crucial data' in support of macroeconomic models and theories – especially, (though not exclusively) those that are micro-founded – can be gathered in the laboratory. Such experimental tests can complement empirical analyses using field data, as in analysis of intertemporal consumption/savings decisions, rational expectations, efficiency wages or Ricardian equivalence. On the other hand, there are many macroeconomic theories, for instance on the origins of money, sunspots, speculative attacks and bank runs for which the data critical to an assessment of the theory are not

> available in the field. In the laboratory we can manufacture such data to meet the precise specifications of the theory being tested. In macroeconomic systems such data include not only individual choices over time, but also frequently involve individual expectations of future variables – data which are not readily available in the field.
>
> John Duffy [forthcoming, pp. 67–8]

In John Duffy's forthcoming survey of laboratory-based experimental macroeconomics, he tells us that 'the most important development in macroeconomics over the past several decades has been the widespread adoption of fully rational, micro-founded, calibrated, dynamic stochastic general equilibrium *models as laboratories* for evaluation of macroeconomic theories and policies' [p. 67, emphasis in the original]. He also says that today there is 'the small but growing research on an alternative methodology, which can be characterized as the use of experimental *laboratories as laboratories* for evaluation of macroeconomic theories and policies' [ibid., emphasis in the original]. Using models as laboratories is what I was discussed in Chapter 6. Here we need to consider the claim that, contrary to popular opinion, one can experimentally test macroeconomic models and theories in the laboratory.

Duffy's distinction about laboratories versus models as laboratories is, I think, misleading. After all, laboratory experimental designs are models – just a different form of model. Both involve the use of behavioural assumptions and both add extra assumptions such that the dreaded Duhem-Quine problem still persists. While Kydland and Prescott's computer models [1996, p. 69] are not really claimed to explain directly some aspect of the economy, experimental designs do – albeit in a sometimes limited way. And the experimental-design type model still cannot avoid the question of external validity.

With all this in mind, how would one design a macroeconomic experiment? Or maybe first we should ask, what is a macroeconomic experiment? Obviously, one would think that such an experiment involves a large number of subjects. However, Duffy claims that 'research has shown that attainment of competitive equilibrium outcomes might not require large numbers of subjects' [forthcoming, p. 3]. Specifically, 'economies with just 10 subjects yield market-based allocations that are indistinguishable from the competitive equilibrium of the associated pure exchange economy' [p. 4]. He thus concludes, 'while more subjects are generally better than fewer subjects for obtaining competitive equilibrium outcomes, it seems possible to establish competitive market conditions with the small numbers of subjects available in the laboratory' [ibid.].

Duffy distinguishes between two different experimental designs, which he calls the 'learning-to-forecast' design and the 'learning-to-optimize' design. As he explains:[7]

> In learning to forecast experiments, one elicits subjects' forecasts only, and a computer program uses those forecasts to solve optimization problems for the subjects. . . . In a learning to optimize design, you ask subjects to choose actions and they learn from repeated interaction what they should do; their forecasts are implicit in their action choices.

Such experiments have helped in developing 'a methodology for assessing whether laboratory time series data are converging toward predicted equilibrium levels' [p. 68].

It appears that most of what is being called experimental macroeconomics is really experimental general-equilibrium economics, which, of course, many continue to think is just a different way of looking at a macro economy whenever one thinks macroeconomics needs micro-foundations. As such, the experiments are designed to deal with simultaneous decisions of many individuals in diverse roles interacting indirectly – in a multiple-market context, for example. And like game-theoretic modeling, the issue is whether one can be sure an equilibrium coordination can be obtained.

Obviously, unlike experimental microeconomics, experimental macroeconomics involves a complexity that is difficult to avoid. However, as Duffy says, 'This complexity issue can be overcome but ... it requires experimental designs that simplify macroeconomic environments to their bare essence, or involve operational issues such as the specification of the mechanism used to determine equilibrium prices' [p. 2]. Nevertheless, he says, 'experimental methods can and should serve as a complement to the modeling and empirical methods currently used by macroeconomists as laboratory methods can shed light on important questions regarding the empirical relevance of microeconomic foundations, questions of causal inference, equilibrium selection and the role of institutions' [ibid.]. Again, critics will say, experimental macroeconomics designs that simplify involve extra assumptions and as such raise the Duhem-Quine problem for any conclusions reached. And no matter what, the question of external validity will not go away.

Despite this, Duffy [p. 4] claims that

> to date the main insights from macroeconomic experiments include (1) an assessment of the micro-assumptions underlying macroeconomic models, (2) a better understanding of the dynamics of forward-looking expectations which

[7] Personal correspondence dated 23 June 2013.

play a critical role in macroeconomic models, (3) a means of resolving equilibrium selection (coordination) problems in environments with multiple equilibria, (4) validation of macroeconomic model predictions for which the relevant field data are not available and (5) the impact of various macroeconomic institutions and policy interventions on individual behavior.

Unlike experimental microeconomics, the development of experimental macroeconomics research methodology is at an early stage, so there is a lot of work to do – particularly toward convincing empirical macro model builders that experimental macroeconomics should be part of their training.

8.6. Models and behavioural economics

At the core of behavioral economics is the conviction that increasing the realism of the psychological underpinnings of economic analysis will improve economics *on its own terms* – generating theoretical insights, making better predictions of field phenomena, and suggesting better policy. This conviction does not imply a wholesale rejection of the neoclassical approach. . . . The neoclassical approach is useful because it provides economists with a theoretical framework that can be applied to almost any form of economic (and even noneconomic) behavior, and it makes refutable predictions. Many of these predictions are tested . . . and rejections of those predictions suggest new theories.

Colin Camerer and George Loewenstein [2003, p, 3]

At the core of most models in behavioral economics there are still agents who maximize a preference relation over some space of consequences and the solution in most cases still involves standard equilibrium concepts. However, the behavioral economists are not committed to what is usually referred to as rational motivations. An economic fable (or a model as we would call it) that has at its core fairness, envy, present-bias and the like, is by now not only permitted but even preferred.

Ariel Rubinstein [2006, p. 246]

Clearly, these emotions have economic implications. . . . By modeling such emotions formally, one can begin to understand their economic and welfare implications more rigorously and more generally.

Matthew Rabin [1993, pp. 1281–2]

Neuroeconomics will remain a hot topic in economics during the coming decade, probably one of the hottest. This is not because of any truth that is waiting to be discovered or some urgent real-world problem that needs to be solved. Rather, the evolution of economics (and probably other disciplines as well) is subject to forces similar to those that dictate the emergence of any other fashion trend.

Ariel Rubinstein [2008, p. 485]

Given the early work of Herbert Simon in the 1950s, behavioural economics has obviously been around for some time. The main characteristic ever since has been the notion that somehow psychology should matter whenever one is explaining any human being's decision making [see Sent 2004]. In simple terms, behavioural economic models are microeconomic models which include extra assumptions that involve a psychological perspective. For Simon, this was merely the claim that in terms of inherent human cognitive abilities it is too difficult to see how any individual could actually perform what is necessary to assure the achievement of simple utility maximization as it is assumed in mainstream economic theory. As Simon observed [1955, p. 101],

> [A]ctual human rationality-striving can at best be an extremely crude and simplified approximation to the kind of global rationality that is implied, for example, by game-theoretical models. While the approximations that organisms employ may not be the best – even at the levels of computational complexity they are able to handle – it is probable that a great deal can be learned about possible mechanisms from an examination of the schemes of approximation that are actually employed by human and other organisms.

Once one is willing to question the realism of the usual behavioural assumptions of microeconomics, experiments are not out of the question. And as is usually recognized, currently there are primarily two types of experiments: laboratory and computer – although some will suggest there are some alternatives such as survey-based experiments, field experiments and 'natural' experiments. In the case of the laboratory-based behavioural economics, the model, as discussed earlier in this chapter, is nothing more than what is assumed in the experimental research design. In the case of the computer-based experiments, the model is the assumptions represented in the computer program.

8.6.1. 'Behavioural' computer models

Most of the discussion today about behavioural economic models is about experimental behavioural economics. One aspect not discussed much today is computer-based evolutionary game theory, which examines interactive behaviour – perhaps by focusing on the evolutionary genetics that supposedly influences behaviour [see Samuelson 2002]. The evolution examined is simply the result of repeated interaction in a game between two (or more) genetic types of individuals [see further Friedman 1991; Boland 2003, chapter 9]. As such, notions of mutations, replications, equilibria as evolutionary stable states and other ideas imported from evolutionary biology are modeled usually as computer programs. Needless to say, it is difficult to see how such computer models can reliably provide external validity. However, evolutionary behavioural economics does not have to be based on either game theory or computer programs, as will be seen in Section 8.7.

8.6.2. Survey-based behavioural experiments outside of economics

Historically, economists have been suspicious of using surveys as legitimate empirical data.[8] Non-economists in fields such as business studies are much less negative in their view of surveys as a form of experiment. For example, one might wonder about whether allowing stockholders to participate in the determination of the compensation of a corporation's CEO will lead to better decisions. Perhaps though, despite the hope of U.S. federal legislation requiring such participation, the effect depends on how knowledgeable are non-professional investors. Can this be tested? Obviously, one cannot conduct an experiment on an actual board of directors or on real investors, but one can simulate the situation using, say, MBA students [e.g., see Kaplan et al, 2013] and survey them by putting them hypothetically in the position of investors,[9] and survey how they would respond to various hypothetical conditions – for example, to what extent does their perception of fairness or due process matter? Of course, just treating the group of MBA students as a substitute for a board of directors amounts to creating a model of a board of directors. Obviously, the experimental design using a survey of substitute subjects is at minimum a form of a model of the intended subject – such as of the board of directors in this example[10] – but

[8] It is not clear that this common view of economists today is ever thought out beyond shear prejudice. Surely one can conceive of survey questions that one could ask individual decision makers – say managers of large companies or corporations – that might be useful for government policy makers. For example, how would the managers respond to various hypothetical changes to a relevant regulation or tax? From the perspective of most behavioural economists, it is not clear that equilibrium-based explanations of management decisions always conform to what is presumed in textbook economic theories of the firm.

[9] Some surveys alternatively put the students in a 'third-person' situation by asking what they think, say, Jack would do if facing such and such condition. Using such an approach begs yet another question. Just what is being tested – one's own attitude or one's opinion of other people's attitude?

[10] And if the question involves an economic or a sociological behavioural theory of the behaviour of members of such a board, it would be a way of building a pre-1980 version of a model.

one suspects that survey-based experiments such as this example too easily invite the question of external validity, let alone the issue of the Duhem-Quine problem.

8.6.3. Natural and field experiments as models of individual behaviour

One type of natural experiment was discussed in Chapter 5. That one involved building microeconomic empirical models which the proponents considered natural experiments [e.g., Angrist and Pischke 2010]. Those experiments were about questions such as the effects of smaller class size or the effectiveness of banning capital punishment. Another published example of a natural experiment was a study of professional golfers on the PGA tour that was concerned with a question about the focusing accuracy of putting when it was for par to avoid incurring a bogey [Pope and Schweitzer 2011]. Field experiments involve deliberately altering some small situation in the field and observing the effects of the change – such as I briefly discussed in Section 8.1, the one proposed by Lloyd using a Hudson's Bay Company store to test consumer theory. Usually, such experiments are not possible, given that they might have real effects on the possibly unaware subjects of the experiment, and as such too often raise questions of ethics. In all of these cases, one is building a micro model of individuals in some sort of social behavioural situation using assumptions from various social sciences either directly, in the case of field experiments, or virtually, in the case of natural experiments. Of course, both cases can be considered tests of behavioural assumptions, and as such, while not obviously subject to questions of external validity – because the observed behaviour is already in the external world – they still will be questionable on the basis of the Duhem-Quine problem since all natural and field experiments involve interpretations based on added assumptions.

8.6.4. Experiments as models of behavioural economics

It is interesting that outside of behavioural economics (and the activities within devoted to testing various economic notions), the old pre-1980 idea that a test of any behavioural theory involved building a mathematical model of it that could be used to confront data econometrically seems dead. The post-1980 view that the notions of a theory and a model are interchangeable now seems commonplace; but this is not the case in either game-theoretic models or experimental economics. That is, it is clear to most of these model builders that a game is built using behavioural assumptions to test those assumptions by building a model of those assumptions.[11] Similarly, any research design for an experimental test of those behavioural assumptions is also building a model of those assumptions.[12] It seems the only difference between these model builders in behavioural economics is a matter of terminology, not methodology. And as has been repeatedly pointed out, the question of external validity and the Duhem-Quine problem (i.e., ambiguity that results from adding modeling assumptions to test any behavioural assumptions) remain.

8.7. Models and evolutionary economics

> Most of the economic evolutionary models are sufficiently complicated so that the modeler or anyone else would have great difficulty in deducing optimizing strategies for all the actors. It is a basic premise of economic evolutionary theory that this state of affairs accurately reflects the problem facing real-world economic actors.
>
> Robert Nelson and Sidney Winter [2002, p. 40]

> Adopting an evolutionary approach in economics does not commit one to the view that it is in the end the economic entities' relative biological fitness that determines what evolves in economic systems. Adopting an evolutionary approach in economics leaves open the possibility that things may happen in economic evolution that are totally unrelated to their repercussions for the biological fitness of the economic agents involved. It is possible that things evolve that have detrimental effects for the biological fitness of the economic agents involved.
>
> Jack Vromen [2004, p. 227]

> Although evolutionary economists often criticise neoclassical economists for conducting analysis which is ahistorical, many, including Nelson and Winter [1982], only provide simulations, rather than models which can address historical data directly.
>
> John Foster [1997, p. 433]

At the end of the nineteenth century, Thorsten Veblen wondered whether economics could become an evolutionary science. But it is likely not until Richard Nelson and Sidney Winter [1974; 1982] began promoting evolutionary economics in the 1970s and 1980s that we began to see serious wide-spread efforts to build models of evolutionary economics.

[11] Assumptions that must be compatible with the mathematics of game theory.

[12] Assumptions that must be compatible with the mathematics of statistical inference, such as the requirements of randomness.

One might naively think that the primary task for any evolutionary model of economics would be to identify the essential aspects of evolutionary biology, such as genes, genetic mutations, replications, selection, and so on, that we usually recognize as essential components of natural selection. In this light, of course, one might claim that the competitive market seems most obviously an analogue of natural selection [cf. Alchian 1950]. The analogue for genetic mutations is also fairly obvious, since in economics innovation seems to fill the bill. Replication is less obvious, as one would find it difficult to think of an analogous form of biological reproduction between firms. But replication usually depends on what is considered the analogue to genes. Nelson and Winter [1974, p. 892] proposed using a firm's internal routines or 'decision rules' that would be the basis for management or production decisions. They go on to explicitly say, 'In our evolutionary theory, these routines play the role that genes play in biological evolutionary theory' [1982, p. 14]. In this sense, an innovation or mutation can be modeled as a change in such rules or routines, perhaps as the result of 'R&D'.[13] But can such an analogue for genes explain evolution? Jack Vromen has argued that 'Even if we were to have complete knowledge of genes and skills, we would still fall far short of being able to predict the behaviour of individuals, of routines and of firms' [2006, p. 545]. In any case, it seems any evolutionary model would need to include assumptions that characterize the necessary evolutionary biological elements or analogues.

In a recent article, Vromen [2012] has identified two alleged different views of Darwinian evolutionary economics based on the ontology of what such evolutionary based theories presume about the role of biological evolutionary perspectives. Here I am more concerned with two (or more) different ways of modeling evolutionary economics. One involves the pre-1980 view of models and the other includes the post-1980 view. The latter includes those which are really versions of behavioural economics, as it focuses on how individuals evolved to make decisions, in particular where their preferences come from.

8.7.1. Two views of evolutionary economic models

Evolutionary economics focuses on the transformation of the economy over time and the consequences this has for the current conditions of production and consumption. The sources of the transformation process are human learning, problem solving, and the accumulation of knowledge and capital. The diversity of

[13] Viz., research and development.

individual efforts and capabilities with respect to both learning and innovation results at any time in the generation and diffusion of a variety of innovative technologies, institutions, and commercial activities that compete with each other. The competition between them, and the economic and social adaptations triggered by that competition, fuel the process of transformation from within the economy.

Ulrich Witt [2012, p. 493]

[E]volutionary economics is not quite unlike the neoclassical theory of the firm *qua* its level of analysis and its technological (rather than organizational) theoretical orientation. But *qua* their key assumptions in their explanatory (or theoretical) framework they are very different. (Static) equilibrium analysis is discarded in evolutionary economics and so are strong rationality assumptions. Agents are boundedly rational at most. They satisfice rather than maximize. What is more, agents, firms in particular, differ with respect to their behavioral properties. There is heterogeneity in this respect. Thus representative agent type of theorizing is rejected. So is equilibrium theorizing. There is no presumption that economies (or industries) are in equilibrium. There is no presumption even that economies tend to move in the direction of equilibria.

Jack Vromen [2012, p. 739]

The primary example of a pre-1980 evolutionary model is that of Nelson and Winter [1974]. Their article was about their evolutionary theory of economic growth, and it reports the results of what amounts to a simulation model linking to data about United States economic growth between 1909 and 1949. Winter [1971] actually presents a formal model roughly based on Simon's 1955 behavioural model. Winter's article presents what amounts to a model of a modified version of the orthodox partial-equilibrium theory of a competitive industry.

Today, evolutionary economics appears either to be more involved with the post-1980 models or instead to be going back to work on the theoretical notions without much concern for building models. Most of the former type of evolutionary economic model is relevant to behavioural economics, such as asking how such basic things as consumer preferences and beliefs have been affected by biological evolution [see Robson 2002]. Those less concerned with building models are those who think we should first try to understand economics without resorting to equilibrium-based explanations [e.g., Hodgson and Knudsen 2006; Witt 2012]. As Vromen [2012, p. 739] explains,

To the extent that the notion of equilibrium serves any analytical purpose at all (as a benchmark, for example) . . . in evolutionary economics, economies may be out-of-equilibrium all of the time. And if an economy converges on an equilibrium, it need not stay there for long. Both exogenous and endogenous changes

> may dislodge the equilibrium. Static (or comparative-static) equilibrium analysis is replaced by dynamic process-analysis. Dynamic process-analysis need not take the form of analytically tractable models that allow for close-form solutions. . . . Attempts are made to make room for endogenous technological change (innovations); attempts that are taken by some to defy closed system theorizing.

It is important to recognize that, unlike Nelson and Winter's approach, one does not have to rely on a Darwinian view of evolution to build an evolutionary model. For example, Kenneth Carlaw and Richard Lipsey [2012] specifically address evolutionary modeling without relying on any Darwinian perspective.[14] For them, 'Economists face two conflicting visions of the market economy, visions that reflect two distinct paradigms' [p. 736]. In one vision,

> the behaviour of the economy is seen as the result of an equilibrium reached by the operation of opposing forces - such as market demanders and suppliers or competing oligopolists - that operate in markets characterised by negative feedback that returns the economy to its static equilibrium or its stationary equilibrium growth path.

In the other vision,

> the behaviour of the economy is seen as the result of many different forces - especially technological changes - that evolve endogenously over time, that are subject to many exogenous shocks, and that often operate in markets subject to positive feedback and in which agents operate under conditions of genuine uncertainty.

The main characteristic that Carlaw and Lipsey are stressing is that what 'distinguishes the two visions is *stationarity*' in the former 'and *non-stationarity*' in the latter. And of course, Darwinian evolution is not the only way to characterize non-stationarity.

8.7.2. Going beyond the evolutionary theory of the individual

While Nelson and Winter [1974] focus much of their evolutionary model on a behavioural model of the firm, evolutionary economics can also be a more macro view of evolution. One obvious issue is population dynamics (which much of the computer-based evolutionary game theory is also about). One might even claim that evolutionary economics is more about change and thus should be seen as a perspective that challenges the old Walrasian general equilibrium view of the macro economy. As such, evolutionary models do not need to delve into biological metaphors or analogues.

[14] They provide an explicitly non-Darwinian evolutionary model in their [2011].

One main issue that evolutionary model builders think needs to be explained is the basic notion of selection – particularly, if one is going to see such a model as the basis for explaining evolutionary change. Is change the result of a process analogous to genetic replication, or is it the result of environmental interaction, or perhaps both? In recent years, many evolutionary economic model builders have turned to what is called the 'Price equation' that was introduced in the work of geneticist George Price [1972; 1995]. The Price equation is claimed to be very useful in modeling evolutionary economics [Knudsen 2004, p. 155] and can be shown to be consistent with the formalization of Nelson and Winter's evolutionary economics. The usefulness of the Price equation for modeling economic evolutionary dynamics is still open to question. But what are most important here are merely the issues we have already seen. If the model of evolutionary economics involves making assumptions that raise the Duhem-Quine problem and then we try to test them, we cannot be sure what will be accomplished. But perhaps this problem can logically be overcome, as will be argued in the next chapter.

9

The logical adequacy of convincing tests of models using empirical data

> The universe we examine through what Spinoza has called the 'the lens of philosophy' – heaven knows what he would have called it had he been, for example, a pudding manufacturer!
>
> 'Professor Walther von der Vogelweide' (a.k.a. Severn Darden [1961])

Throughout this book I have attempted to analyze critically the explicit process of building models of the economy or aspects of the economy. Model building is so widely practiced today that it becomes very difficult to question the soundness of the process. Even when we accept the traditional theories of the textbooks, we still must make decisions regarding the process of applying them to the real world. As such, the process of model building is certainly not automatic. There may be infinitely many potential models that could be built to use any given behavioural hypothesis. However, it does not matter whether we view model building as a process of choosing between existing complete models or a process of building from the ground up, so to speak, assumption by assumption.

As is evident in much of the discussion so far, a model builder must begin by addressing a simple but key question: What is the purpose for building any model? No single model will serve all purposes. The models we build to describe or explain the real world will not necessarily be usable for testing the behavioural hypotheses used in their construction. Similarly, models built for quick application to policy issues may not always be sufficiently realistic for plausible explanations or convincing tests – recall from Chapter 5, this is the distinction Mankiw [2006] was making between engineers and scientists. Sometimes one might suspect that these considerations may not be well understood or appreciated by most economists. Too often it is assumed that a model which has been shown to be successful for one purpose (e.g., description of data) will automatically be sufficient for another (e.g., testing). Of course, in this chapter I will be discussing only models designed for the purpose of testing. However, another distinction is that testing can be on the basis of either singular observations or, as will be discussed in the next chapter, be on the basis of statistical observational data. The distinction between these two bases needs to be kept in mind throughout this chapter as the matter of *logical adequacy* does not necessarily involve statistics, although it is clearly relevant to statistical testing. This chapter is only about testing involving singular observations as that is the best way to make clear the *logical requirements of testing*. Recall, it is the logical requirements that led many, such as Smith and Kirman, to raise the recognition of the so-called Duhem-Quine problem, which makes any conclusion about the cause of a failed model so ambiguous.

The issue of distinguishing between the logical problems of testing and the more familiar statistical problems of testing is usually difficult for those economic model builders trained in the post-1980s view that I have been distinguishing from the pre-1980s view of models. It is particularly difficult for those readers who a priori see the real world as a necessarily 'stochastic environment'. The problem here, as I will explain, is that – outside of the casino – it is our models which are stochastic rather than the world we wish to explain.[1]

Another key question about testing and model building in economics is: Where do we start? Historically, confronting empirical data with a theory or model was the main approach to testing. The purpose was to determine the truth status or even just the reliability of empirical applications and as such has usually been a matter of collecting or observing data to determine if the data does or does not contradict statements that can be logically derived from the theory or model in question. In this case, the first step is to make sure the logical validity is sufficient to perform such a test. Another approach is to collect observed (non-experimental) data to see what needs to be explained. This requires building a model of the data itself to determine its sufficiency for posing significant empirical questions. This chapter is about the former approach – that is, the view that we begin with a model (theoretical or empirical) to determine what data it would take logically to test that model and then look at the data (experimental or non-experimental). The next chapter will be about the latter approach – that is, building models of available statistical data to determine their adequacy

1 I realize that some readers will be quick to point out that in the absence of perfect knowledge, decision makers' choices may be stochastic, but it is such stochasticism that we would be explaining and thus being modeled, and so cannot be used to excuse any failure to explain those decisions.

for empirical analysis and testing. For this chapter, I stress, statistical data will never be at issue and so the problems discussed in the next chapter about the statistical adequacy of observational data will not be relevant here.

In this regard, many of those readers who see models from what I have been calling the post-1980 perspective will initially have a difficulty that I would like them to try to put aside. The difficulty is illustrated by the quotation at the top of this chapter. The quotation there is about Baruch Spinoza, who happened to be a seventeenth-century lens grinder by trade, and thus, as the comedian Severn Darden put it, Spinoza said that we examine the universe through 'the lens of time', but, as Darden says, 'Heaven knows' what he would have called it if Spinoza had been 'a pudding manufacturer'. Here is the problem. I will be talking about testing models of theories but not talking about statistical or otherwise stochastic data. Those who approach models from the post-1980s perspective or almost anyone who sees economics or testing only from the perspective of econometrics will likely be at first unable to see testing without any consideration of statistics and statistical data, which is the subject of econometric theory. In contrast, in this chapter observations will be singularly discrete, not samples consisting of many observations of one or more variables. This is because I will be talking about *non-stochastic* models and theories, and by 'non-stochastic' I am ruling out consideration of stochastic data – observations will usually be considered exact, perfectly accurate[2] – as well as ruling out any behaviour that might be characterized as gambling or otherwise random. For those econometrics-oriented readers, perhaps they can see this as an assumption of leaving errors aside because errors are unobservable and instead just focusing on observables. Either way, the reason for my doing this 'strange' thing is because I wish to focus exclusively on the logic of the relationship between theoretical models and observational reality in terms of the 'informativeness'[3] of the theories or models being tested. A test in this case means identifying what conceivable observations are denied as being

2 I will slightly relax this later on, but it still will not be an issue of statistics or stochasticism.

3 Informativeness is about the amount of conceivable observations that would be *denied* should the theory or model exactly be true. An elementary example would be, if the statement '*all* swans are white' is 100% true, then it would be impossible to observe a non-white swan anywhere in the Universe or at any time – or in other words, there are an unlimited number of conceivable observations that are denied such that one would have to check possibly an unlimited number of swans if the statement is true. A much less informative statement would be '*some* swans are white', which, unless one knows how many swans there are in the Universe, not much is denied as even observing one non-white swan would not contradict the truth of this statement. For more about informativeness, see chapter 6 of Boland [1989].

possible *if* the theory or model is actually 100 percent true. In the next chapter, I will take up today's more common view of data, where we would not usually assume observational data is exact.

9.1. Testing versus mere testability of modern economics

In his PhD thesis, Paul Samuelson [1947/65] set out a manifesto for modern economics. Its keystone idea was that, to be taken seriously, economic propositions or theorems must always be testable – or, in his words, must be 'operationally meaningful' such that a meaningful theorem is simply 'a hypothesis about empirical data which could conceivably be refuted, if only under ideal conditions. A meaningful theorem may be false' [1947/65, p. 4]. And note that Samuelson was talking about observations in exactly the way I will be talking about them in this chapter.

While philosophers and methodologists might see Samuelson's statement as something about what it takes to be 'scientific' [e.g., Blaug 1992], this requirement had nothing to do with such an issue. Instead, as noted in the Prologue, it was a response to the 1930s critics of the growing use then of mathematical modeling in economics. Their criticism was the false claim that the use of mathematics could only produce tautologies. Remember, tautologies are statements which are true regardless of the meaning of the non-logical words in the statements. For example, the statement 'I am here or I am not here' is true regardless of who I am or where here is. Such a statement cannot thus be an empirically meaningful or informative statement, since one cannot ever conceive of data that would refute it. So, if one has an economic proposition that is testable, then one would have a statement that is conceivably false and hence not a tautology. In his thesis, Samuelson goes on to show over and over how testable propositions can be derived from simple mathematical models of ordinary economics. Of course, he thereby proves the critics wrong. He also demonstrates a perspective that will be used in this chapter. Namely, what was mentioned at the very end of the previous section – one can talk about tests and testing without the necessity of talking about statistics or econometrics or, in other words, about probabilities.

Today, economics is characterized by the activities of model builders and definitely not by the debates among economic philosophers and ideologists. Economists today see themselves engaged in an ongoing saga of advances in model building. The basic behavioural hypotheses and behavioural theories that ordinary economists attempt to model may not have changed substantially in several decades, but various models do come and go.

The progress in model building is most visible when it is seen to involve the rejection (rather than empirical refutation) of various modeling techniques. In the 1930s, the use of calculus-based techniques to prove theoretical propositions was commonplace among economic theorists, and so utility or production functions were specified to be everywhere continuous and differentiable in order to complete an equilibrium model. By the beginning of the 1940s, the task among avant-garde theorists was to complete a model of general equilibrium in order to be able to prove the existence of an equilibrium vector of prices or quantities. As discussed in Chapter 2, the functions were specified as such to fulfill the requirements of Brouwer's fixed-point theorem, which was commonly used[4] to construct such existence proofs [see Wald 1936/51]. In the 1950s, calculus was eventually rejected as a basis of general-equilibrium modeling. In later models the continuous utility and production functions were replaced with 'upper semi-continuous' set-theoretic correspondences. These less demanding specifications were allowed by the alternative, Kakutani's fixed-point theorem [see Debreu 1959]. The testing standards – if we wish to see the process in these terms – were the criteria employed by formalist mathematicians. Any model which could not be shown to meet the 'standards of rigor of the contemporary formalist school of mathematics' [loc. cit, p. viii] would be rejected in the same way empirical models are rejected when they do not meet the standards set by the currently accepted empirical testing conventions.

Whether the model builder uses calculus or set theory might have been a hot topic in the 1960s, and today, similarly, there could be other more advanced modeling techniques that one might have to choose between, but (as I will argue in this chapter) there is another type of choice to be made. Specifically, if we are building an empirical model using econometrics, then we have to recognize the choice of any estimation convention is an additional and integral part of one's econometric model. And since it is a matter of choice, it may, of course, give a reason for rejecting a model separate from the results of any particular observational test.

Having said this, however, I do not wish to mislead about the issues in this chapter. Again, the matter of testing in this chapter will be about the logic of a test – specifically, about the logical requirements of the test which involves just a singular observation (one that is logically denied by the truth status of

[4] Although almost exclusively in the non-English-speaking world. In North America, concern for such proofs came later in the 1940s and 1950s when translations became available.

the statement or model being tested) or of the test which involves a sample. The underlying logic of testing applies to both but is made clear and unambiguous if we do not bring up the complications of using statistical or stochastic data since that requires a separate analysis – as will be pursued in Chapter 10.

9.2. The basic logic of model building for the purpose of testing economic hypotheses

Historically, model building in the 1950s and 1960s was a means to determine whether a behavioural hypothesis or theory would work in a given practical situation. As such, the task was to build a 'model' of that behavioural hypothesis or theory much in the spirit of design engineering. As discussed in the Prologue, design engineers might build a small-scale model of a new airplane wing design to test its aerodynamics in a wind tunnel. In other words, engineers commit themselves to specific models. Of course, many different models may be constructed – all based on the same new wing idea (or behavioural hypothesis, in the case of economics) – by varying certain proportions, materials, and so on. Unfortunately, for a long time such opportunities for testing in this manner (i.e., with scaled-down models in wind tunnels) rarely arose in economics when it came to using non-experimental observational data. But, of course, today this to a great extent is no longer the case given the development of experimental and behavioural economics, as I discussed in Chapter 8.[5]

9.2.1. The basic three-stage process of model building

Schematically, whether one is building an engineering model or a model of the economy, one can see model building as a three-stage process. Of course, our concern here is the process of building economic models, but before describing these stages, I need to point out a difficulty for some readers. It

5 As well as the examples I discussed in Chapter 5, such as the empirical microeconomic models that were designed to be small-scale tests of more general questions (e.g., the effects of class size or in a limited way, the deterrence effectiveness of capital punishment). Of course, some macroeconomic model builders [e.g., Lucas, Kydland and Prescott] also see their models as test beds for testing policy questions, but these are only remotely related to the kind of prototype models that engineers once played with since wind tunnels are controlled experiments. I say 'once played with' because, today, engineers more often use computer models of the wing designs to test out an idea using usually nothing but physics principles and known parameters of the materials used.

has to do with the difference between the pre- and post-1980 views of models versus theories. The point is that the pre-1980 view recognizes three separate stages, but the post-1980 view recognizes only two, as it does not distinguish between the first two stages. So, with this in mind, let us now consider the three stages of the process of constructing a model.

The first stage of building a model is rarely discussed today. It starts (explicitly for some and only implicitly for others) with a set of autonomous conjectures as to basic behavioural relationships. And, most importantly, this set must explicitly or implicitly include an identification of the relevant variables;[6] moreover, there must be an indication as to which of them are exogenous and which are not since at root this is fundamental to any (causal) explanation in economics. In very elementary terms, the endogenous variables are, of course, what the model is designed to explain – in the *causal* sense of explanation – and the causes are the exogenous variables.[7] How the exogenous variables cause the particular values of the endogenous variables is what is conveyed by the behavioural hypotheses included in the model.

As we will see, today the next stage of building a model is seen to be fused with the first stage. For this stage, in the past, this would have been as a stage where we would separately add to the posited behavioural relationships some specifying or simplifying assumptions, the nature of which depends on what is being simplified or specified (i.e., on the behavioural assumptions themselves). Moreover, the parameters usually talked about are the result of this specification. As those who come from the pre-1980 perspective will easily see, the main reason why these extra assumptions must be added is that hardly anyone would have wanted to make the behavioural assumptions of the theory of the consumer (or producer) as specific as would be required to make them (or predictions deduced from it) *directly* observable. But, of course, those model builders today who come from the post-1980 perspective would have from the beginning made their behavioural assumptions as specific as would be necessary for the completion of the second stage. In effect for most model builders today, stage one and stage two are fused together.

Finally, if we wish to apply the model to empirical data we must add a set of assumptions designed to deal with the values of the parameters created with the second stage (whether or not the creation was done separately)

6 In a very fundamental sense, identifying a list of relevant variables is the most significant theoretical idea to be modeled, as any posited relationships will be limited to those variables – moreover, any conceivable variable not included is deemed to play no role in the determination of the values of the endogenous variables.

7 For more about the relationship between exogeneity and causality, see further Boland [2010, pp. 533–5].

either directly by specifying them or indirectly providing criteria for measuring them. I will be explaining these stages in turn, but note that in the following discussion I will be keeping the examples as simple as possible in order to avoid having to discuss unrelated complications that one might find in more elaborate models. So, to begin, this three-stage process gives us the following schemata for any model:

(1) *A set of behavioural assumptions* about people and/or institutions. For example, this set may include the simple textbook claim that the level of aggregate consumption (C) depends on the level of aggregate income (Y).
(2) *A set of simplifying assumptions* about the relationships contained in the first set. For example, this set might include, say, a very simple textbook behavioural proposition about aggregate demand, such as $C = f(Y)$, where $\partial C/\partial Y$ is assumed to be positive, or it may go as far to assume that the aggregate demand function stated in the behavioural theory be specified as a linear function, $C = \alpha + \beta Y$, where α is positive and β is between 0 and 1.

For the most part, most model builders would be satisfied with these two sets as a sufficient two-stage characterization (or again, one fused-compounded stage), but, as I said, there is more. Although often taken for granted as a separate issue for statistical methodology, there is the third stage, which involves a set that is either assumed or presumed to deal with how one is to apply the model to empirical data. Specifically,

(3) *A set of assumed parametric specifications* about the values of those parameters created in the second set. This set would either (a) directly assume true values for the parameters or, more likely today, (b) specify criteria for measuring the parameters. For example, (i) we might assume that the parameter β has the value $\beta = 0.33$ (short of this, we might choose to 'calibrate' the model, as discussed in Chapter 2) or (ii) we might instead specify that the above model be deemed to fit the available data according to certain specified statistical criteria.

This third set will be examined more closely later in this chapter, for now we will focus more on the first two stages of model building.

9.2.2. The ambiguity of direct model refutation

Observing that every model is a conjunction of at least the first two sets of assumptions leads to the consideration of some problems concerning what constitutes a successful or failed test. For theoretical models that are designed to explain so-called stylized facts or data, usually we do not need to specify criteria for what would constitute an empirical fit for available observable data. Stylized or not, for now let us accept data as perfectly accurate and hence simply and literally true (i.e., for now, let us rule out all observation error[8]) so that we can clearly define what constitutes a successful or a failed test when considering exact observational data. Specifically, if there is no observation error (and thus no measurement error), whenever it is shown that one of the predictions is false, then, by *modus tollens*[9] we can conclude that at least one of the assumptions (the constituent parts) must be false. Note however, as was discussed in Chapter 8, there is a certain logical ambiguity about *which* assumption and hence which type of assumption is responsible for the false prediction – was it the basic behavioural assumptions of the first stage or was it some simplifying assumption introduced in the second stage? But, regardless, if any one of the assumptions in any stage is false, then some of the possible predictions will be false. Moreover, since an assumption from either set could be the false offending assumption, just noting that one of the predictions is false does not necessarily tell us anything about *which* assumption has 'caused' the false prediction – again, is it one of the behavioural assumptions or just one of those simplifying assumptions we added to build the model? This ambiguity is what Vernon Smith recognized as the Duhem-Quine problem,[10] that I briefly discussed in Chapter 8 (it was also noted there that philosophers refer to this problem of ambiguity with the uninformative label the 'Duhem-Quine thesis'). As will be seen, this is particularly a problem for model builders who are using models to refute behavioural theories or hypotheses (and as such is a problem not unlike the one discussed in Chapter 8 for anyone trying to use experiments to refute behavioural theories or hypotheses or to produce credible experimental exhibits).

Alan Kirman [1992] makes the point specifically about macroeconomic models which include the simplifying assumption in the form of the representative individual when building and testing macroeconomic models. What Kirman is talking about is the addition of the simplifying assumption whereby a single agent is used to represent all individuals in an entire

[8] Today, many econometricians would say 'measurement error', but in this chapter I will refer to 'observation error' since it is more general and allows for simple observations. Moreover, observation error includes measurement error.

[9] For an explanation of *modus tollens*, see note 3 in Chapter 8.

[10] In chapter 8 of Boland [1989] I labeled this problem as the Ambiguity of Direct Model Refutation, which is a lot more informative.

macro economy. He tells us that when using the representative individual 'as a model for empirical testing, the representative agent presents a peculiar disadvantage.... [I]f one rejects a particular behavioural hypothesis, it is not clear whether one is really rejecting the hypothesis in question, or rejecting the additional hypothesis that there is only one individual' [1992, p. 118]. As quoted at the top of Section 6.4 of Chapter 6) he specifically notes, 'when the conclusions of such a model are tested with empirical data ... and should they, by chance, be rejected, this may simply reflect the fact that the assumption that the economy could be represented by a single individual was erroneous' [p. 125]. He goes on the say, 'In other words, whenever a representative agent model is tested, one is testing a joint hypothesis: the particular behavioural hypothesis one is interested in and the hypothesis that the choices of the aggregate can indeed be described as the choices of a single utility-maximizing agent' [ibid.].

9.3. Overcoming the ambiguity of direct model refutation

Contrary to the views of some philosophers of economics, ordinary practicing economists (who see their task as one of building and applying models of macro- or microeconomics) will testify that the occurrence of *model* refutation is a common experience. Nevertheless, spending one's time refuting particular models without ever addressing the question of testing some particular behavioural hypotheses themselves seems less than satisfactory even though ambiguities discussed earlier in Section 9.2 might give one pause if one wishes to perform a convincing test. But surely one can go beyond the ambiguity inherent in the Duhem-Quine problem. In the remainder of this chapter I present an approach to testing which to some significant extent does overcome the ambiguity that constitutes the Duhem-Quine problem. However, for anyone trying to refute one or more behavioural hypotheses, a little extra effort will be required before they rush off to employ the latest modeling techniques.

9.3.1. Critical interpretations are merely models

In this chapter, the central concern is the issue of testing behavioural hypotheses (or behavioural theories) with models or models that include such hypotheses. So far, I have argued only that the falsification of a *model* of a behavioural hypothesis does not necessarily imply the falsification of the behavioural hypothesis itself (i.e., the Duhem-Quine problem). The methodological problem at issue concerns the logical relationship between models and behavioural hypotheses and the limitations imposed by the principles of ordinary logic. In this light, I have noted that all testing involves the conjunction of the behavioural hypothesis being tested and some necessary extra assumptions involved in what I have called stage two. That is, it involves building a model using the behavioural hypothesis in order to test the behavioural hypothesis. Specifically, however, one cannot expect to be able to observe just one false model[11] and thereby prove the behavioural hypothesis itself to be false. If one thinks that hypotheses or theories are refutable in this way, then one's job would appear to be much too easy. For example, one could always append a known false extra assumption to a behavioural hypothesis and thereby construct a model which is automatically false. Certainly, such testing would be 'unfair' at best. Just as surely, we would have no reason to expect that proponents of the behavioural hypothesis would accept such a 'refutation' of their hypothesis. So, in what way does building a model of a behavioural hypothesis constitute a test *of the hypothesis*?

Many economists once seemed to think that the act of building a model always constitutes a test of a behavioural hypothesis or theory because the act of specification amounts to an interpretation of the theory. For example, in a critique of Milton Friedman's famous 1953 essay on methodology,[12] Tjalling Koopmans claimed that if any one interpretation of a theory is false then the theory must be false [Koopmans 1957, p. 138; cf. Boland 1997, chapter 2]. This method of criticism presumes that 'interpretation' is a process equivalent to a logical derivation from a set of given postulates without the addition of any other assumptions. Probably only a pure mathematician would make such a claim since the pure mathematical models used by economists are always presumed to be logically complete. With complete models, the only possibility of a false interpretation would be due to an error in the logical derivation. Surely, there are other ways to produce a false interpretation. If so, under what circumstances does a possibly false interpretation of someone's view constitute a criticism of that view?

Despite Koopmans's presumption, the ordinary sense of the word 'interpretation' (like 'model building') always involves additional assumptions (e.g., 'I assume by this word you mean . . .'). Moreover, any assumption

[11] To 'observe a false model' means treating the model as a conjunction of all of the assumptions into a compound sentence. If any assumption in the conjunction is false, the compound statement as a whole is false.

[12] Friedman's essay claimed that the only relevant test is a test of the predictions of the theory and not of the assumptions. This may be acceptable to those with an engineering perspective but certainly not to those with the perspective of a scientist that Mankiw [2006] was discussing.

could be false. Putting numbers in place of letters in mathematical models is an overt (stage three) act of 'specifying' the equations.[13] Most interpretations require such specifications of the variables. Such specification involves at least an assumption about their dimension or scale and this type of specification, too, involves possibly false assumptions. In other words, a model is merely a mode of interpreting behavioural hypotheses or theories. More important, a model or an interpretation can lead to a successful direct criticism (or test) only when what has been added is known to be true – remember, one *assumes* when one does not know. This is the root of the problem. Testing behavioural hypotheses by adding assumptions and finding that the resulting model does not 'fit the data' does not usually allow us to conclude that the behavioural hypotheses (rather than the additional assumptions) were at fault since our added assumptions may not be true. And again, any interpretation of behavioural hypotheses or theory involves adding extra assumptions and thus is just a model.

Some readers may say that the real root of this problem is that it is always difficult or impossible to determine when any assumption is true. They may be right, and I will consider how model builders cope with this question later. But for now, let us assume that it is possible to make true observations such that there is no ambiguity concerning whether a model 'fits the data' so that I can eventually show that testing behavioural theories or hypotheses by building models using them is not completely impossible. I will subsequently show that the apparent impossibility of testing behavioural theories or hypotheses using models is due entirely to not going far enough. It will be argued subsequently that if one builds a model of the behavioural hypothesis or theory and also builds a model of a conceivable counter-example[14] to the *behavioural hypothesis or theory* in question using the same simplifying and specifying assumptions, then, using ordinary test conventions, convincing tests can be performed!

9.3.2. Testing with models of counter-examples

Prior to discussing the difficulties encountered when performing a convincing test in this way, we will need to investigate what constitutes a counter-example (i.e., a set of conceivable but logically denied observations) and when a model of a counter-example constitutes (logically) a refutation of the behavioural theory or hypothesis.

[13] Today, some would see this specification as the calibration that was discussed in Chapter 6.
[14] Or, in the words of Binmore [2011], a 'counter-factual', as was discussed in Chapter 4.

First, to determine what would constitute a counter-example, we need to decide what we want to test. Are we testing the truth status of a single behavioural hypothesis or is it the truth status of the stage-two specification assumptions? In both cases, rather than building a model of a behavioural hypothesis to see whether it 'fits' the available data, considering counter-examples amounts to another approach to testing behavioural theories or hypotheses by means of building models. If it is a single hypothesis we wish to test, before we proceed to build a model using it by adding what I earlier called 'simplifying assumptions' (the stage-two extra assumptions concerning the specific form of the functional relationship between the endogenous and exogenous variables recognized by the behavioural assumptions), we might try to identify one or more statements or propositions that are directly logically denied by the behavioural assumptions alone[15] (i.e., without benefit of the further stage-two specifications). If, instead, it is a test of a stage-two specification assumption, then a failure to fit will not allow us to blame the assumptions of either the stage-one or the stage-two since this runs up against the Duhem-Quine problem[16] – but for those model builders who are interested in testing specific alternative stage-two ways of modeling a particular behavioural hypothesis, this would not matter as one would simply presume that the hypothesis is true or at least not open to question. Nevertheless, my discussion here will be limited to testing only stage-one behavioural assumptions in order to draw sharp distinctions.

At first this counter-example approach to testing may seem too easy. Consider a behavioural hypothesis which has just one relationship involving two endogenous variables but only one exogenous variable. We could say that any two observations of the values of the endogenous and exogenous variables which show that the values of the exogenous variable did not change, but also show that just one of the endogenous variables did change, constitutes a refutation of that theory. For an endogenous variable to change consistent with the model, at least one exogenous variable must change – after all, that is the purpose for distinguishing between endogenous and exogenous variables. We can thus say that the observation of changes in an endogenous variable without changes in the posited exogenous variables

[15] For example, if the statement 'All swans are white' is literally true, then it would be impossible to observe a non-white swan. That is, observing a non-white swan is denied by the truth of the 'All' statement.

[16] To avoid this, and depending on how the model is specified, one might consider a non-nested hypothesis test [see Pesaran and Deaton 1978 or Pesaran and Dupleich 2008], which is more appropriate for testing stage-two modeling specifications – I will discuss this type of test later.

logically constitutes a counter-example for the theory in question. In the performance of this test, we can see that it is possible for just two observations (of all variables) to constitute a refutation.

There are other conceivable counter-examples which may require more observations (perhaps for vectors of variables). When we consider behavioural hypotheses involving several relationships or which recognize many exogenous variables, things get much more complex and the minimum number of observations can grow large. Nevertheless, as I have shown in chapters 2 and 3 of my 1989 book, for simple algebraic system-of-equations models the minimum number of observations can be determined based on the number of endogenous and exogenous variables (and the algebraic nature of the assumed relationships). Obviously, more of either of these increases the minimum number of observations.

If the question of how many observations it takes to form a counter-example is not obvious to the reader, consider the following well-known geometry principle. Let us say we are given three points plotted on a graph. Obviously, any given two points would establish a straight line. But if the third plotted point is not on the extension of that straight line, then we know the three points cannot represent a linear relationship (remember, here we are always assuming the points represent exact observations). So, in this case, we can say that the minimum number of observations (represented by points on the graph) that it would take to refute a claimed linear relationship is simply three.[17] What I provided in the 1989 book was just an elaborate extension of this principle – namely, a formula for calculating the number of observations needed to constitute a counter-example based on the number of exogenous and the number of endogenous variables.[18]

What constitutes a counter-example is also limited by considerations of quantificational logic. To use the philosopher's example, if our theoretical claim is merely that all swans are white, then the observation of just one non-white swan would constitute a decisive counter-example. If our theory were, instead, that there is at least one pink swan, then the observation of a counter-example is impossible. The counter-example in this case amounts to a collection of observations sufficiently large to prove that all swans are

[17] And note, if one is only specifying a positive correlation, it would only take two observations to form a counter-example.

[18] Since the formula was being constructed for testing entire models, it also involved the degree of the algebraic equations assumed in the second stage of the model construction. What this means is that, when the degree of the equations is increased, the minimum number also increases.

non-pink – which at minimum is impractical since without limiting the claim temporally or spatially, it refers to all swans that may exist anytime (present or future) or anywhere (in the Universe!).

Strictly speaking, one does not directly observe a counter-example. Instead, one builds a model of a conceivable counter-example *relevant* for the behavioural hypotheses being tested such that verifying the counter-example model would necessarily (i.e., as a matter of logic) refute the behavioural hypotheses. Obviously, to be relevant, the model of the counter-example must be built using the same stage-two specifications, but the question of relevance extends beyond techniques of model building.

The requirement of relevance is apparently not widely appreciated. It is often violated in the old discussions of Giffen effects.[19] Would the observation of the Giffen effect logically ever be considered a refutation of traditional ordinal demand theory (however modeled)? At first blush everyone might answer 'yes'. But on logical grounds such a question is very misleading since it would presume that we have a complete theory of the downward-sloping demand curve – i.e., of the so-called Law of Demand. It once may have been the intended purpose of demand theory to explain why demand curves are always downward sloping [see Hicks 1956, p. 59], but ordinal demand theory never succeeded in doing so [Samuelson 1953, pp. 1–2]. Simply stated, the existence of a Giffen effect is not completely denied by ordinal demand theory; hence, its observation cannot be considered a refutation [see Samuelson 1948b].[20]

In general terms, whether a particular observation constitutes a test (i.e., a refutation or a verification) of a given theoretical proposition

[19] This effect refers to a commonly claimed observation that the nineteenth-century statistician Robert Giffen made about the potato famine in Ireland when, supposedly, although the price of potatoes went up, so did the demand. This is deemed a counter-example to the so-called Law of Demand, which claims demand curves are always negatively sloped.

[20] Alternatively, it can be argued that Giffen effects are contrary to our traditional theory of prices [see Boland 1977a]. Demand theory itself is traditionally offered as logical support for our equilibrium theory of prices. Elsewhere I have gone further to argue that downward-sloping demand curves are necessary for a stable equilibrium in a world of truly independent decision makers [see Boland 1977b, 1986]. In this sense, ordinal demand theory is intended to be a complete set of reasons for why demand curves are downward sloping. In particular, those reasons are required to be consistent with independent decision making. As is well known, the traditional demand theory is only able to tell us when Giffen effects will occur (e.g., the implications of the Slutsky relations – a Giffen effect implies a counter income effect that is stronger than the substitution effect of a change in price). Thus, apart from price theory, Giffen effects are not logically denied and the simple observation of a Giffen effect alone would not constitute a test of ordinal demand theory, no matter what one means by 'testing'. Such testing in this case is simply not relevant.

necessarily depends on what that proposition logically affirms or denies. Such dependence (or 'relevance') is never a matter of judgment. In the case of exact (non-stochastic) variables, it is always a matter of logic. What constitutes a test always depends on what is put at stake by the theoretical proposition being tested. Whenever any behavioural theory is claimed to be true and informative, it must be denying conceivable specific observations. The more informative the theory, the more conceivable observations denied. This connection between informativeness and the number of conceivable counter-examples was the keystone of Samuelson's methodology of searching for 'operationally meaningful propositions'. But more important, it is the significance of what is denied by a theory that determines how much is at stake.

Let us temporarily assume away some of our possible irritants. Let us assume (1) that relevance is not a problem, (2) that we can directly test behavioural hypotheses – that is, without having to build models – and (3) that, for the sake of argument, the logical consistency of the set of behavioural or institutional assumptions constituting the theory or model has *not yet* been established. Now let us consider a *simultaneous test* of a behavioural theory and one of its many counter-examples. On the one hand, it is impossible to verify a theory by showing that the theory 'fits' one observation of all of its variables – that is, by finding a 'good fit' with the available data, since there is no guarantee that more observations tomorrow will also 'fit'.[21] On the other hand, if a counter-example does 'fit' the data (e.g., an observed change in endogenous variables without a change in the exogenous variables), then, so long as we accept the observations as true statements, we would have to admit that any logically complete and consistent theory which denies the possibility of observing the counter-example in question has been empirically and logically refuted. That is, in any combination of the behavioural theory and this counter-example, both cannot be true.

Consider now four possible outcomes of a combined simultaneous test of the behavioural theory (which can be just one behavioural hypothesis or a conjunction of more than one) and one of its logical counter-examples. If neither the theory nor the counter-example fits the available data then we could easily argue that the theory may not be logically consistent. Similarly, if both the theory and its counter-example do fit the available

[21] For example, observing only white swans to date does not assure us that tomorrow we will not see a non-white swan.

data, then again it is easy to argue that the theory could not be consistent.[22] Of course, these conclusions are based on the acceptance of the observations as true (viz. zero observation error). If the theory is logically consistent, then we would expect that any combined simultaneous test of the theory and one of its counter-examples will yield a fit of either the theory or its counter-example – that is, at least one – but not both. When it is the counter-example that fits, the theory is obviously refuted – either directly because the counter-example is 'verified' or indirectly by saying that even if the theory somehow fits, it would have revealed an inconsistency. When the theory fits but the counter-example does not, then not much has been accomplished with respect to the truth status of the behavioural hypotheses being tested. On the one hand, such an event is a minimum condition for logical consistency. On the other hand, it is still only a single fit, and (as I have already noted) there is no guarantee that the theory will fit future observations (or whether or not other possible logical counter-examples will fit the current data).

What is important about this combined approach to testing is that, whenever we accept the observations as being true, we can overcome the difficulties of the Duhem-Quine problem. To see this we need to recall the arguments of Section 9.2, in which it was noted that showing that a specific model using a particular behavioural theory or hypothesis does not yield a 'good fit' will not (by itself) prove that this theory or hypothesis being modeled is false because one has to prove that there does not exist any other model that uses this same particular behavioural theory or hypothesis which does yield a 'good fit'. While a bad fitting model *of any behavioural theory* does not constitute a refutation (even though we accept the observations as true), a good fitting model *of the counter-example of the theory* may constitute a refutation when the observations are considered true. To see this, let us again assume the behavioural hypothesis is logically consistent so that either the hypothesis is true or its counter-example is true but not both. When we are using the same data (i.e., the same set of exact observations), there are, again, four possible outcomes of a combined simultaneous test of the model of the hypothesis itself and a model of one of its counter-examples. Whenever models of a behavioural hypothesis (or theory) and its counter-example both fit the data, we know there is something wrong with the modeling. If they both do not fit then not much

[22] These two are not new ideas; they are just the implications of *modus ponnens* discussed in previous notes.

has been accomplished since a bad fit of either the hypothesis (or theory) or the counter-example runs afoul of the Duhem-Quine problem.

Whenever the model of the counter-example of the behavioural hypothesis fits and the model using the behavioural hypothesis itself does not, then this is a strong case against the theory, although we cannot be sure there is no modeling problem. Avoidance of a refutation would require at least a critical examination of the modeling methodology. When the model using the hypothesis fits but the model of the counter-example of the hypothesis does not then we have what some philosophers call 'corroboration' [e.g., Popper 1965, p. 220]. Specifically, we can say that corroboration would occur whenever the combined simultaneous test of a behavioural theory and its counter-example runs the risk of yielding a refutation but the theory manages to survive. The occurrence of corroboration means that a refutation could have occurred but did not. These four outcomes are summarized in Table 9.1.

Table 9.1 *Test model of:*

Test result	hypothesis	*counter-example*
model inconsistency	good-fit	good-fit
corroboration	good-fit	bad-fit
refutation	bad-fit	good-fit
ambiguous	bad-fit	bad-fit

9.4. Stochasticism and econometric models

> [T]heories are often being compared with data which cannot at all be considered as observations obtained by following the design of experiments we had in mind when constructing the theory.
>
> Trygve Haavelmo [1944, p. 15]

Having argued that convincing refutations are logically possible – at least, in principle – we should now see whether my argument is compromised by actually considering all observations as accurate data and hence true. Any refutation of a theory based on a model of a counter-example still requires the acceptance that the refuting observation or evidence is true. As noted many years ago by Professor V. Kerry Smith [1969], one of my early critics, 'The quest for truth and validity is indeed a noble venture. However, the economist exists in a stochastic environment' [p. 81]. To facilitate subsequent discussion, I will label the view that claims that our models of the economy *must* be considered stochastic: 'stochasticism'.

9.4.1. Stochastic models versus stochastic worlds

Many economic model builders are very fond of claiming (like Professor Smith) that the world is a 'stochastic environment'. As I said in the first paragraph of Section 7.1[23] of Chapter 7, based on the origin of the word 'stochastic',[24] it is easy to explain away an error when throwing a dart at the dartboard by claiming that the board moved rather than that it was bad throw. In effect, claiming the environment is stochastic amounts to the same thing unless the reason for the target's movement is also completely explained. Before examining the significance of stochasticism for my argument (namely, that logically convincing tests are possible when we include simultaneous tests of counter-examples), I offer a brief theory of stochasticism in modern economics. My purpose is to show that stochasticism is a specific version of model building since it requires an explicit modeling assumption which is possibly false, and thus stochasticism should not be taken for granted. Following this, I will use my brief theory to briefly discuss how econometricians deal with stochasticism, and postpone a deeper discussion of the statistical aspects of econometrics until the next chapter. Specifically, while later I will be discussing observational errors that need to be recognized, in this chapter I will not be discussing statistical errors made when making an observation (perhaps as part of a sample). That is, observations in this chapter are *singular.* In the next chapter we will take up statistical sampling that may be used to form an observation. A sampling error is not the same as an observation or a measurement error of singular observations.

First, let me stipulate that there are two 'worlds': the 'real' world, which we observe, and the 'ideal' world of the theory or mathematical model, which we construct. When we say the behavioural theory (or model) is 'true', we mean that the real and the ideal worlds exactly correspond.[25] Many will argue that, even with true theories and models, there are obvious

[23] Which some readers may have skipped.

[24] Which, as I said, is based on the Greek word Στόχος that refers to a target.

[25] That is, with respect to the variables identified in the model. Unlike models in this chapter, for any model with an assumption about a probability distribution of conceivable observations, it would be the distribution that would have to exactly correspond with regard to the distribution's parameters.

reasons why the correspondence will not be exact (e.g., errors of measurement, irrational human behaviour, etc.). For these reasons, economists have for many years been building 'stochastic models' which explicitly accommodate the stochastic nature *of the correspondence.* For example, this would mean that for our stage three or third step of specifying my schemata for a model, we can assume that the measurement errors leave the observations in some distribution about the true values of the ideal world. This means that the correspondence itself is the stochastic element of the model.

It should be noted, thus, that it is the model which is stochastic rather than the world or the 'environment'. Any test of a stochastic model is as much a test of the assumed correspondence as it is of the behavioural theory or hypothesis itself. And most important in this regard, *one can choose to see the world as being necessarily stochastic only if one assumes beyond question both that one's model is true (and fixed) and observations are exact and thus that any variability of the correspondence is due entirely to the unexplainable changes in the real world.* Thus, from this perspective, stochasticism can be seen to put the truth of our behavioural theories or hypothesis beyond question.

I think there is always potentially a serious danger of intellectual dishonesty in asserting that the environment is stochastic. Again, we assume that the 'assumptions' of our behavioural theory or model are true because we do not know them to be true. Avoiding facing this reality seems to be the purpose of presuming stochasticism (i.e., that the 'target moved'). But not knowing is not the same thing as stochasticism, and the truth status of our assumptions should never be put beyond question – after all, that is why we test our models or their assumptions in the first place. Yet, stochasticism itself is put beyond question in the study of econometric models. In other words, not knowing the truth status of our models does not mean that one must thereby claim that the environment is stochastic rather than just our models being stochastic.

9.4.2. Econometrics as applied stochastic models: some historical considerations

Econometrics is a research program founded in the early 1930s to address the obvious need to be able to confront (stochastic) statistical data with exact models of economic theories. The usual statistical analysis that one would have learned in a typical mathematics department was not always appropriate for the intended research program. In the early 1940s an entirely different approach was proposed. The idea then was to make the statistical analysis part of economic theory itself [Haavelmo 1944; see also Koopmans 1941, Mann and Wald 1943 and Haavelmo 1943]. While there is some danger in seeing this as an endorsement of stochasticism,[26] Haavelmo was quite aware of the limitations of such an approach and was careful to stress that the approach necessitated separating our stochastic models from our exact theoretical models. Moreover, he stressed that his approach required a thorough commitment to stochastic modeling with no hope of returning to the world of exact models [see Haavelmo 1944, pp. 55–9].

If one restricts econometric model building to practical problems (i.e., in the engineering rather than the scientific perspective) then one would have to say, in Milton Friedman's 1953 instrumentalist[27] terms, that the truth status of the model is less important than the *usefulness* of the results of its application. If one restricts econometrics to instrumentalist methodology, then there may be no need to separate internal inaccuracies introduced by specification errors from the external inaccuracies caused by observation errors. However, if the truth status of our theoretical models does matter, then econometric modeling which does not treat observation and specification errors separately will not obviously be an appropriate tool for analysis. Stated another way, whenever the truth status of our theoretical and modeling assumptions is at issue, *the only acceptable means of accounting for errors is the recognition of external 'observation errors'*. Moreover, when the truth status of a model matters, specification errors are always unacceptable and always imply a false *model* (but not necessarily one or more false behavioural hypotheses that were used in the model, as I noted in Section 9.2).

9.5. Asymmetries in tests based on stochastic models

Hopefully I have shined some critical light on stochasticism that might at least encourage some readers to be a bit skeptical about how easily stochasticism is invoked in empirical discussions. Let me nevertheless

[26] As I explained in Section 7.1.1 of Chapter 7.

[27] Instrumentalism is the view promoted in the early eighteenth century by Bishop George Berkeley in his effort to shield the Church's doctrine from the claims of philosophers who said the success of Newton's mechanics obviated the need for the Church. The Bishop merely said that we should consider Newton's theory to be a useful tool or instrument that one could use to describe the movements of the planets around the Sun. One did not have to declare it to be some universal truth as such provision is the providence of the Church. In economics, we know this view as that advocated in Friedman's famous 1953 methodology essay – see Boland [1979 or 1997, chapter 2]. This issue of using models in an instrumentalist fashion will be discussed further in Chapter 11.

accommodate minimally stochastic models in my theory of convincing tests. As mentioned earlier, a stochastic model can be one that recognizes that our observations of its variables may not be 100 percent accurate. And, it is important to remember in this chapter the discussion is still just about inaccurate singular observations and not necessarily about statistical errors that might occur in sampling. For the purposes here, it is enough that an observation is inaccurate without concern for why it is inaccurate. The central question here is just whether the recognition of *stochastic models* undermines my theory of convincing tests or instead, as I shall argue, actually emphasizes the need for combined simultaneous tests using counter-examples.

The key question that necessitates the recognition of stochastic models is still the acknowledgement that observation statements are seldom exactly true. Perhaps, of course, this is just a matter of measurement error, but recall that my discussion in Sections 9.2 and 9.3 temporarily *assumed* that observation statements were without error; that is, they were assumed to be (exactly) true. Given that assumption, whenever a model of the counter-example – using the same modeling assumptions as the model being tested[28] – was said to fit (i.e., exactly correspond to) the available data, we knew that the compound statement formed of the counter-example plus those modeling assumptions was a true statement. Since the truth of the behavioural hypothesis would deny the possibility of our ever building a relevant model of a counter-example of that behavioural hypothesis which would fit the data, it was concluded that, whenever the counter-example did fit, the behavioural hypothesis must be false. Now, the question to consider is what happens when the determination of a good fit is not exact (due to inaccuracies of the observations, such as the measurements used to determine the fit).

9.5.1. A simple example with observational errors

Consider the following one-equation model, which represents some behavioural theory in which the level of observable Z is claimed to be a *linear* function of the level of another observable Y:

$$Z = \alpha + \beta Y$$

The question at issue will now be whether the specification of a two-variable linear model represents the true relationship between Z and Y.

[28] The point of using the same (simplifying and specifying) assumptions is, of course, to isolate the behavioural hypothesis from those modeling assumptions.

However, for the purposes of this elementary discussion, let us say we know that conceivably there are no other relevant variables so that the *only* issue is the linearity of the model. Let us also say we have made three observations to determine if the linear relationship holds. With two observations we could deduce values for α and β which are the same for both observations – that is, we solve the pair of simultaneous equations (one equation represents one observation):

$$Z_1 = \alpha + \beta Y_1$$

$$Z_2 = \alpha + \beta Y_2$$

The third observation is used to test the deduced values of α and β. The question is whether the calculated Z, which equals $(\alpha + \beta Y_3)$ also equals the observed Z_3? Ordinarily, if we are were not talking about stochastic models, any difference between the calculated Z and the observed Z would both constitute a counter-example and be immediately interpreted as a refutation of the model. But of course, that would be primarily due to our prevailing assumption that our observations were always exactly true.

Let us now relax this assumption somewhat by saying the observations are not exact, but, unlike the ordinary presumption about data in econometric modeling, let us also say we have some independent knowledge of the possible observation errors. If we *knew* the singular observations could be wrong by no more than 10 percent,[29] then our criterion for interpreting the third observation must accommodate errors of as much as 10 percent. Before going on, I need to explain such knowledge of errors as this would not be a common perspective in economics but one I wish to use at this point. The type of knowledge in question is what would be common in civil and mechanical engineering when testing materials. In those cases, one knows the accuracy (i.e., tolerances) of the measuring instruments and thus knows how far off a measurement can be but no more. We do not usually have this measurement luxury in economics, but to keep things simple and separate I will pretend that we do. Later, we will consider what kind of observational and measurement errors we deal with in economics.

Now, most important, if we allow for errors in the determination of whether the third observation constitutes a refutation of the linearity of the equation, we will run the risk of incorrectly claiming that the counter-example fits and thus falsely claiming a refutation of the theory. Similarly,

[29] For now I will only mention that it is interesting that economists use data for which they have no idea about how accurate their data is.

we run the risk of incorrectly claiming that the third observation *confirms* the linearity assumption when in reality the relationship is non-linear. What needs to be appreciated when there are errors in observations is that *failure to confirm the behavioural hypothesis or theory may not constitute a confirmation of a counter-example.* With errors in observations, both the behavioural hypothesis or theory and its counter-example could fail to be confirmed by the same observations whenever we make allowances for errors.[30] This will depend now on how we decide what criterion we are to use to determine if we have a confirmation.

To illustrate this asymmetry, let us say that we ourselves make two correct observations, but all subsequent observations will be made by our friend and are subject to errors of as much as (but no more than) 10 percent.[31] Now, let us say we correctly have observed that $Z_1 = 10$, $Y_1 = 20$, $Z_2 = 12$ and $Y_2 = 30$, then using our given behavioural hypothesis and assuming linearity we can deduce that $\alpha = 6$ and $\beta = 0.2$. But let us say that at the time of our third observation the (unknown) true value of Y_3 is 40 but our friend's observation is *inaccurate* such that the third observation says that $Y_3 = 44$. At the same time, the friend also observes that $Z_3 = 12.6$. Both observed variables are off by about 10 percent. If the true relationship is linear then the true value for Z_3 would be 14, but, of course, if the true relationship is non-linear, then the true value of Z_3 could differ from 14. Assuming linearity is true, the calculated Z will be 14.8, which differs from our friend's *observed* Z by more than 17 percent, even though neither observation is more than 10 percent wrong. Depending on how we choose to interpret this, when allowing for an observational error of 10 percent, we might incorrectly conclude that Z and Y are not linearly related when in reality they are.

For the sake of discussion, let us say we doubt that *both* singular observations would be off by as much as 10 percent so we will interpret a 17 percent calculated difference as a 'bad fit' with regard to our linearity assumption. However, a bad fit in this case does not mean that we have proven that the true model is non-linear. All that we can conclude is that the linearity assumption is *not confirmed*. For us to conclude that the linearity assumption is false we have to decide what would constitute a counter-example as well as a good fit for a counter-example.

30 This is in contrast to what we can say when, as was previously assumed, that observations were exactly true. In the previous case, not true is the same as false and not false is the same as true. Now, with inaccurate observations, we cannot say that – even though it is assumed that we know how inaccurate that can be.

31 Perhaps, let us say, our friend has a history of making observational errors but never more than 10 percent.

9.5.2. Disconfirming versus non-confirming observations

In my example I said that it is known that singular observations by our friend could differ from the true values of *Z* and *Y* by as much as 10 percent, and thus, when making the third singular observation, the calculated and observed values of *Z* could be found to differ by as much as 17 percent without necessarily proving that the true relationship is non-linear. By recognizing that non-confirmations of linearity are not necessarily confirmations of non-linearity, it is always possible when adopting conservative test criteria based on single observations that both the behavioural hypothesis (linearity) and the counter-example (non-linearity) will fail to be confirmed. Thus a test based on a single observation is not usually considered a very convincing test. This is so even though a single observation of, say, a 20 percent calculated difference in our simple example would constitute a refutation, while a zero error does not constitute a proof that the relationship is linear, since the next observation might not be errorless.

Anything short of the maximum possible error in the calculated difference leaves the results of the test doubtful. Nevertheless, we may wish to interpret the test based on any notions we might have about the acceptability of errors. Specifically, we might think that a claim that linearity is confirmed based on a 17 percent allowable error is too risky. Even a 15 percent error might be considered too risky for a confirmation of linearity. We might take the position that while a 15 percent error does not constitute a proof that the model is not linear, such an observation casts serious doubt on the model's linearity. Let us call this interpretation (of the observation) a 'disconfirmation' of the linear model. Similarly, an error of 5 percent may be too risky for a conclusion that the counter-example is confirmed and thereby that the assumption of linearity is definitely false. In this case, the observation may be interpreted as a disconfirmation of the counter-example.

Now some readers may find all this tedious, but such is the way of the logic of testing with less than accurate observational data. So please bear with me. It is important here not to confuse the disconfirmation of a behavioural hypothesis with the confirmation of its counter-example. Equally important, we ought not to confuse 'not disconfirmed' with 'confirmed'. While a calculated difference greater than 18 percent may constitute a proof of non-linearity when we know the observations cannot be more than 10 percent wrong, using 18 percent as a test criterion seems too severe. So we need to choose a convenient standard to interpret the calculated difference.

On the one hand, if we are looking for a confirmation of the counter-example, we may wish to say that a calculated error of 15 percent is sufficient for us to conclude that the linearity assumption is false but an error of less than 10 percent is not sufficient, and thus the counter-example is not confirmed. If we are looking for a disconfirmation of the counter-example, we might say an error of less than 5 percent leads to the conclusion that the counter-example is disconfirmed, but an error of more than 10 percent leads us to declare the counter-example to be not disconfirmed. On the other hand, a similar disparity can be created when we are directly assessing the linearity assumption. If we are looking for a confirmation of the linearity assumption, we may wish to say that a calculated error of less than 2 percent is sufficient for us to conclude that the linearity assumption is confirmed, but an error of more than 10 percent is not sufficient, so in that case the linearity assumption would be declared to be not confirmed. If we are looking for a disconfirmation of the linearity assumption, we might say an error of more than 15 percent leads us to conclude that the linearity assumption is disconfirmed, but an error between 5 and 10 percent leads us to declare the linearity assumption to be not disconfirmed.

Here, of course, I am arbitrarily assigning numbers to the allowable or required criteria for the purposes of discussion. Any actual criteria would be decided on the basis of what we know about the nature of the observation errors and the nature of the actual behavioural hypothesis being tested. As my simple example illustrates, it is easy to adopt very different criteria of rejection or of acceptance. I am using the words 'confirmed' and 'disconfirmed' rather than 'true' and 'false' to bring out the essential asymmetry. In the true-false case, 'not-true' means false and 'not-false' means true (so long as we do not deny the axiom of the excluded middle[32]). Here, it should be clear that 'not confirmed' does not necessarily mean disconfirmed and 'not disconfirmed' does not mean confirmed whenever there is a wide range of possible errors.

In terms familiar to those who have read any elementary statistics book, we have to decide which is more important: avoiding the rejection of a true assumption or avoiding the acceptance of a false assumption. Statisticians

[32] Recall, the 'excluded middle' was explained in Chapter 4, note 7. It refers to one of three axioms of logic. It was actually Aristotle who said that, in order for an argument to be logical, its premises must not violate any of his three axioms of logic, which, as I explained, are the *axiom of identity*, viz., different statements within the argument cannot use different definitions of the same words; the *axiom of the excluded middle*, viz., no statements that cannot be true or false, or can be something else, are allowed; and finally, the *axiom of non-contradiction*, viz., statements cannot be allowed to be both true and false. Thus, any argument that contains such prohibited statements cannot qualify as a *logical* argument [see further Boland 2003, p. 205].

usually refer to these as Type I and Type II errors. What criterion is used to define Type I or Type II errors is still a matter of judgment with a heavy element of arbitrariness. Selecting a criterion which makes it easier to avoid one type of error will usually make it easier to incur the other type of error. Furthermore, whether we use a criterion of 5 percent or 10 percent as allowable deviation in calculated values may be determined more by the economics of the situation than by one's philosophy of science. The cost of making one type of error based on a narrow range of 5 percent may be greater than the other type of error based on a range of 10 percent. When dealing with matters of social policy it may be considered safer to have low standards of accepting a false linearity assumption and high standards for rejecting a true linearity assumption. Since there is usually ample room for doubt, linear models are often easier to apply to practical problems. It all depends on what we are looking for or are willing to accept.

My distinction between disconfirmations and non-confirmations (or maybe even between confirmations and disconfirmations) may not be clear to those familiar only with the concept of hypothesis testing found in statistics textbooks. Textbooks too often say that, whenever one has chosen to avoid, say, Type I error, any failure to confirm the counter-example is automatically interpreted as a confirmation of the theory.[33] Furthermore, exclusive concern for Type I error leads to the exclusive use of confirmation criteria. Concern for Type II error would have us use disconfirmation criteria instead. If for any reason we are unwilling to choose between Type I and Type II error, then we will need to be able to distinguish between disconfirmations and non-confirmations.

9.5.3. Confirmation versus disconfirmation test criteria

The possible asymmetry between confirmation and disconfirmation criteria needs to be seen against the background of the problems I have already discussed concerning the process of testing behavioural hypotheses using models of those behavioural hypotheses. Even when we considered observations to be without errors, we still could not expect to be able to refute a behavioural hypothesis by refuting just one singular model of that behavioural hypothesis (as stage-two modeling assumptions may be false while the stage-one hypothesis is true). However, I showed in Section 9.3.2 that if

[33] And one might suspect that this applies to the use of the common Null-Hypothesis test, but that is not the issue here.

we simultaneously test a model of a theory and a model of its counter-example, it is possible to say what would constitute a refutation of a behavioural hypothesis. Specifically, a refutation would occur when the model of the behavioural hypothesis fails to fit the data while the model of a counter-example does fit (of course, all this requires using the same data and the same criteria). Now, it might be asked, what is being added to this by entertaining the known extent of possibility of errors when making singular observations?

If we were to base our combined simultaneous test on a single observation of the behavioural hypothesis and a coincident observation of its counter-example, we would be wise to adopt rather conservative criteria of acceptance or rejection – maybe, as in my simple example, something like 2 percent for confirming observations of linearity versus 15 percent for a confirmation of an observation of the counter-example. The difficulty here is that a singular observation test is one-dimensional. It is necessary then to distinguish between a 'confirming observation' and a 'confirmation', which may require many confirming observations. Similarly, a 'disconfirming observation' is distinguished from a 'disconfirmation', which may require many disconfirming observations.

Since observation errors are possible and we might not wish to jump to a conclusion on a single observation, let us now repeat the third observation (of *Z* and *Y*) 19 more times. This new dimension (the number of repeated observations) raises a new question for decision: how many non-confirming observations will we allow in a confirmation? No more than 1 in 20? Maybe 2 in 20? This is a question of statistical adequacy rather than just a question of the number that has to be observed. And remember, we are still not talking about stochastic observations (i.e., observations hypothetically generated by some sort of stochastic 'generator'). This will be the topic for the next chapter, where the nature of statistical data will be the modeling issue. For now, we will just stick with considering it a question about the number of singular observations needed to allow for a definitive confirmation.

Perhaps readers familiar with all the complications involved in econometric estimation will find this kind of discussion of observation error and criteria frustrating, but, I think, too often these issues of the underlying logic of testing are overlooked in the rush to be able to declare a model acceptable or not. So, I invite these readers to bear with me as I continue to postpone addressing the issues involved in econometric estimation until the next chapter. For now, we are still looking at singular observations rather than any statistical characterization of a sample, such as its mean or variance.

So, given that errors in singular observations are possible, let us consider alternative postures concerning how to interpret the results of 20 observations.[34] Our test criteria and our posture must, of course, be decided before making the observations if we wish to avoid unnecessary skepticism. The following represent four different and illustrative postures that employ only confirmation/non-confirmation criteria for the assessment of the results of singular observations:

(1) We might say that whenever 5 or more of the 20 observations are convincing *confirming observations* of linearity (no more than 2 percent calculated difference, as discussed in Section 9.5.1) we will conclude that the linear model is *confirmed*, otherwise it is *not confirmed.*
(2) We might say that whenever 5 or more of the 20 observations are convincing *confirming observations* of non-linearity (at least 15 percent calculated difference) we will conclude that a model of a counter-example of the linear model is *confirmed*, otherwise it is *not confirmed.*
(3) We might say that whenever 5 or more of the 20 observations are not convincing *confirming observations* of linearity (more than 2 percent calculated difference) we will conclude that the linear model is *disconfirmed*, otherwise it is *not disconfirmed.*
(4) We might say that whenever 5 or more of the 20 observations are not convincing *confirming observations* of non-linearity (less than 15 percent calculated difference) we will conclude that a counter-example of the linear model is *disconfirmed*, otherwise it is *not disconfirmed.*

Given that our criteria for convincing observations might be considered extreme (2 percent or less in one case and at least 15 percent in the other), it may be reasonable not to expect a large proportion of observations to be

[34] As I mentioned in Section 9.3.2, in chapters 2 and 3 of my 1989 book I addressed the question of just how many singular observations it would take logically to form a decisive refutation of a simple macroeconomic model – specifically for models consisting of algebraic equations, such as I have been using for examples here. As a matter of algebra, I was able to construct a polynomial formula for that number, which I called P-dimension. The formula was just a generalized version of what I discussed Section 9.3.2, where I noted that it takes three exact observations to refute the assumption of linearity. The calculated P-dimension depends on the total number of exogenous variables, the total number of endogenous variables, and the maximum degree of the constituent equations. Increases in any of these numbers increases the number of observations necessary. Note that requiring a minimum sample of 20 stochastic observations to play the same role as one non-stochastic singular observation means that a stochastic version of a non-stochastic model which has a P-dimension of, say, 30 would now have an effective P-dimension of 600. This means a model for which it may have taken at least a year of data to construct a refutation would now require at least 20 years to refute!

meeting either criterion. Thus, there is an asymmetry between the confirmation of a counter-example and a disconfirmation of the behavioural hypothesis itself. Even though we have employed a confirmation/non-confirmation criterion (to assess observations), in order to define the four interpretation postures there is still a need to decide whether we are more interested in finding disconfirmations or confirmations, although there may not be any non-arbitrary way to do so.

Let me illustrate the possible consequences of all this for combined simultaneous tests of the model of a behavioural hypothesis and a model of its counter-example. If it is recognized that 'not confirmed' does not imply disconfirmed, then to illustrate the possible outcome, depending on whether we are looking for confirmations or disconfirmations as defined in statements (1) to (4) above, two tables are needed. In Table 9.2, the presumption is that the socially acceptable testing conventions only identify a confirmation, as in the case of desiring to avoid Type I errors. And in Table 9.3 it is presumed that only disconfirmations are identified (avoiding Type II errors).

In Tables 9.2 and 9.3 I have indicated that all corroborations or refutations must be considered conditional. The condition is that the interpretation of the result is always dependent on the acceptance of the specified test criteria used. In the case of my simple example above, the criteria involve the possibly extreme limit of a 2 percent acceptable error between the calculated and

Table 9.2 *Confirmation-based test model of:*

Test result	hypothesis	*counter-example*
inconclusive	confirmed	confirmed
weak conditional corroboration	confirmed	not confirmed
conditional refutation	not confirmed	confirmed
inconclusive	not confirmed	not confirmed

Table 9.3 *Disconfirmation-based test model of:*

Test result	hypothesis	*counter-example*
inconclusive	not disconfirmed	not disconfirmed
conditional corroboration	not disconfirmed	disconfirmed
weak conditional refutation	disconfirmed	not disconfirmed
inconclusive	disconfirmed	disconfirmed

observed Z. Other criteria are possible, such as limiting the ratio of acceptable to unacceptable errors in the given number of observations made. In both tables, the inconclusive results may cause one to question the test criteria in a single equation model. In multiple equation models, inconclusive results might also suggest that the model could be either incomplete or inconsistent.

As long as one is willing (a) to not demand unconditional refutations, (b) to adopt standard views of testing and thus commit oneself to which type of error (I or II) to avoid and (c) to commit oneself to use either a confirmation or a disconfirmation criterion for the evaluation of observations, then I think by making all tests of a behavioural hypothesis combined simultaneous tests of the model of the hypothesis and of at least one counter-example to the behavioural hypothesis, refutations in economics are in principle possible, albeit conditional.[35]

9.5.4. The irrelevance of the probability approach for the issues raised in this chapter

So far, I have not said anything about probabilities. Many readers will find this irritating because they think probabilities are essential for a discussion of conclusions drawn from inaccurate observations, that is, from stochastic models. While the probability approach to economics [e.g., Haavelmo 1944] may appear to solve some of these problems, it too often masks from view the logical structure that defines the methodological problem at hand. If one wishes to discuss things in probability terms then, instead of saying that errors of observation could be as much as 10 percent, one could *assume* that when one repeatedly makes the third observation, the possible errors for this observation will be assumed to be distributed in some manner (usually we associate this with the Gaussian 'normal distribution' when appropriate, but whether that is an adequate or appropriate characterization is a question to be discussed in the next chapter). If one also assumes that the average value of the observations represents the true observation, then the formal mathematical properties of such a distribution can be used to calculate the

[35] Several years ago, some of my PhD students made elementary applications of this approach to testing in economics. What is most striking from their applications, where they have repeated previously published tests of mainstream economic theories, is that in almost every case the published reported results do not correspond to the decisive categories but to the inconclusive results. For another explanation of this approach to testing and how it can be used, see Robert Bennett [1981]; Chris Jensen, Sham Kamath and Robert Bennett [1987].

probability that the observations will be incorrect in more than, say, 5 percent of the observations. In doing so, one would facilitate a calculation of potential damage done by incorrectly accepting a fit. If there is no reason to assume that errors are normally distributed, or if one knows something about the observation process independent of both the model and the testing process, then some probability presumptions may be a major source of difficulty. I suspect that the primary reason for promoting probabilistic approaches to economics is that they provide a basis for formalizing the arbitrary decisions regarding the choice of confirmation or disconfirmation criteria. Some people simply feel better when necessary arbitrariness is formalized.

Nevertheless, for some practical problems in which the assessment of benefits and costs are unproblematic (and there is no independent means of assessing the accuracy of observations), characterizing the occurrence of errors to be governed by a given probability distribution can be very helpful. But if we do not know how the errors are distributed, more questions may be begged than are answered [cf. Swamy, Conway and von zur Muehlen 1985; see also Spanos 2010]. I think, for the purposes of understanding the difficulties in forming conclusions when there are errors in observations, it is better not to confuse stochastic theoretical models with theoretical probabilistic models. As I have attempted to show in this section, the problems and means of avoiding the Duhem-Quine problem *do not require* a probabilistic approach to testing stochastic models, unless, of course, the behavioural hypothesis being tested is itself a probability statement.

10

The statistical adequacy of convincing tests of models using empirical data

'What is the use of testing, say, the significance of regression coefficients, when maybe, the whole assumption of the linear regression equation is wrong?' This is just the type of arguments we have discussed.

Trygve Haavelmo [1944, p. 66]

Without some idea of the power of statistical tests against interesting alternative hypotheses and/or some metric for evaluating the extent to which the data are inconsistent with a maintained hypothesis formal statistical tests are uninformative.

Science proceeds by falsifying theories and constructing better ones. Falsifications of hypotheses based on overidentifying restrictions ... are unenlightening in two senses. First, they provide little insight into whether the reason for the theory's failure is central to its logical structure or is instead a consequence of auxiliary assumptions made in testing it. ... While in principle it would be possible to explore a range of possible assumptions, this type of 'data mining' is usually condemned by those who favor formal approaches to empirical work.

Larry Summers [1991, p. 135]

[S]ome of the methodological problems that contribute to the mountains of untrustworthy evidence could have been avoided if only textbook econometrics paid a bit more attention to some of the key methodological ideas in Haavelmo [1944].

Aris Spanos [2011, §4.3]

Chapter 9 was primarily about the logic of testing with exact, singular observations, although I did raise the issues of having to use stochastic data that, of course, are not exact. In this chapter, testing econometrically using statistical data will be the main issue. But, keep in mind that the underlying logical issues remain relevant – often reappearing in the form of the requirements for convincing statistics-based tests – particularly, the ambiguity caused by having to add assumptions.

In this chapter, an additional type of model will be introduced, this one will be about modeling the nature of the available data. As noted in

Chapter 9, to conduct an empirical test one must know something about the available data. Unlike my illustrative examples using singular observations, usually in empirical economics the available data are in the form of non-experimental statistical data. The main obstacle for using statistical data in economics (either for forecasting or for testing) is that one must in effect specify (i.e., create) a statistical model by making assumptions about the nature of that data in order to determine the best estimator – that is, the statistical method needed (one that captures the statistical information in the data) to use for the forecast or test. Specifically, what do we know about the nature of the errors in that data?

Unfortunately, for non-experimental data, we know very little – we do not know the probabilistic structure of the possibly different types of error. Errors could be simply measurement errors, but they could be sampling errors. However, for experimental data, we can by design neutralize other effects in order to render the error white noise. So, we might ask, are data normally distributed such that samples of the data have errors with constant means and constant variation and are independently and identically generated? If the method to be used, for example, requires normally distributed errors but the data are not normally distributed – or more importantly, the data are not independent and identically distributed[1] – we would have to say that any statistical model or estimation method, such as classical linear regression, that requires normally, identically and independently distributed errors would be statistically inadequate for the intended forecast or test, as the data are misspecified for such a regression.

As will be explained later, the question that must always be addressed is: What should we do when the assumed statistical model is mispecified (some of its assumptions are false) vis-à-vis the data? Today, there seem to be two basic approaches to answer this. One approach would try to correct the statistical inference procedures by making them 'more robust' and the other would instead try to learn more about the probabilistic structure of the stochastic process underlying the data that would have rendered one's initial choice of assumptions inappropriate.

10.1. The purpose of testing with 'robust' statistical estimation

Because researchers are not in a position of knowing with certainty that the assumptions used to justify their choice of estimator are met, it is tempting to protect oneself against violations of these assumptions by using an estimator

[1] Identically distributed here refers to a constant mean and a constant variance.

whose properties, while not quite 'best', are not sensitive to violations of those assumptions. Such estimators are referred to as *robust* estimators.

Peter Kennedy [2008, p. 345]

Since the early 1950s, prestigious econometric journals are overflowing with a bewildering plethora of *estimation* techniques, and their associated asymptotic theory based on invoking mathematically convenient assumptions that are often non-testable. Even in the case where some of these assumptions are testable they are rarely checked against the data.

Aris Spanos [2011, §4.1]

In keeping with the discussion in previous chapters, I will continue to focus mostly on the 'Forest' rather than the 'Trees' and thus leave the technical issues of robust estimation or non-parametric techniques to econometrics textbooks [e.g., Kennedy 2008, chapter 21; Mittelhammer et al. 2000, chapter 15; Moore, McGabe and Craig 2012, chapter 15] – although, 'Tree' examination is sometimes necessary in order to talk about the 'Forest'. It is always important to note that errors of a non-normal distribution are not the errors considered to be caused by human or mechanical errors of observation that are deemed to 'contaminate' the data. In this regard – that is, using uncontaminated data – the goal of a robust estimator, according to Kennedy, is for the inferences to be insensitive to violations of one or more of the assumptions about how the data was generated, and, in particular, robust estimators are usually designed to avoid the effects of assumptions that would render the estimator unreliable.

When the observation or measurement errors are correctly specified as normally distributed, an ordinary least squares (OLS) estimator of a Classical Linear Regression (CLR) model is usually considered the best among all unbiased estimators, and they are fully efficient – meaning that it has the smallest variance among all possible estimators.[2] If any of the error assumptions are false – say, not normally distributed – only an OLS estimator can be the best among linear and unbiased estimators. If the error distribution frequently produces relatively large errors (i.e., the distribution is 'fat-tailed'), requiring linearity would be asking too much. While an OLS estimator is

[2] That is, from the 'Tree' perspective, they coincide with the Maximum Likelihood Estimators (MLE). The Gauss-Markov (G-M) theorem – that the OLS estimators in the CLR model are the Best Linear Unbiased Estimators (BLUE) – does not invoke normality, and thus the OLS estimators without normality are BLUE. That is, they have the smallest variance among the class of linear and unbiased estimators – they are relatively (not fully) efficient. The G-M theorem is practically useless as the result depends on 'the linearity of the estimator' which is clearly a dodge as nobody includes linearity among the good properties of estimators and so one cannot use the theorem to do any reliable inference, not even to test if a coefficient is zero [see Spanos 1999, chapter 13].

the best linear unbiased estimator (BLUE), it is not as good as some other non-linear estimators that are called 'robust estimators' particularly when the distribution of errors is fat-tailed [Kennedy 2008, p. 346].

10.1.1. Dealing with fat-tailed error distributions

Usually, when facing what appears to be a 'fat-tailed' distribution, one would search for 'outliers' – that is, apparently large observation errors that do not fit the pattern of the other observations.[3] But one cannot use OLS estimators to determine this pattern [Kennedy 2008, p. 346]. The reason for identifying outliers is that they can exaggerate OLS estimates. It should be noted that unusually large observational errors is just one of two possible reasons for the outliers. The other may be simply that the variable being observed has itself deviated from the observed pattern. Such a deviation could indicate something worthy of attention. Both types of outlier are considered 'influential observations' [ibid.]. Such influential observations might indicate the need to modify the statistical model's specification, so it is important to determine whether it is possible that they are the result of human errors, such as incorrectly entered data. But they might be due to some extraordinary event that would lead one to consider modifying the theory or model being tested to allow for such observations.[4]

10.1.2. Types of robust estimators

My late colleague Peter Kennedy identified five general types of robust estimators [2008, pp. 247–8]: (1) M-estimators (i.e., Maximum Likelihood Estimators), which use different weights than OLS uses; (2) Adaptive estimators, which might view the distribution by 'implicitly assuming that outliers come about because of non-normally distributed errors, rather than

[3] An observation deemed an outlier for one distribution, might be perfectly regular for another distribution. Hence, wading into the 'Trees', one needs to distinguish between observations from genuine fat-tailed distributions, such as the Cauchy distribution, and Student's *t* distribution, from any false typing of the numbers. The remedies in the two cases are drastically different. If the underlying distribution is non-Normal, say it is Student's *t*, then the estimator that is more robust simply throws that crucial data information away and leads to unreliable inferences. For an example that demonstrates this, see Spanos [1995a].

[4] It can be argued that departures from the statistical model's assumptions should be viewed as a blessing not a hindrance because they signal to the modeler that there is additional systematic information in the data that, when utilized, can improve all inferences considerably – possibly make them more reliable and precise.

because of data contamination' [p. 348]; (3) L estimators, which involve 'linear combinations of sample order statistics' such as regression quantiles [ibid.]; (4) Trimmed least squares, which throws away some observations; and (5) Bounded influence estimators, which are 'designed to limit, or bound, the influence an aberrant observation can have on the coefficient estimate. . . . Such estimators are operationalized by defining what is meant by "influence" and choosing a bound' [ibid.].

10.1.3. Dealing with outliers and 'influential' non-experimental observations

Much of the effort devoted to robust statistics and estimators is deemed necessary whenever the data being used is non-experimental observations. Obviously, one of the main purposes for conducting a controlled experiment can be to produce data that can be easily modeled as normally distributed and thus amenable to classical statistical methods. If one is dealing with data with possible outliers or influential observations, perhaps one should test for non-normality of the errors – that is, test for misspecification of the statistical model of the observational data. More will be discussed about misspecification tests in Section 10.2, but from Kennedy's perspective [2008, p. 353],

> All the methods of searching for outliers and influential observations . . . involve looking at summary statistics; a natural alternative to this is to look at the data themselves through graphical means. Numerical summaries focus on expected values whereas graphical summaries focus on unexpected values.

Not everyone thinks we should view this as an ingredient of robust estimation.

10.2. Statistical adequacy of non-experimental data

> Viewed in the context of the error-statistical perspective . . . experimental economics attempts to bridge the theory-data gap by bringing the data closer to the theory. . . . Instead of using observational data . . . one generates experimental data under 'controlled' conditions that aim to correspond closely to the conditions envisaged by economic theory. These data can then be used to evaluate theoretical predictions concerning economic behavior. In this sense, the structural (estimable) model – in view of the data – is often much closer to the theory model than in the case of observational data. Despite this *important difference*, the statistical modeling of experimental data in economics – with a view to learn about economic phenomena – raises the same issues and problems of reliability as for observational data, where the primary differences are in emphasis.
>
> Aris Spanos [2010a, p. 220]

One can easily see the main purpose of an experimental-design model to be that of producing empirical data upon which one would apply classical statistical methods – specifically, apply methods that usually require the data to be normally distributed and where samples of the data have constant means and constant variation and are independently produced. But non-experimental data can be less accommodating, as one cannot reliably presume that the data is normally, independently and identically distributed.

There are two basic ways to view available (observational) data. On the one hand, theoretical and empirical model builders almost always see the situation as one where we first build a model and then test it with observational data. As I complained in Chapter 9, rarely do such model builders know much about the data they intend to use to test their models other than what is included (or not) in the list of the endogenous and exogenous variables. On the other hand, some econometrics theorists today [e.g., Hendry 2011; Spanos 1995a, 2010b] think we should also be building statistical models of the available data before or at least separately from our considering using that data to test a model or a behavioural hypothesis. These latter theorists start from the perspective of the data being produced by an unknown and independent data generating mechanism[5] to which our models and theories are to be applied – that is, empirical and the related statistical models are seen to be restrictions[6] placed on the data produced by the actual generating mechanism. The adequacy of each model is assessed very differently. A statistical model is adequate when one can demonstrate that the data in question could have been generated by the model in question. Statistical adequacy is the price one has to pay for using reliable statistical inference procedures – the actual error probabilities approximate closely the assumed ones. Adequacy in the case of a theoretical or empirical model refers to what the econometrics theorist, Aris Spanos, usually calls 'substantive' adequacy, which refers to whether the theoretical or empirical model in question actually explains (or describes) the phenomenon of

[5] That is, again, from the 'Trees' perspective, these theorists distinguish between the actual and statistical data generating mechanisms. The former refers to the actual mechanism behind the phenomenon of interest that the empirical model aims to explain or represent. The latter is built directly on the (vector) stochastic process underlying the data by postulating a probabilistic structure so as to render the data a typical realization thereof. The two mechanisms are related by choosing a parameterization of the statistical model, so as to nest the empirical model parametrically.

[6] Some econometricians like to think of an empirical model as a set of restrictions placed on the observable data. That is, each equation of the model is specifying how the data must have been generated.

interest – or (as he would probably not say) is true. As to the statistical adequacy perspective, the key question is, can we learn anything about the data before using the data to test one's theories or models? If we hope to have convincing and reliable tests using the data, at least we do need to know about what kind of statistical errors to expect of the data. We particularly need to know that the assumed statistical model is adequate vis-à-vis the data so as to ensure the reliability of any econometric test of our theoretical or empirical models.

As was discussed in the previous section, some econometricians see any deviations from error free, normally distributed sampling data to be something to fix so as to make the inference more 'robust'. Critics counter that tests performed using such 'robust' inference procedures are considered by some unlikely to be either convincing or reliable. An inference procedure such as an estimator or a test is said to be robust to a certain departure from the statistical model assumptions when it is not very sensitive to these departures – that is, its relevant error probabilities are not too inferior to those of the optimal procedure under the correct specification.

So, let us look at the main alternative to fixing the statistical model to produce 'robust' inferences. Specifically, I will review some of the relevant work of Spanos [1995a], who promotes a promising alternative to the textbook idea of fixing misspecified statistical models to make the resulting inferences 'robust'.

10.2.1. Dealing with misspecified statistical models

> Very few theories have been abandoned because they were found to be invalid on the basis of empirical evidence. Irreconcilable theories seem to coexist happily because the available empirical evidence is inadequate for the purposes of choosing between them. . . .
>
> The fact that observational (nonexperimental) data are analyzed using an approach better suited for experimental data raises a number of problems the most important of which are:
>
> (a) the gap between theoretical models and the information in the available data and
> (b) the problems of statistical model specification and statistical adequacy: ensuring that the postulated probabilistic assumptions are appropriate for the data in question.
>
> The theory relies heavily on *ceteris paribus* clauses evocative of controlled experiments, but the available data are often the result of an on-going, uncontrolled market process. This gap raises serious doubts about the sagacity of the specification of statistical models by attaching white noise error terms to

> theoretical models. This approach often leads to statistically misspecified models which cannot be used as a basis for reliable theory testing.
>
> Aris Spanos [1995a, pp. 189–90]

We must keep in mind that we need to know how the observed data differ from the data that would be generated from a statistical model. For example, a statistical model might assume that the data in question constitute a realization of a normal, independent and identically distributed stochastic process. Any deviation from such a realization would lead to misspecification errors that would invalidate a test of the theoretical or empirical model. Rather than fixing the statistical model by modifying some of its assumptions about errors or choosing inference procedures which are less sensitive to particular departures, as discussed in the previous section, one first might try to understand the extent of the errors so that one can respecify the model to account for any departures from the original statistical model's assumptions. Using a respecified model of the data would allow for more reliable and decisive tests of the theoretical or empirical model being tested. So, before one can respecify the model whose statistical generating mechanism – David Hendry [2011, p. 117] calls it the 'data-generating process' and I will straddle by calling it a 'data-generating mechanism' – one needs to determine in which ways the model's assumptions are false for the available data.

As briefly noted in Chapter 9, every model implicitly or explicitly begins with a list of endogenous and exogenous variables (which does not include any of the parameters or coefficients since they are properties of the structural assumptions that make up the model[7]). It is at this juncture – that is, before considering a posited relationship between variables – that one can build the model of the statistical- or data-generating mechanism involving all of the posited observable variables in the list. Critics might claim that looking at the data at this stage amounts to 'data mining' [Lovell 1983; Chatfield 1995] and is thus subject to 'pre-test bias' [Kennedy 2008, pp. 205 and 210], both of which are possible, but they are not necessary outcomes, as will be argued in Section 10.3. After all, nothing prevents separately developing one's model independently of the data, as is usually done with the theoretical models that were discussed in Part I. For now, let us just consider what is usually expected of available non-experimental data.

[7] Otherwise, they should be considered exogenous or endogenous variables.

10.2.2. Textbook view of observational data

The textbook view of observational data usually begins with the presumptions of classical statistics that were developed to deal with experimentally produced data. As I have already noted, experimental data are presumed to have been produced such that samples of data are usually normal, independent and identically distributed. This presumption is at least appropriate if one were discussing experimental economics, where if the data were not so distributed, it would indicate something wrong with the experimental design. Obviously, such an option is not open to the model builder who wishes to explain non-experimental data. All this is particularly important if one wishes to test a theory or model using observational data regardless of whether the data are experimental or non-experimental.

As I discussed in Chapter 9, limited knowledge about how data were produced – particularly there when using singular observations to test a model – limits what one can reliably conclude from the results of such a test. If one rejects any attempts to make the collected data 'more robust' by 'fixing' the data, then what does one do to make the test results more reliable than would be the case if one were to stick with the textbook view of data? First, one needs to determine how the available data deviate from the textbook view.

10.2.3. Determining how the data generation model is misspecified

Generally speaking, from the 'Forest' rather than the 'Trees' perspective, determining how the data deviate from what is presumed initially in the textbook view is a matter of case-by-case testing. But before any deviations from the textbook's initial view of data can be assessed, one needs to preliminarily specify the presumed data-generating mechanism. With this initial model, one tests the assumptions underlying this model of the data by examining the data – Spanos [1995a, pp. 211–12] provides some examples for the case of a normal autoregressive model. As Kennedy suggested, in some cases it is merely a matter of examining plots of the data. Spanos [1999, 2010b] provides many examples where plots are examined to determine the extent of deviation from textbook presumptions about data generation. What Spanos [1995a, p. 209] thinks is important here is that, when we are postulating a statistical model, we are not looking for a theory in the data – instead we are looking for 'probabilistic patterns'. As a result [ibid.],

> the modeler is strongly encouraged to look at data plots in order to avoid meaningless searches for statistical regularities. Observational data are assumed to be generated by stochastic variables and the specification of statistical models is based primarily on the probabilistic structure of these observables.

As with my discussion in Chapter 9 of allowable errors with singular observations to be used to test a model or its counter-example, one needs to draw the line beyond which the type of observation is deemed to be an acceptable or unacceptable confirmation or disconfirmation. When examining plots of the statistical data, the plots can be similarly assessed.

10.2.4. Respecifying a misspecified model of the data generation mechanism

> The presence of departures from the assumptions of the postulated statistical model is considered as a blessing and not a nuisance, because they indicate the presence of additional systematic information which will improve the appropriateness of the statistical summary when accounted for. In this sense a *robust estimator* is an estimator which is insensitive to systematic information in the data; such an estimator is not a blessing but a nuisance. ... The presence of misspecification is dealt with by respecifying the statistical model to account for the systematic information ignored by the previous model, not by 'concealing' its existence.
>
> Aris Spanos [1995a, p. 214]

A misspecification test that leads to the rejection of one or more assumptions of the initial specified model of the data-generating mechanism can indicate that there is more systematic hence useful 'probabilistic' information in the data than initially presumed. If the available non-experimental data whose generation is being modeled for the that data is to be used to provide a reliable test, then the model (not the individual assumptions) needs to be respecified to account for the occurrence of this information in the data. Specifically, Spanos [1995a, p. 209] says:

> The concept of 'probabilistic information' gives operational meaning to the notion of 'systematic information in the data' to be accounted for by the theory. When a statistical model is chosen (postulated), the idea is to summarize the probabilistic information in the data, adequately.

Again, what needs to be respecified is a matter of a case-by-case assessment of the apparent probabilistic information about *how* the available data differs from the usual textbook's probability presumptions for testing.

Spanos [2010b, pp. 1446–51] provides several examples in which a model of the data-generating mechanism is respecified using available non-experimental data concerning the typical Keynesian consumption function. What is important here is that the respecified assumptions for the model of the data-generating mechanism relate only to the probability structure of the available data 'without invoking any substantive information' [loc. cit. p. 1445] about any theory that might be used to explain that data.

Once the model of the data-generating mechanism is determined to be statistically adequate for representing the available data, we can use the data to test any theories or models of interest. Spanos adds [1995a, p. 215]:

> Given that statistical models are just convenient summaries of the data, they are data-specific and they seldom have a direct theoretical interpretation. On the other hand theoretical models should not be data-specific, in order have generality. Hence, we go from the statistical to the theoretical model by *reparameterization/restriction*. The more restrictions we impose on the statistical model, the more informative and less data-specific the theoretical model is.

This is true whether the testing is being devoted to the textbook, Neyman-Pearson 'Null Hypothesis' type testing or to the logic of testing that I presented in Chapter 9. In both cases, the respecified model of the data-generation mechanism is used to apply the data to both the Null Hypothesis and the Alternative Hypothesis just as was done with applying singular observations to both the model being tested and the implied counter-example.

One difference in this chapter is that we are discussing using statistical data and thus have to determine the appropriate econometric methods for using the respecified statistical model. In effect, 'The decision to accept or reject the theoretical model is based on whether the restrictions it imposes on a statistically adequate summary (statistical model) are data-acceptable' [1995a, p. 215]. The test here is of the restrictions being placed on the observable statistical data. But, like the discussion in Chapter 9, since the Neyman-Pearson type test would be only about the null hypothesis, rejecting the null usually would not indicate acceptance of the alternative hypothesis – both have to be tested with the same data. However, according to Spanos, there is another important difference. For the traditional Neyman-Pearson framework, 'In the present context the alternative is the statistical model in question whose data-acceptability has already [been] established. Indeed, the statistical adequacy of the latter ensures the validity of the test' [ibid.; see also 1995b].

10.3. Data mining and pre-test bias?

> [F]ailure of the pre-test estimator to achieve the properties of the OLS estimator using the correct specification is called *pre-test bias*. ... The most dramatic implication of the pre-test bias phenomenon occurs when econometricians use

> sequential or 'stepwise' testing procedures (sometimes called 'data mining') in which a large number of different hypotheses are tested to select a relatively small set of independent variables out of a much larger set of potential independent variables, greatly increasing the probability of adopting, by chance, an incorrect set of independent variables. This problem has been exacerbated by the advent of the computer.... A straightforward corollary of the pre-test bias phenomenon is the fact that researchers should not use the same sample evidence for both generating a hypothesis and testing it.
>
> Peter Kennedy [2008, pp. 205 and 210]

Critical claims of data mining have been around since the seventeenth century when the philosopher Francis Bacon was concerned with people choosing data solely with the purpose of proving that their favourite theoretical claims are true. He said, in effect, that we need to let facts to speak for themselves – that is, we should collect observations without bias (pre-test or otherwise) and then *logically induce* our theoretical claim using only those observations. That would obviously be a wise strategy except for one thing: there is no logic that can do that if we want to have our theoretical claim to be proven true without exceptions (probability 1.00).[8] We always have to conjecture an explanatory hypothesis which, if true, would allow us, with the help of observable data, to deduce true explanatory statements – that is, statements that exactly correspond to the observed data. Doing so is merely what we call explaining observations or observational regularities. Exceptions require further explanation.

10.3.1. Misspecification tests and pre-test bias?

Now, unlike Chapter 9's discussion of the logic of testing a conjectural behavioural hypothesis or model involving misspecification tests and pre-test bias, the approach of Spanos discussed in this chapter considers the model of the data-generating mechanism separately from testing a model or hypothesis. For this reason, critics may see his approach to testing as either data mining or subject to pre-test bias.

Spanos [2012, pp. 374–5] provides several reasons for why this criticism is wrong. His requiring misspecification testing is being misinterpreted

[8] Unfortunately, as I noted earlier, economists too often call an argument (or inference) 'inductive' simply because it argument includes observational data. The probable source of this mistake is a notion that induction and deduction are analogous forms of logic [see further, Sugden 1998]. The problem is that there is no such thing as inductive logic if one means by it that there is a corresponding *modus ponnens* that I discussed in the notes to Chapters 8 and 9. It probably is also based on the false notion that deductive arguments never use observational data.

'by recasting it as a decision-theoretic estimation problem' [p. 374]. When a misspecification test supposedly selects the alternative to the null hypothesis, implicitly the inference presumes that the alternative is statistically adequate and as such commits a logical error, as was discussed in Chapter 9 – disconfirming the null does not confirm the alternative. Similarly, when the null is supposedly selected, it is being presumed that the null is statistically adequate. On this basis, Spanos [pp. 375–6] suggests that, rather than 'devising ways to circumvent the [logical] fallacies of rejection and acceptance to avoid erroneous inferences' in any misspecification testing,

> the pre-test bias argument embraces these fallacies by recasting the original problem . . . formalizes them . . . and evaluates risks . . . that have no bearing on erroneously inferring that the selected model is statistically adequate. The pre-test bias charge is ill-conceived because it misrepresents model validation as a choice between two models come what may.

10.3.2. Misspecification tests and data mining?

> It is ironic that the data mining procedure that is most likely to produce regression results that appear impressive in terms of the customary criteria is also likely to be the most misleading in terms of what it asserts about the underlying process generating the data under study. . . . Data mining is inevitable; the art of the applied econometrician is to allow for data-driven theory while avoiding the considerable dangers inherent in data mining.
>
> Peter Kennedy [2008, pp. 84–5, 365]

Instead of following the approach that Spanos advocates – that is, first build a model of the data-generation mechanism appropriate for the available data – we could follow the typical approach to empirical model building and first build our theoretical model and then use the available data econometrically to estimate the values of the parameters of our model. Sometimes, of course, this yields estimates with the wrong signs, yields an insignificant coefficient for a variable of particular interest, or maybe indicates the strong possibility that some of the key assumptions are false. If any of this happens, what does one do next?

Too often, the model builder might try different estimation methods, or perhaps try different subsets of the data until finding a subset that yields results that are closer to what is expected. This approach to unexpected results is sometimes called 'error fixing' and can involve estimating many variants of our original theoretical model by making modifications to its assumptions. Hopefully, one of these modified models will be found to overcome the shortcomings of the original estimated (unmodified) model.

Having tried out several modifications and/or several different subsets of data, we are supposedly able to pick a modified model or particular subset of data, one that yields the 'best' outcome. But, as Spanos [2012, p. 381] points out,

> When such statistical 'error-fixing' recommendations are tried out, one is supposed to keep one eye on the 'theoretical meaningfulness' of the estimated variants and choose between them on the basis of what can be rationalized both statistically and substantively. It is widely acknowledged that these 'error-fixing' strategies constitute problematic forms of data mining.

Clearly, searching over various theoretical models until one finds a 'best' outcome according to the available data is at best questionable and certainly not what is meant by testing a model. If one chooses to try different estimators (ordinary least squares, generalized least squares, Instrumental Variables, Generalized Method of Moments, non-parametric methods, etc.) in hopes of finding an 'optimal' one for each deviation from the various assumptions of the presumed data-generating mechanism, it is too easy to misdiagnose the anomalous deviation, and thus 'the ad hoc "fixes" of specific error assumptions lead to exacerbating (not ameliorating) the reliability of inference' [Spanos 2012, p. 382]. Such 'error fixing' too often ends with another misspecified model of the data-generating mechanism. Moreover, as a basis for estimating the model's coefficients, such fixing gives unreliable inferences concerning the theoretical meaningfulness of any chosen theoretical model. Viewed from the approach to testing he recommended, Spanos [ibid.] adds,

> [E]ach step in the . . . 'error-fixing' strategies fosters further errors, and ignores existing one . . . with the modeler unwittingly worsening the overall trustworthiness of the evidence these strategies give rise to. Moreover, the modeler focuses on 'saving the theory' by retaining the systematic component and ignoring alternative theories which might fit the same data equally well or even better. By focusing the 'error-fixing' strategies the textbook perspective overlooks the ways the systematic component may be misspecified. In addition, incomplete specifications of statistical models . . . are not conducive to securing statistical adequacy. This should be contrasted with warranted 'data mining', such as the use of graphical techniques and [misspecification] testing . . . where they enhance the reliability of the inferences reached.

In particular, his approach to testing suggests that once one has determined that there are deviations from what is assumed in the original model of the data-generating mechanism, one should not use the actual error probabilities, as would be the case with textbook 'error fixing', 'but to respecify the original model and construct a new optimal inference procedure based on the respecified model' [p. 383].

10.4. Putting things together

My main point in this chapter is simply that, given the logic of convincing tests, as I explained in Chapter 9, the approach promoted by Spanos fits the need perfectly. It does not involve data mining in the usual sense, as the analysis of the data is done separately from the model or its counter-example that we wish to test. It does not involve double-use of data since the model and the counter-example are being tested separately, albeit with the same data as intended for the logic of the test.

What must be kept in mind when testing behavioural hypotheses or models using the hypotheses is that, if one is honest about testing, then one is not looking to repair one's model but to reject it if it is false. If a model of the theory fails the test, one needs to go back to the 'drawing board' and rethink the substantive claims of the constituent assumptions of the model. But, of course, some readers will dismiss this viewpoint as being too philosophical. Perhaps this is the case, so in the next chapter, I will take up some of the philosophical aspects of model building in economics.

PART IV

METHODOLOGICAL CONSIDERATIONS

11

Model building from a philosophy of science perspective

[W]e look upon economic theory as a sequence of conceptional *models* that seek to express in simplified form different aspects of an always more complicated reality. . . . Each model is defined by a set of postulates, of which the implications are developed to the extent deemed worthwhile in relation to the aspects of reality expressed by the postulates. The study of the simpler models is protected from the reproach of unreality by the consideration that these models may be prototypes of more realistic, but also more complicated, subsequent models.

Tjalling Koopmans [1957, pp. 142–3]

Treating the development of modelling as an epistemic genre – that is, as a practical mode of reasoning to gain knowledge about the economic world – does help to part the clouds that obscure the historical gaze. It reveals to us that mathematics grew up in two styles of reasoning in economics at more or less the same time in the late nineteenth century: the method of mathematical postulation and proof and the method of hypothetical modelling using mathematical models. . . .

No doubt, there were both descriptive and analytical aims for the early economists who created models, but there came a marked divergence after the interwar period so that statistical (econometric) modellers concentrated on theoretically informed descriptions that could be used for measurement and hypothesis testing, while mathematical modellers concentrated on providing accounts that established concepts and sparked hypothesis formation and theory development.

Mary Morgan [2012, pp. 18 and 388]

It is not clear what Morgan means by 'theory development' here, given her (I think correct) claim that modelling has become the primary way of doing economic science. If modelling is what economists mean by theory, how can there be a stage of theorising that progresses beyond modelling? It is easier to understand the claim that economics engages with the real world through econometrics. Presumably, econometrics is 'theoretically informed' when it is informed by the kind of modelling that is the subject of Morgan's book. But how do models provide *information* to econometricians, unless there is some reason

> to expect similarities between properties of models and properties of the real world? I cannot see how the practice of modelling can have scientific value unless models can provide genuine explanations of the phenomena of the real world.
>
> Robert Sugden [2013, p. 113]

In my 1989 book about the methodology of model building in economics, I was approaching the subject from the perspective of what here I have been calling the pre-1980 view of models. As I discussed in the Preface and the Prologue, the pre-1980 view was the view promoted by economic theorists, as illustrated by the quotation from Koopmans [1957] at the beginning of this chapter. As I discussed in Chapter 9, the concern in my 1989 book was the commonplace notion that models can be used to test behavioural theories and hypotheses. I specifically focused on the common philosophical notion held by almost all economic model builders from the 1950s onward – namely, that the true test of whether a model or theory is *scientific* is whether it is 'testable'. Hardly any non-methodologist today thinks this is a question worth spending any time on to the extent that the question of testability now seems a historical relic of early criticism of using mathematics in economics to build models. As noted in the Prologue, critics in the late 1930s naively thought that mathematical models could only provide tautologies. As I explained in Chapter 9, Samuelson's 1941 PhD thesis [1947/65] apparently was intended to provide a clear demonstration that the critics were wrong.

Neither Paul Samuelson nor I were writing for an audience of philosophers or for those today who call themselves philosophers or even philosophers of economics.[1] Our concern was the methodology of economic model building. I think Samuelson's concern was to demonstrate straightforwardly the methodology of model building, and as such he was devoted to understanding the 'Trees' in the 'Forest'. The concern of my book was much less ambitious as it was only about learning why model builders assume what they assume. In particular, my book was written from a 'Forest' perspective when it came to the models themselves. However, I did examine some of the many 'Trees' that philosophers might recognize – particularly when I discussed the logic of testing from the perspective that practicing models builders would hopefully understand. Unfortunately, that is not a perspective that most philosophers seem to appreciate. There seems to be a cultural gap between the kind of methodological questions that interest philosophers of economics (so-called big-M methodological

[1] As many methodologists have noted, Samuelson never mentions the name of a philosopher when making his pronouncements about methodology.

questions) and the kind of methodological questions that interest economic model builders (so-called small-m methodological questions) at least to the extent that they must be dealt with. In this chapter I will discuss how philosophers try to understand the small-m issues about model building in economics.

11.1. Types of model recognized by philosophers of economics

> The question: 'How do economists use models?' is, in one sense, easy to answer: they ask questions with them and tell stories! Or more exactly: they ask questions, use the resources of the model to demonstrate something, and tell stories in the process.
>
> Mary Morgan [2012, pp. 217–18]

> [M]odels in economics serve many purposes and are of many kinds. Models . . . are crutches or pedagogical devices rather than conceptual innovations. Such models . . . simplify features of more general models and make them vivid. They are particularly useful for illustrating or evaluating more general models . . .. 'Model' is a particularly apt term for such constructions, because they resemble descriptions of the physical models that engineers build. Just as one can illustrate, develop, teach, and test claims about the properties of airplanes by means of scale models, so one can illustrate, develop, teach, and test features of theories and general models by means of special case models.
>
> Daniel Hausman [1992, pp. 80–1]

> In several accounts of what models are and how they function a specific view dominates. This view contains the following characteristics. First, there is a clear-cut distinction between theories, models and data and secondly, empirical assessment takes place after the model is built. In other words, the contexts of discovery and justification are disconnected. . . . Model building is like baking a cake without a recipe. The ingredients are theoretical ideas, policy views, mathematisations of the cycle, metaphors and empirical facts.
>
> Marcel Boumans [1999, pp. 66–7]

The idea of an economic model or a model of the economy is not new, of course. Historically considered [see Morgan 2008; 2012], the first explicit idea of what today is considered a 'model' of an economy is usually credited to Jan Tinbergen, and his macro-econometric models which were intended to be fitted to available data in the late 1930s. Once such a model was fitted to the data, it would be used to represent a macro economy. But the idea of representing economic data or economic ideas with some abstract object preceded Tinbergen's macro models. Simple examples are, of course, diagrams such as Marshall's market demand and supply curves that we still use in beginning economics classes. A more recent and persistent example is the

IS-LM diagrams of most elementary macroeconomics textbooks. A less well known example is due to Irving Fisher [1892/1925], who in the late nineteenth century built a physical, hydraulic model to represent an economy with three goods demonstrating a general equilibrium system in process. He saw this as the dynamic working of an economy that could be seen in action.

Although today one would more likely find design engineers using a computer monitor to see the workings of a new design, as the philosopher Daniel Hausman suggests in the quotation at the beginning of this section, producing models that we can see and feel was once a major activity of design engineers with their physical prototype models. As I have mentioned before, one would test a new design for the shape of an airplane wing or an automobile body by building a scale model and putting it to test in a wind tunnel. And like building models in economics, building a scale model involves making simplifying assumptions in addition to the theoretical assumptions involved in the design itself.

In my 1989 book, I identified two general categories of models: *Pure or abstract* models, which are representations of the underlying logic of the theory being modeled, and *applied models*, which are explicit, simplified representations of more general theories and which are designed to apply to specific real-world problems or situations. Both were considered separately from the theoretical notion both types of model were based on. Perhaps today, from the post-1980s view of models, this methodological distinction seems to correspond to theoretical versus empirical models, as was discussed in Parts I and II. But it is important to acknowledge that today, among post-1980 economists, apparently there is little if any distinction recognized between what is considered a theory and what is considered a model. And, as I have been discussing so far in this book, what is considered a model today is almost always some form of mathematical model with the possible exception noted with Chapter 8's identification of an experimental design as a type of model.

When I began working on this book I thought the difference between the pre- and post-1980 views was about two different ideas of what constitutes a model in economics. But it now seems to me more apparent that these are two different views of what constitutes a theory. In the pre-1980 view, a theory is an object that one can talk about separately from how it might be represented – whether that be by means of a diagram, mathematical equation, or system of equations, or in Fisher's case, a hydraulic machine. The post-1980 view sees the theory as nothing more than the model itself – a theory is just one of the possibly many ways of interpreting the model.

11.2. Philosophy of science's only relevance to economic model builders

> Older treatments in the mainstream philosophy of science defined models in terms of their logical and semantic connections with theories, where the latter are the real focus of interest. . . . The more recent structuralist account applies the term 'models' to the logical structures that the scientific theory describes. . . . These philosophical definitions of models in relation to theories have proved grist for the philosophical mill, but do not properly address the problem of why economists might use or need the things that they call 'models'.
>
> Mary Morgan [1998, p. 316]

> Models are not themselves empirical applications, but they have the same structure. Economists are often concerned with developing applications of theory, not theory itself . . . and they are concerned with particular, albeit often stylized, circumstances. In these regards they are more like chemists than physicists.
>
> Daniel Hausman [1992, pp. 80]

It would appear from the writings of many, perhaps most philosophers and methodologists of economics[2] that their view of economic models and theories is stuck (as I was in 1989) in the pre-1980s perspective.[3] A commonly held view of the role of models in economics (perhaps opposed to that in natural science) is that of a tool or instrument created for the purpose of measurement or empirical investigation [e.g., Klein 2001; Boumans 2001, 2005, 2012; Morgan 2001, 2012; Morgan and Morrison 1999]. This of course includes building models either to represent the hypothesis so that it can be tested, as discussed in Chapter 9, or to quantify a theoretical hypothesis in order to express the hypothesis in terms of parameters and coefficients that can be 'measured' using data, as discussed and questioned in Chapter 10. But the idea of a theoretical model being an instrument is a very old idea that precedes modern economic model building by almost two centuries. Philosophers of science call this old view 'instrumentalism'.

11.2.1. Eighteenth-century instrumentalism in modern economics

> In the past few decades, model building in economics has yielded many powerful, clear results with rigorous demonstrations. . . . The assumptions of these models often do not seem even remotely accurate as descriptions of an actual economy, and the happy consequences of some models of perfect competition do not match our experience. . . .

2 For more on this, see chapter 7 of Hands [2001].

3 Although this now seems to be changing [e.g., Morgan and Knuuttila 2012].

> Can models with unrealistic assumptions . . . be of any use in understanding the world? We think they can be. . . . The question we should be asking is: In what ways can a model help in understanding a situation in the world when its assumptions, as applied to that situation, are false?
>
> Allan Gibbard and Hal Varian [1978, pp. 664–5]

> [I]nstead of explaining how it is that economic models can actually provide understanding, despite the falsity of their assumptions, [Gibbard and Varian] have brought into sharper focus the puzzle of why it is that economists have continued for so long to use models with false assumptions, and indeed with the very same false assumptions, not just for decades, but for more than a century, even though they purport to be engaged in an attempt to understand the world.
>
> Alexander Rosenberg [1978, p. 683]

> People often wonder why economists analyze models whose assumptions are known to be false, while economists feel that they learn a great deal from such exercises. We suggest that part of the knowledge generated by academic economists is case-based rather than rule-based. That is, instead of offering general rules or theories that should be contrasted with data, economists often analyze models that are 'theoretical cases', which help understand economic problems by drawing analogies between the model and the problem. According to this view, economic models, empirical data, experimental results and other sources of knowledge are all on equal footing, that is, they all provide cases to which a given problem can be compared.
>
> Itzhak Gilboa, Andrew Postlewaite, Larry Samuelson and David Schmeidler [2011, abstract]

As I noted in Chapter 9, instrumentalism has a long history going back at least to Bishop Berkeley at the beginning of the eighteenth century.[4] It may even go back to the seventeenth century when Cardinal Bellarmino suggested that Galileo would be wise to consider his heliocentric view of the planets to be a convenient instrument and nothing more than a supposition or a mathematical hypothesis.[5] But the common view of instrumentalism is the one due to the Bishop's attempt to corral the growing interest in Newton's mechanics. Again, the problem the Bishop was addressing was that some philosophers were using Newton's theory to claim its authority to demonstrate that the Church was no longer needed to truly understand the Heavens and Earth. Berkeley simply argued that Newton's theories should be considered mere tools or instruments for measuring and predicting such things as the movements of planets, and as such, they need not be

4 Specifically, I briefly explained this in Chapter 9, note 27.

5 Thanks to Axel Leijonhufvud for pointing this out to me. It should however be noted that Cardinal Bellarmino was not necessarily an instrumentalist like Berkeley [see Popper 1963, p. 98, note 2].

considered true or even competitors for the universal truths that Berkeley thought were the responsibility of the Church.

While the role of the Church no longer seems at issue, the idea of seeing economic models as instruments does bring up a similar issue concerning whether theories or models should be considered true representations of the economy or *just* tools or instruments for measuring the economy. In the early nineteenth century, eminent philosophers, such as Sir John Herschel [1830], considered Isaac Newton's theories of physics to be true because they were thought to be rationally based inductively only on observed facts, just as Francis Bacon had prescribed for scientific method. The eighteenth-century beliefs in the power of rationality were implicitly, if not always explicitly, based on the presumed pure inductive basis of Newton's physics. Those beliefs led to the extreme view and perhaps the hope that all knowledge can be rationally based solely on experience. However, as I explained in Chapter 2, the philosopher and economist David Hume shot down this hope with what can be characterized as a simple self-referencing question: How do you know *all* knowledge is based solely on experience? To which the only consistent answer is 'by experience', which of course leads to the question: How do you know that you know all knowledge is based solely on experience? And this, of course, leads to an infinite regress. One possible response to Hume's recognition of the failure of Bacon's inductive scientific method is, in effect, to retreat to Berkeley's version of instrumentalism since it would deny that theories or models have to be true to be useful.

Today in modern economics we recognize eighteenth-century instrumentalism as Milton Friedman's methodology, promoted in his 1953 methodology essay. Critics of Friedman's methodology in the 1950s and 1960s were too eager (ideologically?) to dismiss his methodology, but none seemed to see that his methodology was nothing more than a modern version of Berkeley's instrumentalism. As I explained at the end of my 1979 *Journal of Economic Literature* article about the various criticisms of Friedman's essay, the only effective criticism of his methodology is to point out that his *only* consistent response to the critics was to invoke instrumentalism itself, which at best leads to a circular defense and which I think means that the sagacity of Friedman's essay should at least be considered questionable. Perhaps the best that one can say is that Friedman's methodology seems to be stuck in the early eighteenth century.

While Friedman's methodology is rarely invoked openly to justify viewing models as instruments, it is not uncommon to see economists knowingly creating or defending the known false assumptions they used to construct their models. For example, consider Robert Aumann's view of the truth status of economic theories and models [1985, pp. 31–2, 34]:

> [I]n my view, scientific theories are not to be considered 'true' or 'false'. In constructing such a theory, we are not trying to get at the truth, or even to approximate to it; rather, we are trying to organize our thoughts and observations in a useful manner.
>
> One rough analogy is to a filing system in an office operation, or to some kind of complex computer program. We do not refer to such a system as being 'true' or 'untrue'; rather, we talk about whether it 'works' or not, or, better yet, how well it works. . . .
>
> Some philosophies deny altogether the existence of objective truth, but for my purposes this is not necessary, and I do not wish to insist on it. The concept of truth applies to *observations;* one can say that such and such were truly the observations. It also applies to all kinds of everyday events, like whether or not one had hamburger for dinner yesterday. It does not, however, apply to *theories.*

So, it easy to see how philosophers and methodologists can think of models as instruments even without the mention of Berkeley or Friedman.[6]

11.2.2. Seventeenth-century inductivism versus modern economics

> [A] relevant aspect of logical empiricism is the change from an inductive to a *hypothetical-deductive* view of the structure of scientific theories. . . . According to logical empiricism, only the deductive consequences of a scientific theory were relevant to its empirical support. . . . One reason for adopting the hypothetical-deductive method was to avoid the inveterate 'problem of induction'. This problem, originally articulated by David Hume, is the philosophical problem of *justifying induction.*
>
> D. Wade Hands [2001, pp. 84–5]

Today, not only do philosophers of economics usually not mention Bishop Berkeley, they rarely even mention instrumentalism itself. Instead, most will talk about something like what they call the hypothetical-deductive method,[7] which is usually seen to be the best characterization of the practice of model building in economics – that is, as being that of employing

[6] Technically speaking, Aumann's view, like those of most economists today, is a mixture of instrumentalism and what some philosophers call conventionalism. The latter merely holds out for an eventual inductive proof of our theories or hypotheses (perhaps in the very long-run), but until then we must accept that the best we can do is make sure they are true to the limit of the conventional criteria – that is, one accepts the best theories or hypotheses in accordance with convention. In this sense, many philosophers of economics consider instrumentalism to be merely an extreme version of conventionalism.

[7] Usually used to characterize the logic of testing [see Guala 2012, p. 601].

hypotheses to produce explanations of observable data. The hypothetical-deductive method is usually identified with the 1930s view of scientific explanation. It is also seen as a way to avoid resorting to instrumentalism as an alternative to seventeenth-century Baconian inductivism and as an alternative to addressing the question of the realism of the proffered theories or models of an economy or the economic behaviour of the decision makers that make up the economy. Instead of declaring the truth status of an assumption to be irrelevant, the most common version of this alternative is usually to invoke probabilities as an acceptable truth-status substitute.

In the 1940s, a slightly different view of scientific explanation was promoted that was called the deductive-nomological model of explanation. It saw explanations being based on so-called known covering Laws rather than mere conjectural hypotheses. The format, however, is logically the same for all practical purposes.

Now it must be recognized that both the deductive-nomological model's and the hypothetical-deductive method's characterizations of model building in economics are based on the pre-1980 view of models and theories and, especially, their logical relationship with data. Philosophers also address the issue of whether, in this relationship with data, the theories or models are to be considered *explanations* or just *descriptions* of the data. About this Wade Hands [2001, p. 85] notes:

> According to classical empiricism and early logical positivism, scientific theories *do not explain at all*; the scientific domain is the domain of empirical observation and the purpose of a scientific theory is to reliably describe those empirical observations. The commonsense view of science that science should 'explain' what we observe in the world by uncovering deep, underlying, not directly observable, causal mechanisms, is a view that is alien to strict empiricism.

He goes on to explain [p. 86]:

> The logical empiricist's answer to the problem of scientific explanation is the deductive-nomological (or D-N) model. ... According to the D-N model, a particular observed event (say entity x exhibiting property y) is 'explained' by subsuming the event under a general law (say x is an instance of z, and all zs exhibit property y).

But he then points out that [p. 87]:

> As it currently stands, the D-N model has been harshly criticized, but no other alternative model has gained enough support among philosophers of science to be seriously regarded as a viable replacement. The D-N model remains the standard, if highly criticized, characterization of scientific explanation.

There was a time many decades ago when practicing academic economists were openly well versed in the latest view of the philosophy of science, but, needless to say, few if any economic model builders today see themselves in engaging in such an explicit philosophical program such as that which philosophers and would-be philosophers of economics[8] today spend so much time discussing.

11.3. Black boxes versus transparent boxes

> [A]n experimental system is always opaque to a certain extent, because the builder/experimenter has left some degree of freedom of expression in the system that will teach us something previously unknown. This opaqueness may be the principal source of misinterpretation of the experimental result, but is a resource for at least two reasons. (1) because it can teach us something new . . . but also (2) because it allows one to use some systems as 'black boxes' that we do not understand perfectly, provided we are confident that the same basic principles (whatever they may be) are at work in the target.
>
> Francesco Guala [2012, p. 611]

Let us consider how we explain the behaviour of a single agency, such as a firm or a single individual, if we are not going to consider our behavioural and situational assumptions as literally true (i.e., not consider any of them as something with a probability equal to 1.00). To keep it obvious, let us just consider a firm (whether privately owned or a public corporation). We could always view the firm as a 'black box' – black in the sense of being opaque. In this sense, the data to consider is limited to the externally viewed or measured inputs and outputs. Our behavioural or modeling assumptions are only about the unseen contents of the black box. What do we expect of our model as an explanation based on the inputs and outputs of a black box? This question arises regardless of whether we see it from the pre- or the post-1980 view of theories and models.

Obviously, the black box characterization of the object that a model is to explain invites an instrumentalist viewpoint. That is, given such a characterization and given the observed inputs, so long as the observed output matches (by some acceptable criterion) the model's predicted output, does it matter whether the behavioural assumptions of the model (or the underlying theory, if that is your perspective) are true (or even probably true, if that is your perspective)? If your answer is 'Yes', then of course you accept

8 For a discussion of a recent effort to promote the study of the philosophy of economics, see Boland [2013].

the limits to the usefulness of instrumentalism. If it is 'No', is instrumentalism then the only alternative?

If the black box perspective is unacceptable, then one is asking for some sort of transparent box instead. In effect, most model builders engaged in experimental and behavioural economics, as was discussed in Chapter 8, are rejecting the black box perspective. The discussions in Chapters 9 and 10 were not clearly endorsing or rejecting the black box perspective. It all depends on what one would do with a test that shows the predicted output does not match the observed output. In Chapter 9, our deciding it was a refutation was a bit more elaborate, since a convincing refutation requires a failure of the model's predictions to match observed data, but it also requires that the model of the counter-example matches the relevant observed data (a statement, by the way, that may or may not have anything to do with inputs or outputs). In Chapter 10 (as well as Chapter 9 in a more limited sense), it is a matter of establishing the adequacy of the observed data concerning the inputs and outputs – that is, it depends on what we know about the data and what we do if the data turns out to be inadequate for testing the model of the box regardless of whether it is treated as a black or a transparent box. As to the type of model discussed in Part I – that is, theoretical models – the issue of empirical methodology does not arise given the purpose of such models. However, everything I have said about the discussions in Chapter 9 and particularly Chapter 10 apply to the types of model discussed in Part II – that is, empirical models – if observable data are really to be our concern. It is all a matter of attitude, particularly as to whether instrumentalism is an acceptable philosophical or methodological stance regarding the contents of the box. All this sounds a lot like what was considered in Chapter 5 with regard to what Mankiw was saying concerning a difference between macroeconomics as science and macroeconomics as social engineering, as the latter is fundamentally instrumentalist while the former does not need to be. But it should be noted that any question of attitude and purpose can be dependent on some important sociological considerations. It is this question that I will turn to in the next chapter.

12

Choosing model-building methods

Macroeconomic model builders always face a choice of how to go about building models, although far too many North American model builders are unaware of the options. There are many reasons for the lack of awareness, but they fall into three categories: sociological, historical and methodological. Few graduate students are given any training in how to go about choosing a modeling method. Instead, they are encouraged to follow their teachers' examples of demonstrated successful modeling. Needless to say, for a decade or more the sub-discipline of the history of economic thought has not been considered an essential part of anyone's graduate economics training; consequently, there has been little opportunity to become of aware of historical debates about the best or most appropriate model building methods. An obvious sociological reason is that beginning professors need to worry about their careers. Which modeling method is chosen will be the one that helps in obtaining tenure and promotions. Today, too often, the criterion employed for such promotion and tenure decisions is the quantity of publications. So, if one were aware of several alternative modeling methods to choose between, clearly it would be sensible (dare we say rational?) to choose the method that will maximize the number of published papers within the time allotted before the next tenure or promotion decision – or perhaps just the next salary decision. Methodology-oriented critics of the lack of awareness of alternatives point to the methodological issue of the unrealism of the models created – in particular, models that are the easiest to publish are often ones that disregard the unrealism of the assumptions of the model. In other words, critics of the methods practiced in North America say that too often convenience is put before the time-consuming problem of building realistic models.

Macro-econometric models are a case in point. Recently, a relatively new web-based journal (www.economics-ejournal.org) published a special econometrics issue discussing various alternative modeling methods. Included was an informal debate between the historian of thought David Colander and the econometrics theorist Aris Spanos. The debate was about two alternative econometric methods of modeling macroeconomics. One is a method that has been promoted by some economists in Europe; the other is the method that prevails in North America. These are given various names by the two main participants in the debate. Colander [2009] sometimes calls the European method the 'general-to-specific approach' and at other times the 'cointegrated vector auto regression (CVAR) approach' (which I discussed in Chapter 6). He sometimes calls the North American method the 'theory-comes-first approach' and at other times he specifically identifies the theory that comes first as being the one based on the 'Dynamic Stochastic General Equilibrium (DSGE) approach', which I also discussed in Chapter 6. Spanos [2009] instead calls the North American method the 'pre-eminence of theory perspective'. I will use Colander's more descriptive nomenclature (theory-comes-first).[1]

The technical mathematical differences of these approaches to modeling are not the issue here since the debate in that journal raised more interesting issues regarding sociological, historical and methodological bases for the choice of methods and in particular the issue of the dominance of the theory-comes-first method in North America.

12.1. Sociological implications of a choice of modeling methods

The particular situation that Colander focuses on in the debate involves the North American economists' use of a particular econometric model-building technique. He asks why the general-to-specific approach as developed in Europe has had only limited success in North America where the theory-comes-first approach dominates. The reason he gives is that, as a tool for doing empirical macroeconomics, the European approach requires the researcher's judgment to be part of the analysis, which involves spending the extra time needed to examine data, as I discussed in Chapter 10. In contrast, the North American researcher is required to be more focused on the

[1] Colander recognizes that the North American perspective has been making inroads in many European universities, and so many might find this dichotomy somewhat artificial, but, nevertheless, I think it is useful for illustrating the sociological issues that face many beginning economic model builders today – perhaps even in Europe.

journal publication quantity criterion for career advancement, which discourages any subjective and time-consuming research methods. Specifically he says, 'The bias against judgment is inherent in a blind peer review system' [2009, p. 5], which is, of course, a major aspect of 'the current academic economics institutional environment of "publish or perish" (in the right journals)' and thus 'there are very few incentives for top young economists to reflect on the overall economic research process, but there are strong incentives for them to focus on narrow technical issues' [pp. 6–7].

So, Colander's main argument is sociological in that the institutional environment surrounding career advancement provides incentives that favour the North American theory-comes-first approach, which he claims facilitates quick and frequent publications. However, as he points out, there are problems inherent in any measurement such as the quantity of publications; any measure used in an assessment will be adversely manipulated by the participants so that it does not achieve what it was meant to achieve. Given this institutional environment, not much publishable research would ever be produced if a North American researcher were to follow the method Colander says is often practiced[2] in Europe. It is a method whereby one would be expected to exercise one's judgment as well as do the extensive research[3] that is needed to determine the statistical adequacy of the data before developing elaborate econometric models to explain those data. As a result, if the European general-to-specific approach were dominant, the quantity of published research would not be a very useful criterion for promotion or tenure, and instead a more subjective criterion would have to be used. But in North America, subjective criteria have not been relied on since the 1960s. One reason might be the fast growth of universities both in size and number during the 1960s. Graduate programs grew in response with the obvious consequence that the size of the community of economists in North America became too large for any one member to know much about all but a very few other members of their academic community. Even some economics departments are too large to expect any one member of their tenure and promotion committees to know much about the work of every candidate. While weight might be given to solicited reference letters, it is even difficult to be sure that the letters are honest if one does not know the referee personally.[4] As a result, most departments have resorted to counting

2 Or at least advocated.

3 Such as was discussed in Chapter 10.

4 And in this regard, some universities are banning as unethical any personal contact with the referees or contacts at other universities! At my university, this applies to all appointment decisions.

publications. Even worse, this means that the essential judgment is being made not by one's colleagues but instead by journal editors – but that is another topic.[5]

While avoiding the use of subjective criteria may solve a problem of unreliable promotion and tenure assessments, it seems to result in another problem – the other one Colander identifies. In the North American system, the obvious aim for those wishing to advance their careers in the economics profession should be to maximize the number of publications. Since the mid-1970s we have seen an explosion in the supply of specialized publications in economics. This has facilitated the widespread counting of publications and thereby the ubiquitous careerism by providing the needed opportunities for publication.[6] Add to this the now common tactic of allowing PhD theses to be composed of several (publishable) essays and worse the tactic of multiple authors for published articles – thereby increasing the number of publications for the same effort – and you have the adverse manipulation Colander calls 'gaming' the system and thereby maximizing the number of publications regardless of any assessment of quality beyond conforming to the currently accepted modeling methods. And all of this is done without any concern for the thorny question of the truth status of the assumptions used in the models.

Parenthetically, there is another issue that would-be promotion or tenure candidates should consider but was not discussed by Colander in his debate with Spanos. Specifically, there exists a somewhat newer criterion for promotion or tenure that encourages the theory-comes-first perspective. With less money coming to North American universities from governmental agencies, many universities are now relying more and more on research grants to finance their graduate programs. As a result, not only is the quantity of a candidate's published articles being considered in many economics departments, but so is how much research money a promotion or tenure candidate brings in. Unless the research granting agencies encourage the European approach to modeling economics, the theory-comes-first approach may continue to dominate for a long time. Moreover, given that the academics who sit on promotion and tenure committees are the same academics who sit on the boards that award the research grants, things do not look good for the European approach in the near future.

5 See Grubel and Boland [1986].

6 For more on careerism in economics, see the preface and epilogue of my 1997 book.

12.2. Historical implications of a choice of modeling methods

In the debate, Spanos takes issue with Colander's diagnosis of the sociological situation concerning the choice of model building methods. Spanos does not deny the dominance of the theory-comes-first approach or, as he calls it, the pre-eminence-of-theory approach. Instead, he argues that the history of the dominance started long before there was a concern for careerism on the part of model builders. Specifically, Spanos asks 'Why does the pre-eminence of theory . . . perspective currently dominate US empirical macroeconomic modeling?' [2009, p. 2]; and he says, 'The short answer is, arguably, it "represents the *status quo*" with a very long history in economics going back to [David] Ricardo (1817)'. Moreover, he says, 'A case can be made that [it] has dominated economic modeling for the last two centuries'. He says, today, 'The conventional wisdom underlying this perspective is that one builds simple idealized models which capture certain key aspects of the phenomenon of interest, and uses such models to gain insight concerning alternative economic policies'. From this perspective, Spanos says, 'the role of the data is only subordinate in the sense that it can help to instantiate such models by quantifying them'. I would state this in another way: it can be said that most North American economic model builders see their research methodology as a matter of a developing a *sequence of models* [Koopmans 1957, p. 142; Weintraub 1979, p. 15; Boland 2003, p. 228]. As a result, raising a question of the realism of assumptions in 'simple idealized models' at an early stage is considered counter-productive or, at minimum, premature.

As to the long, 200-year history of the pre-eminence-of-theory approach, Spanos says [2009, p. 3] 'The primary difference between the 19th and the later part of the 20th century is that the developments in statistical inference, associated with the Fisher-Neyman-Pearson . . . model-based approach that culminated in the 1930s, helped to shed illuminating light on the role of data in empirical modeling in ways which were unknown to [John Stuart] Mill or Marshall'. But, he says, 'Unfortunately for economics, some of the key elements of the [Fisher-Neyman-Pearson] statistical perspective, including the importance of statistical model validation, never made it into modern econometrics, primarily because the Cowles Commission literature[7] solidified the [pre-eminence-of-theory]

[7] Which, as was discussed in Chapter 6, was merely the perspective of multi-equation structural models regularly promoted by Koopmans.

perspective in econometric modeling'. The technical details of all this are not at issue here.[8]

It is all too easy for the practitioners of the theory-comes-first approach to dismiss criticism of the sort identifying the incentive-based choice of method instead of a realism-based choice that Colander identifies by simply claiming that all models are to some degree unrealistic. And all too often the simple criticism implicit in the European approach – that data should matter as much if not more when making modeling decisions – is answered by saying that focusing on data before one has a model sounds like the old methodological argument for 'measurement without theory' [Koopmans 1947] or even, as was discussed in Chapter 10, like promoting 'data mining' [Lovell 1983; see Hoover and Perez 1999].

Again, the main point that I think Spanos and the discussion in Chapter 10 is making concerning the apparent dispute between the 'theory-comes-first' and what looks like the 'data-comes-first' is that it reflects a misunderstanding or a lack of appreciation for the proper use of statistics in the development and assessment of economic models. Advocates of the theory-comes-first perspective conflate (a) the realism of the *substantive* assumptions regarding the phenomenon of interest to be explained by the theoretical model in question, with (b) the inappropriateness of the *probabilistic* assumptions regarding the data in question for the statistical model that defines the underlying premises for data-based inferences.

As will be familiar from the discussion in Chapter 10, Spanos[9] thinks 'the distinction is important because the presence of statistical misspecification will undermine any prospect of reliably probing potential substantive errors and/or omissions'. So, he says, 'securing statistical adequacy is not just another optional criterion; it is the price one has to pay for employing statistical inference because it is *necessary* for the reliability of any inductive inference pertaining to substantive questions of interest, including assessing the [realism] of the theory-model in question'. Furthermore, he says,

> Without statistical adequacy no *learning from data* is possible because one effectively renders statistical inference tantamount to a crystal ball procedure by rescinding its reliability! This is because the reliability of statistical inferences – measured in terms of the relevant error probabilities – is totally unbeknown to the

[8] For an excellent explanation of the Fisher-Neyman-Pearson statistical perspective and the related technical issues involving economics, consult the 2008 *New Palgrave* entry on 'Statistics and economics' by Spanos. Most will recognize this perspective as involving the usual Null-Hypothesis approach to testing.

[9] In personal correspondence to me dated 27 September 2009.

> modeler. The surest way for an inference to lead one astray is to use a 5% significance level test whose actual type error probability is closer to 100%; something that can easily happen when the statistical model is misspecified vis-à-vis the data.

As I observed earlier in this section, Spanos [2009] thinks the apparent dominance of the theory-comes-first approach is not necessarily just a matter of the career incentive choices made but is more a matter of a long-standing *status quo*. And the *status quo* survives because too many econometric model builders do not understand the proper role of data in drawing reliable inferences. Contrary to what Colander suggested, Spanos thinks the European general-to-specific approach is not an issue of subjective judgments but of appreciating the need to be concerned with the statistical adequacy involved in the relationship between data and models. That is, there are matters of judgment, of course, but, as was discussed in Chapter 10, the judgments need not be subjective, as they can be based on a proper technical assessment of whether the data collected satisfy the probabilistic assumptions of the statistical model underlying the inferences for the purposes at hand.

So, a choice of method may have to be made as Colander argues, but there is no need to ignore the realism of the models constructed if, as Spanos says,[10] one also understands 'the need to secure the statistical adequacy of such models vis-à-vis the data in question in order to ensure the reliability of inferences concerning the primary questions of interest'. But it can be argued that this would require reconciliation between these alleged competing approaches to building macro-econometric models. And what are the prospects of such reconciliation? If Colander is right, it does not look promising given the demands of careerism. Nevertheless, Spanos [2009, p. 11] remains 'optimistic that the new generation of econometricians will eventually grow out of esteeming technical dexterity and begin to reflect on the serious methodological issues undermining the trustworthiness of the evidence produced by the prevailing econometric modeling practice'.

12.3. Methodological implications of a choice of modeling methods

The one thing that both Colander and Spanos seem to agree on is that one should be concerned with the realism (or as Spanos would say, at least 'the

[10] In personal correspondence to me dated 27 September 2009.

substantive adequacy') of one's models while allowing for the sequence-of-models perspective, for which practitioners wish to avoid premature refutation that would preclude progress in model building. However, according to Spanos,[11] the realism question cannot even be posed to the data before one secures the 'statistical adequacy of the estimated model in question'.

The fundamental issue is a familiar one: whether a model builder should be concerned with the realism of the assumptions employed or instead be concerned just with the logical adequacy of the model and its assumptions. Since too many economists in North American universities see no immediate need to worry about the realism of their assumptions, as Colander's criticism of careerism suggests, they can easily turn out all sorts of theoretical models in order to maximize the number of publications. At best, their objective is to use their models to explain empirical evidence that has been collected, but usually without regard for the 'trustworthiness of such evidence', as Spanos would claim, or for the quality of the evidence,[12] as I would say – at worst, it is to explain only what some model builders call 'stylized facts'.[13] As Spanos [2008] put it, such 'stylized facts' are easily called into question on statistical adequacy grounds. In other words, 'stylized facts' are simply not verifiable reports of observations, but instead, simplified or abstracted (and thus assumed) states of an economy. This is another version of the theory-comes-first approach to macroeconomic research. Again, the excuse used to postpone any questioning of the realism of the assumptions is just the promise offered by the progressive sequence of models.

At a deeper level, all model builders must make a choice regarding the realism of their assumptions. On the one hand, many take the view that models (and their assumptions) should not be judged as either true or false but only as better or worse according to the currently accepted conventional criteria. Sometimes it is even claimed that all theories or models are false [e.g., Solow 1956, p. 65], even though this is a theory of theories itself and thus self-contradictory! On the other hand, other model builders seemingly follow Friedman's famous 1953 methodology essay and claim that the truth status of the assumptions – as instruments or tools – does not matter so long as they work. Surprisingly, econometricians are sometimes clearly unaware that they are following Friedman's view of methodology.[14] But, in either

11 In personal correspondence to me dated 27 September 2009.

12 See Chapter 9, Section 9.5.

13 See Boland [2008b].

14 As I explained in my 1997 book [pp. 283–4].

case (i.e., as conventional truths or as mere tools), the question of the realism of assumptions is either postponed or ignored.

It could be claimed that since econometrics is used to test economic theories or models, we should not be so quick to criticize. After all, such tests are intended to determine the truth status of the theories or models in question. However, as I explained in Chapters 9 and 10, it is not clear that econometrics-based tests can always do this.

12.4. Concluding remarks for honest model builders in economics

It would seem clear that model building can be useful for career purposes, but one should not blame model building or even models for their misuse in this regard. Models are obviously indispensable in modern economics. Nevertheless, the time has surely come for honest economic model builders to start being concerned with the realism of their assumptions and the relevance of their models for the economic problems of the day. If this time has come, it may also be the time for model builders to be interested in learning about the methodology of model building in general or at least in the history of economic model building or, better still, in the history of economic thought in general.

Epilogue: Against putting ideology ahead of realism

In this Epilogue, I will be talking about methodology but also about ideology. By methodology I am not talking about the kind of issues philosophers consider methodology to involve, such as how to (or the need to) justify one's knowledge claims. Instead, I always mean the low level questions about why economic model builders assume what they assume. As I noted in Chapter 9, my PhD thesis was about the most popular methodological concern among economic model builders of the 1960s – specifically, the view that, to be taken seriously, mathematical models must be testable. A lot of people then thought that this concern was due to the writings of the philosopher of science Karl Popper. This was a common mistake. The concern was not due to Popper; instead, it was due to the work of the economic theorist Paul Samuelson. And again, Samuelson's concern for testability was a response to the late 1930s critics of the use of mathematics in the development of economic theory. As I have also noted, with his famous 1941 PhD thesis [1947/65], *The Foundations of Economic Analysis*, Samuelson set about demonstrating how one can construct economic models that are testable. As he stated in this thesis, he would always have the methodological question of testability in mind when building his economic models.

Unlike Samuelson, I, of course, did not receive a Nobel Prize for my PhD thesis, but mine, nevertheless, was also concerned with testability of economic models. At the time, I naively thought economic model builders were not just talking about the logical problem of testability, but instead I thought they were actually talking about the process of collecting sufficient empirical data to perform a test of a model. However, as I explained in Chapter 9, even with simple Keynesian models, the number of observations necessary to construct just one single observation-based test of such a model would far exceed what is realistically possible in the real world. Interestingly, as I noted in the Preface, one particular example stood out: I showed that any model that assumes its production function is Cobb-Douglas in form can require[1] a quarter million observations!

Ideology was not a concern in Samuelson's PhD thesis, nor was it in mine. Today, however, some of those who see themselves as engaged in developing 'heterodox' economic models may admit that they are deliberately attempting to engage mainstream economists in ideological issues. But, whenever you ask young model builders in the mainstream of economics why they assume what they do, their answers usually involve only technical mathematical matters, or they simply answer 'because that's what everyone does' and so rarely would they claim that their assumptions were guided by ideological concerns. Nevertheless, too often, only one set of ideological implications are assured by the assumptions mainstream economists make, even if they are unaware of such implications. Of course, sometimes many mainstream model builders consciously promote ideology with their assumptions, but from what I have encountered, that is not the usual case. Either way, I will end this Epilogue with consideration of such implications.

1. Remembering the 1960s, 1970s, and 1980s

When I began teaching microeconomic theory in the 1960s and then continuing through the 1970s, many students at my university were motivated by their sociology teachers – these were teachers who were actively promoting Marxism (although few of them ever read Karl Marx, of course). Whenever I was teaching an economics principles class, I particularly remember spending a lot of our class time explaining the virtues of the market system. But by the early 1980s, things changed dramatically. Then and for the next decade, I had to explain to the beginning economics students the possible virtues of government involvement in the economy. In both cases, I was dealing with ideological concerns and propaganda rather than well-thought-out economic theories. But at least in the 1970s and 1980s such concerns were put on the table for open consideration.

Of course, some economics students may still *explicitly* presume that the market can solve all problems. Nevertheless, among students today, economics is no longer controversial, nor is it seen in ideological terms, as it was in the early 1980s. That is to say, today's students simply presume

[1] That is, to form just *one* singular refuting vector of observations of the variables of the model.

everyone agrees that the market can solve all problems, and thus there is no apparent need to consider government involvement or any need to examine such a presumption. I will try to explain this situation here.

2. It is all about assumptions

As I said, my concern as a methodologist is understanding why model builders assume what they do. As such, I am only interested in small-m methodology questions, and I am definitely not interested in the big-M methodology questions that (economic) philosophers typically pursue [see McCloskey 1994, chapter 19]. In this regard, I have argued for many years that the most interesting methodological problems are caused by what we take for granted – particularly when we are making assumptions.

Let me illustrate the issues at hand by stating a few of the assumptions too often taken for granted when building economic models. Do we assume all prices are equilibrium prices? Do we assume that only individuals make decisions – that is, things don't decide, only people decide? Do we assume that all decision makers have sufficient knowledge to guarantee that their choices will maximize profit or utility or whatever? Are all decision makers maximizers, or are they satisficers, as my late friend Herbert Simon would have us assume? Do all production functions exhibit constant returns to scale? Does every indifference curve form a border for a strictly convex preferred set? Are all production functions continuously differentiable? Do all investors respond to lowered interest rates? Or, similarly, do demanders always buy more when the price drops? Do all game players know all the rules of the game? Or do all the players in any specific game even see the game the same way? And so on.

So, there are a lot of assumptions we must make to build a model or to form and justify any policy recommendation. And, of course, policy recommendations are sensitive to the assumptions we make, but rarely do proponents of an economic policy ever tell you everything they have assumed.

3. Elementary logic and realism

Before I go on, I need to be explicit about some simple elementary facts about logic and realism. Whenever I refer to 'elementary logic', I am only talking about basic explanations whereby one provides reasons for why some explicit statement about an observed (or conceivable) event or about some predicted event is true. For such an explanation we rely on the inherent property of any logically valid argument – this property (which I explained in footnote 3 of Chapter 8) is called, *modus ponens*. As I explained, this inherent property says that every logically valid argument consists of a conjunction of statements – that is, a conjunction of what we call assumptions – and whenever all of the assumptions are true, it is necessarily the case that any and every statement that can be logically deduced using these assumptions must also be true. If it turns out that one of these deduced statements does not 'fit' (in some sense) what we observe, then we know that at least one of our assumptions must be false – that is, at least one of our presumptions is unrealistic.[2]

Now, I am sure almost everyone today knows all about this elementary logic stuff. But it is always amazing how so many economists have the notion that, whenever many observably true statements can be deduced from their model, the observed realism of those deductions somehow tells them something about the realism of their model and its assumptions. However, as a matter of elementary logic, this common notion is simply false. You cannot work back from the observed truth of one's deductions to the guaranteed truth status of the assumptions used to form those deductions. Similarly, if you know one of your assumptions is not true, you do not thereby have a right to claim that any of your deductions which use that assumption are false.[3] For those who might disagree with me on all this, let me give a simple example to illustrate. Consider the following assumptions for a syllogism that could be used to explain why my house pet was a cat:

If it is true that:

1. *All cats have five legs; and that*
2. *Only cats have five legs; and that*
3. *My pet had five legs.*

Then it must also be true that:

4. *My pet was a cat.*

Of course, all three assumptions are false, yet the logically derived conclusion is in fact true.[4] Stated another way, as a matter of elementary logic, even

[2] As I explained in that note, this elementary logical property is also the basis for criticizing explanations by indirectly testing the proffered assumptions. And I also said in that note that using the logic of an argument for criticism is called *modus tollens*, and, unfortunately, if an explanation involves two or more assumptions, whenever at least one deduced statement has been shown to be false, we still do not know which of the assumptions is thereby known to be false – this, of course, is the ambiguity that creates the infamous Duhem-Quine problem, discussed in Chapters 8 and 9.

[3] Other than that assumption itself, of course.

[4] Heuristically speaking, we could say that truth status can be passed forward but not backward, and, similarly, falsity can be passed backward but not forward.

though one of our deductions from our assumptions is true, it is still the case that *all* of our assumptions can be false. So, clearly, just because our model can logically explain an observably true statement, such a logical success tells us nothing about the realism of our model's assumptions.

4. Friedman and instrumentalism

This then brings us to the point where all of this first mattered for modern economists – namely, the publication of Milton Friedman's 1953 methodology essay, 'The methodology of positive economics', which I discussed in Chapter 11. His essay prompted a long list of critiques, yet it still had and continues to have many adherents. However, the critiques of it were not trivial, as they were authored by some of the biggest names in economics – for example, the Nobel Prize winners Paul Samuelson, Herbert Simon and Tjalling Koopmans, as well as other big names of the day, such as Eugene Rotwein, Daniel Orr, Donald Bear, Jack Melitz and Louis de Alessi. As I explained in my 1979 *Journal of Economic Literature* article about the critiques of Friedman's essay, in almost every case, the published critiques involved unfairly redefining the words 'test' or 'testing' in ways not intended by Friedman, and then all go on to criticize their invented unfair version of Friedman's essay. As such, I think this type of unfair criticism is ineffective even though, particularly in the case of Samuelson's critique, many of those who rejected Friedman's ideology or his economic policy recommendations eagerly accepted Samuelson's critique as successful.

With my 1979 article, my purpose was to clear the deck of ineffective and logically defective critiques so that an effective and logically valid critique could be formed. It is always interesting and puzzling to me that so many readers of my article think I was defending Friedman and agreeing with his methodology. That certainly was neither my purpose nor what I said in my article. But I guess that at one level and for purely logical reasons it is easy for someone who accepts *any* critique of Friedman's essay to not care whether Samuelson' critique is actually unfair. Similarly, for ideological reasons, anyone who wants to be armed so as to be able to fend off the various popular critiques will like to think my article is a sufficient defense of Friedman's essay. However, if all of these readers actually read my 1979 article to its last page, they will see that I offered a logically adequate and fair critique of Friedman's essay.

My criticism of Friedman's 1953 essay, as I explained in Chapter 11, was that he was merely presenting an argument for what some philosophers call 'instrumentalism'. Moreover, as I said, my argument in response to all of the critiques of his essay was that its *only* defense would be to invoke instrumentalism itself – a consistent defense, maybe, but certainly a circular one – at best.

As I noted in Chapter 11, instrumentalism has a long history going back at least to the beginning of the eighteenth century when Bishop Berkeley attempted to corral the growing interest in Newton's mechanics. I suspect Friedman was similarly motivated – in this case, in corralling the growing influence of the economics of Keynes and maybe even that of Walras. In this regard, Friedman argued that the only test of a tool is whether or not it works. And, if it works, one need not worry about whether it is a true representation of reality. To illustrate this apparent denial of a need to worry about realism, in my 1979 article, I referred to the situation facing a typical TV repairman. When we take our failing TV to be repaired, we do not quiz the repairman to determine if he understands the latest theories of electromagnetism. For all we know, he may believe there are little green men in the transistors and the TV has failed merely because one of the little green men has died. So long as he replaces the appropriate transistor (the one with the supposedly 'dead little green man', of course) *and* the TV now works, we are happy. In other words, instrumentalism just says that, so long as one's theory works, it does not matter that it has employed false assumptions. The question that must be asked is, can you *honestly* claim to *understand* some phenomena if your understanding is based on *known* false assumptions? But, unfortunately, that question rarely comes up, so let us move on.

While there are many economic methodologists today who still want to argue about Friedman's essay, that is not my purpose here. I raise the notion of instrumentalism for discussion because, despite their public denial of agreeing with his essay, many economic model builders today still invoke instrumentalism to justify their use of patently unrealistic assumptions.

In my 1997 book, I recounted a relevant event that took place at a 1983 Cambridge conference celebrating Keynes's 100th birthday. At the end of the conference, I had the fortunate opportunity to do a survey of some Keynesian econometricians about their view of methodology. I outlined for them the fundamental notions of Friedman's instrumentalist methodology but without ever mentioning his name. When I asked who in the group agreed with these fundamental methodological notions, all of the econometricians held up their hands. When I then asked who among them agreed with Friedman's methodology, they all denied any agreement with Friedman's instrumentalist methodology. Was this inconsistency evidence of hypocrisy or of mere ignorance of methodology? As I will explain here, it continues to be a common problem with econometricians and other model builders who seem completely unaware of the implications of what they take for granted when it comes to methodology.

5. Mathematical modeling: When the left hand does not know what the right hand is doing

The econometrician David Hendry long ago observed that too often econometric model builders make assumptions with their left hands to build their underlying model, but with their right hands they apply theorems from econometric theory that are inconsistent with the model's assumptions. It is this perspective that motivated Chapter 10 and it will be driving what I am talking about here.

There once was an ongoing debate among a few methodologists as to whether Friedman's 1953 essay is responsible for our excessive and growing dependence on using heavy-duty mathematics to build models. That debate does not seem relevant to me, particularly given my 1983 survey of Keynesian econometricians. I would think many (maybe even most) of today's young economic model builders have never read Friedman's essay. Moreover, the early promoters of the use of mathematics, such as Samuelson, actually rejected Friedman's essay. Nevertheless, once mathematics got a minimal hold on the methodology of doing economics, the realism of assumptions seemed to have taken a back seat. However, this relegation is not because of any explicit endorsement of instrumentalism. Let me explain.

For those of you who have spent any time in a typical university mathematics department – or, better, if you have taken a graduate course in a mathematics department, you will immediately understand my explanation for what I have just said, namely about there not being any explicit endorsement of instrumentalism when building mathematical models. I have a colleague who has two PhDs, the first one in mathematics and the second in economics. As he explained to me one day, the culture of the mathematician is that when building a model one's objective is to construct a proof and to do so *by any means whatsoever*. The realism of one's assumptions is not important; what is important is whether the proof is logically sufficient and then – and most important – whether one's proof is deemed *elegant*. Unfortunately, it seems the culture of the mathematician has gotten a significant foothold in today's economics departments.

6. The institutionalization of the mathematician's culture

By itself, the invasion of the mathematician's culture would not be enough to explain why today's young model builders' left hands do not know what their right hands are doing. As economists well know, it is all about incentives as well as constraints on achieving one's objectives. For the question concerning the cultural behaviour of academic economists, the issue of incentives is all about the criteria behind promotions and tenure.

As I explained in Chapter 12, in the debate with the econometrician Aris Spanos, the historian of economic thought David Colander has addressed this in the context of differences between how European and North American macro-econometric model builders go about constructing their models. One issue is simply the question of what counts for obtaining promotions and tenure. As explained in this regard, most North American universities encourage counting publications, and this appears to be the main source of the problem. If a model builder has to choose between two different methods of building a model, then – as most economists would suggest – it would be rational to choose the method that yields the most and quickest publishable papers.

Colander, as I explained, identified two distinctly different methodological approaches to building macro-econometric models. One was characterized as the European approach, which he says students and followers of Hendry supposedly advocate and which Colander called the 'general-to-specific approach'.[5] The other one he characterizes as the North American method approach, which he calls the 'theory-comes-first' approach.[6] Recall, the difference between these two methods concerns whether or not one spends a lot of time collecting or assessing data *before* constructing one's model. The general-to-specific approach requires spending the needed time, but the theory-comes-first approach instead starts by constructing a model and only then turns to applying it to data. Needless to say, from this latter perspective, any given model can be applied to many collections of data and this turns out to allow for the generation of many different papers.

So far, there is nothing obvious about this institutional situation that involves ideology. The ideology enters with the easy-to-use theoretical models that can be employed to quickly address an empirical question with an econometric model. Almost always these theoretical models are

5 Again, the 'general-to-specific' approach is what is today primarily represented by the 'Cointegrated Vector Auto Regression (CVAR)' approach [see Juselius 2006].

6 Again, the 'theory-comes-first' approach is today primarily represented by models using the Dynamic Stochastic General Equilibrium (DSGE) macro theory.

equilibrium models, and often they are ones that would be accepted only by the so-called Chicago School economists.[7] Rarely, today, will you find an *orthodox* Keynesian model being built. And by orthodox Keynesian, I don't mean the neo-Keynesian models that are almost always general equilibrium models; instead, I mean those based on what John Maynard Keynes had to say in his 1937 *Quarterly Journal of Economics* article, in which he was responding to the critics of his 1936 book. Keynes was specifically recognizing the need to see that participants in the capital investment markets lack sufficient knowledge to behave in a textbook maximizer mode, and, as such, any presumption of equilibrium is much too unrealistic. Interestingly, even Friedrich Hayek [1937] argued that any equilibrium-based explanation requires at least an explanation of how the participants in the market know what they need to know to achieve the equilibrium.

By itself, the incursion of the mathematician's culture would not explain the hidden ideology embedded in economic model building today – although obviously it facilitates Friedman's instrumentalist methodology. And, by itself, the urgency of publishing created by the institutional structure of North American universities also does not explain the insidiousness of some underlying ideological presumptions. But when we put them together, we get the picture I have been trying to paint here. Model builders today are engaged in the industry of producing models that satisfy the needs of the institutional structure, but naively are producing equilibrium models that implicitly can only be used to support one particular ideology – the ideology that presumes that the market by itself can solve all problems once the equilibrium has been reached, and hence any government activity in the economy is always seen to be unnecessary at best and destructive at worst.

It is all too easy to see what can happen under the governmental leadership of someone like a conservative president or prime minister or anyone who simplistically and uncritically follows the old ideological views of Chicago-School-inspired economists[8] and thereby sets about minimizing the role of government. As is now apparent to many observers, we can be led to the kind of economic crisis we began experiencing in 2008. However, I am not saying that such a government has to employ only or even any Chicago-School-trained economists – to the contrary, none of them have to be employed. All that would be needed are recently trained PhDs who are very good at building equilibrium-based econometric models.

7 That is, those who follow the ideological pronouncements of Friedman or his followers.

8 Or perhaps just an Ayn Rand inspired libertarian economist.

7. The textbook theory of the firm versus the ideology of the market economy

Despite what I have said so far, I am not trying to blame the purveyors of econometric model building. Nor am I blaming young model builders. Instead, all of this has happened backstage, out of sight, without anyone planning it. Once convenience is put ahead of concern for realism, a lot can happen without anyone designing the outcome. Let me list some of the ways that ideology gets built in – and again, it is without anyone making a decision to do so.

Above all, we still have the popular economics joke mentioned in Chapter 2 about the drunk who lost his keys in the dark part of the street but spends all of his time looking for his keys under a street light because the light is better. This old joke was designed to be a critical comment on the state of economic model building. In particular, as I said, it was about using equilibrium models, which are always easier to construct than non-equilibrium models – if for no other reason, the mathematics is easier.

Then there is the matter mentioned earlier. As I said, in the 1960s and 1970s, almost all of the faculty at my university who claimed to be Marxists never actually read Marx – except maybe the *Manifesto* but certainly never *Das Kapital*. Similarly, today, members of conservative think tanks who promote Adam Smith's views – usually to justify the notion that the market can solve all problems – rarely read all of his *Wealth of Nations* and particularly not the parts that explain the need for taxes and for government involvement [see Saul 1995].

Interestingly, both advocates and critics of mainstream neoclassical economics think the textbook's theory of the firm shows why a private enterprise is always more efficient than a government-owned enterprise. Do textbooks really show that? I have been teaching microeconomics for most of my career and so have examined a lot of textbooks, and except for a few that are deliberately promoting an ideological line of argument, the textbook theory of the firm never requires our saying anything about who owns the firm. Typically, the firm is treated as a black box which transforms inputs into outputs – nothing more. One could go so far as to say that even Adam Smith's division of labour – as a source of production efficiency – does not have to say anything about who owns the firm expanding its use of labour.

In the 1980s, I taught a graduate microeconomic theory class during which one of the students – who was from Czechoslovakia – explained to us what happened with Alexander Dubček's aborted 1968 revolution. For this, he explained how the Central Planning Committee went about organizing the economy. It occurred to the class that what he was describing for us sounded an awful lot like how General Motors goes about doing its business of designing and producing automobiles. It also sounded a lot like how my university was doing its business then. In other words, despite the ideological claims that major differences exist between private and public enterprises, if one's ideological glasses were removed, it might be that these are distinctions without a difference in many cases. One might also see that this is exactly what Joseph Schumpeter was predicting more than a hundred years ago.

8. Concluding remarks

Obviously by now you can see that I am primarily advocating that model builders should be more concerned with the realism of their assumptions, but, of course, some will say we should still allow for a sequential development of models – one that necessarily begins with highly unrealistic assumptions at its early stages. In other words, perhaps model building for model building's sake should be allowed – but, I say, only if we do not just stop there and admire our elegant models. Specifically, my concern is that, before one starts making policy recommendations to governments, the realism of one's model must be addressed and that widely used unrealistic assumptions must be rejected regardless of their mathematical elegance. Of particular concern is the failure to recognize the need to explain how decision makers acquire the needed knowledge they would have to have if one is going to assume the existence of an equilibrium or even presume that an equilibrium will be reached in real time. Such a failure is not trivial – particularly since it encourages an ideological perspective that can be very dangerous, as we have seen in recent years. It turns out, even the former chairman of the U.S. Federal Reserve – the once libertarian, pro-free market believer Alan Greenspan – now recognizes he made a mistake assuming that the financial market did not need regulation [Leonhardt 2008; Beattie and Politi 2008]. The question today is, has anyone learned from Greenspan's admitted mistake about the realism of his assumptions?

Bibliography

Albert, M. [2001] Bayesian learning and expectations formation, in Corfield, D. and Williamson, J. (eds.), *Foundations of Bayesianism* (Boston: Kluwer), 341–62.

Alchian, A. [1950] Uncertainty, evolution and economic theory, *Journal of Political Economy, 58*, 211–21.

Allen, W. R. [1977] Economics, economists and economic policy: modern American experiences, *History of Political Economy, 9*, 48–88.

An, S., Chang, Y. and Kim, S.-B. [2009] Can a representative-agent model represent a heterogeneous-agent economy, *American Economic Journal: Macroeconomics, 1(2)*, 29–54.

Angrist, J. and Pischke, J.-S. [2010] The credibility revolution in empirical economics: How better research design is taking the con out of econometrics, *Journal of Economic Perspectives, 24*, 3–30.

Armstrong, J. S. [1978] Forecasting with econometric methods: Folklore versus fact, *Journal of Business, 51*, 549–64.

Arrow, K. [1959] Toward a theory of price adjustment, in Abramovitz, M. (ed.), *Allocation of Economic Resources* (Stanford: Stanford University Press), 41–51.

Arrow, K. and Debreu, G. [1954] Existence of an equilibrium for a competitive economy, *Econometrica, 22*, 265–90.

Aumann, R. [1985] What is game theory trying to accomplish? in Arrow, K. and Honkapohja, S. (eds.), *Frontiers of Economics* (Oxford: Basil Blackwell), 28–76.

Aumann, R. [1987] Game theory, in Eatwell, J., Milgate, M. and Newman, P. (eds.), *The New Palgrave: A Dictionary of Economics*. (London: The Macmillan Press), *1*, 460–82.

Aumann, R. [1995] Backward induction and common knowledge of rationality, *Games and Economic Behavior, 8*, 6–19.

Aumann, R. [1996a] Reply to Binmore, *Games and Economic Behavior, 17*, 138–46.

Aumann, R. [1996b] Reply to Binmore and Samuelson, in Arrow, K., Colombatto, E., Perlman, M. and Schmidt, C. (eds.), *The Rational Foundations of Economic Behavior* (London: Macmillan), 130–1.

Aumann, R. [1998] On the Centipede Game, *Games and Economic Behavior*, 23, 97–105.

Banks, J., Olson, M., Porter, D., Rassenti, S. and Smith, V. [2003] Theory, experiment and the federal communications commision spectrum auctions, *Journal of Economic Behavior & Organization*, 51, 303–50.

Barro, R. and Grossman, H. [1971] A general disequilibrium model of income and employment, *American Economic Review, 61*, 82–93.

Beattie, A. and Politi, J. [2008] 'I made a mistake,' admits Greenspan, *Financial Times*, 23 October.

Becker, G. [1965] A theory of the allocation of time, *The Economic Journal, 75*, 493–517.

Bennett, R. [1981] *An Empirical Test of some Post-Keynesian Income Distribution Theories*, PhD thesis, Simon Fraser University, Burnaby, B. C.

Bicchieri, C. [1993] *Rationality and Coordination* (Cambridge: Cambridge University Press).

Binmore, K. [1996] A note on backward induction, *Games and Economic Behavior, 17*, 135–7.

Binmore, K. [1997] Rationality and backward induction, *Journal of Economic Methodology, 4*, 23–41.

Binmore, K. [2007] *Game Theory: A Very Short Introduction* (Oxford: Oxford University Press).

Binmore, K. [2011] Interpreting knowledge in the backward induction problem, *Episteme, 8*, 248–61.

Blanchard, O. [2000] What do we know about macroeconomics that Fisher and Wicksell did not? *Quarterly Journal of Economics, 115*, 1375–409.

Blaug, M. [1992] *The Methodology of Economics* (Cambridge: Cambridge University Press).

Boland, L. [1971] An institutional theory of economic technology and change, *Philosophy of the Social Sciences, 1*, 253–8.

Boland, L. [1977a] Giffen goods, market prices and testability, *Australian Economic Papers, 16*, 72–85.

Boland, L. [1977b] Testability, time and equilibrium stability, *Atlantic Economic Journal, 5*, 39–47.

Boland, L. [1978] Time in economics vs. economics in time: the 'Hayek Problem', *Canadian Journal of Economics, 11*, 240–62.

Boland, L. [1979] A critique of Friedman's critics, *Journal of Economic Literature, 17*, 503–22.

Boland, L. [1982] *The Foundations of Economic Method* (London: George Allen & Unwin). http://www.sfu.ca/~boland/book1pdf.htm

Boland, L. [1986] *Methodology for a New Microeconomics* (Boston: Allen & Unwin). http://www.sfu.ca/~boland/book2pdf.htm

Boland, L. [1989] *The Methodology of Economic Model Building: Methodology after Samuelson* (London: Routledge). http://www.sfu.ca/~boland/book3pdf.htm

Boland, L. [1992] *The Principles of Economics: Some Lies my Teachers Told Me* (London: Routledge). http://www.sfu.ca/~boland/book4pdf.htm

Boland, L. [1997] *Critical Economic Methodology: A Personal Odyssey* (London: Routledge). http://www.sfu.ca/~boland/book5pdf.htm

Boland, L. [2003] *The Foundations of Economic Method: A Popperian Perspective* (London: Routledge).

Boland, L. [2008a] On the economist's view of inductive reasoning, paper presented to the 35th Annual Meeting of the History of Economics Association, York University, 28 June 2008.

Boland, L. [2008b] Stylized facts, Durlauf, S. and Blume, L. (eds.), *The New Palgrave Dictionary of Economics, 2nd Ed.* (London: Palgrave Macmillan) http://www.dictionaryofeconomics.com

Boland, L. [2010] Cartwright on 'Economics', *Philosophy of the Social Sciences*, *40*, 530–8.

Boland, L. [2013] Review of Mäki [2012], *Erasmus Journal for Philosophy and Economics*.

Borrill, P. and Tesfatsion, L. [2011] Agent-based modeling: the right mathematics for the social sciences? in Davis and Hands [2011], 228–58.

Boumans, M. [1999] Built in justification, in Morgan and Morrison [1999], 66–96.

Boumans, M. [2001] Measure for measure: How economists model the world into numbers, *Social Research*, *68*, 427–53.

Boumans, M. [2005] *How Economists Model the World into Numbers* (London: Routledge).

Boumans, M. [2012] Mathematics as quasi-matter to build models as instruments, in Dieks, D., Gonzalez, W. J., Hartmann, S., Stöltzner, M. and Weber, M. (eds.), *Probabilities, Laws and Structures* (New York: Springer) 307–18.

Box, G. E. P. [1953] Non-normality and tests on variances, *Biometrika*, *40*, 318–35.

Bridel, P. (ed.) [2011] *General Equilibrium Analysis: A Century after Walras* (New York: Routledge).

Camerer, C. and Loewenstein, G. [2003] Behavioral economics: Past, present, future, in Camerer, C., Loewenstein, G. and Rabin, M. (eds.) *Advances in Behavioral Economics* (Oxford: Princeton University Press), 3–51.

Carlaw, K. and Lipsey, R. [2012] Does history matter?: Empirical analysis of evolutionary versus stationary equilibrium views of the economy, *Journal of Evolutionary Economics*, *22*, 735–66.

Chang, Y. and Kim, S-B. [2006] From individual to aggregate labor supply: A quantitative analysis based on a heterogeneous agent macroeconomy, *International Economic Review*, *47*, 1–27.

Chang, Y. and Kim, S-B. [2007] Heterogeneity and aggregation: Implications for labor-market fluctuations, *American Economic Review*, *97*, 1939–56.

Chari, V. and Kehoe, P. [2006] Modern macroeconomics in practice: How theory is shaping policy, *Journal of Economic Perspectives*, *20*, 3–28.

Chatfield, C. [1995] Model uncertainty, data mining and statistical inference, *Journal of the Royal Statistical Society. Series A (Statistics in Society)*, *158*, 419–66.

Clements, M. and D. Hendry [2008] Economic forecasting in a changing world, *Capitalism and Society*, *3*, 1–18.

Clower, R. [1959] Some theory of an ignorant monopolist, *The Economic Journal*, *69*, 705–16.

Clower, R. and Due, J. [1972] Microeconomics (Homewood, IL: Richard D. Irwin, Inc.).

Colander, D. [2009] Economists, incentives, judgment and the European CVAR approach to macroeconometrics. *Economics: The Open-Access, Open-Assessment E-Journal*, *3*, 2009-9. http://www.economics-ejournal.org/economics/journalarticles/2009-9.

Colander, D., Howitt., P., Kirman, A., Leijonhufvud, A. and Mehrling, P. [2008] Beyond DSGE models: Toward an empirically based macroeconomics, *The American Economic Review, Papers and Proceedings*, *98*, 236–40.

Cowell, F. [2006] *Microeconomics: Principles and Analysis* (Oxford: Oxford University Press).

Crawford, V. and Iriberri, N. [2007] Level-*k* auctions: Can a nonequilibrium model of strategic thinking explain the winner's curse and overbidding in private-value auctions? *Econometrica*, *75*, 1721–70.

Crawford, V., Costa-Gomes, M. and Iriberri, N. [forthcoming] Structural models of nonequilibrium strategic thinking: Theory, evidence and applications, *Journal of Economic Literature.*

Darden, S. [1961] Short Talk on the Universe, *The sound of my own voice (and other noises)* (LP record: Mercury OCS 6202, OCLC No. 12851697).

Davidson, P. [1972] *Money and the Real World* (New York: Wiley).

Davidson, P. [1977] Money and general equilibrium, *Economie Appliquee, 30,* 541–62.

Davidson, P. [1991] Is probability theory relevant for uncertainty? a post-Keynesian perspective, *Journal of Economic Perspective, 5,* 129–43.

Davis, J. B. and Hands, D. W. (eds.) [2011] *The Elgar Companion to Recent Economic Methodology* (Cheltenham and Northampton, MA: Edward Elgar).

Dawes, R., Fildes, R., Lawrence, M. and Ord, K. [1994] The past and the future of forecasting research, *International Journal of Forecasting, 10,* 151–9.

Debreu, G. [1959] *Theory of Value: An Axiomatic Analysis of Economic Equilibrium* (New York: Wiley).

Debreu, G. [1974] Excess demand functions, *Journal of Mathematical Economics, 1,* 15–21.

Duarte, P. G. [2011] Recent developments in macroeconomics: the DSGE approach to business cycles in perspective, in Davis and Hands [2011], 375–403.

Duffy, J. [forthcoming] Macroeconomics: A survey of laboratory research, in Kagel, J. and Roth, A. E. (eds.), *Handbook of Experimental Economics, Vol. 2* (Princeton: Princeton University Press).

Eddington, A. [1928/58] *The Nature of the Physical World* (Cambridge: Cambridge University Press).

Einstein, A. and Infeld, L. [1938/61] *The Evolution of Physics: The Growth of Ideas from Early Concepts to Relativity and Quanta* (New York: Simon and Schuster).

Farmer, R. and Guo, J. T. [1994] Real business cycles and animal spirits hypothesis, *Journal of Economic Theory, 63,* 42–72.

Ferguson, C. E. [1969] *Microeconomic Theory* (Homewood, IL: Richard D. Irwin, Inc.).

Fisher, F. [1983] *Disequilibrium Foundations of Equilibrium Economics* (Cambridge: Cambridge University Press).

Fisher, F. [1987] Aggregation problem, in Eatwell, J., Milgate, M. and Newman, P. (eds.), *The New Palgrave: A Dictionary of Economics* (London: The Macmillan Press), *2,* 53–5.

Fisher, I. [1892/1925] *Mathematical Investigations in the Theory of Value and Prices* (New Haven: Yale University Press).

Flores, B. and Pearce, S. [2000] The use of an expert system in the M3 competition, *International Journal of Forecasting, 116,* 485–96.

Foster, J. [1997] The analytical foundations of evolutionary economics: From biological analogy to economic self-organization, *Structural Change and Economic Dynamics, 8,* 427–51.

Franses, P. H., McAleer, M. and Legerstee, R. [2012] Evaluating macroeconomic forecasts: A concise review of some recent developments, *University of Canterbury, Working Paper 12/2012,* 1–29.

Friedman, B. [1979] Optimal expectations and the extreme information assumptions of 'Rational Expectations' macromodels, *Journal of Monetary Economics, 5,* 23–41.

Friedman, D. [1991] Evolutionary Games in Economics, *Econometrica,* 59, 637–66.

Friedman, D. [1998] Monty Hall's Three Doors: Construction and deconstruction of a choice anomaly, *American Economic Review, 88*, 933–46.

Friedman, M. [1953] Methodology of positive economics, in *Essays in Positive Economics* (Chicago: University of Chicago Press), 3–43.

Frisch, R. [1933a] Propagation problems and impulse problems in dynamic economics, in *Economic Essays in Honour of Gustav Cassel* (London: George Allen & Unwin), 171–205.

Frisch, R. [1933b] Editor's Note, *Econometrica, 1*, 1–2.

Frisch, R. [1936] On the notion of equilibrium and disequilibrium, *Review of Economic Studies, 3*, 100–105.

Frydman, R. and Phelps, E. (eds.) [1983] *Individual Forecasting and Aggregate Outcomes: 'Rational Expectations' Examined* (Cambridge: Cambridge University Press).

Fudenberg, D. and Levine, D. [1993] Self-confirming equilibrium, *Econometrica, 61*, 523–45.

Fudenberg, D. and Levine, D. [2009] Self-confirming equilibrium and the Lucas Critique, *Journal of Economic Theory, 144*, 2354–71.

Georgescu-Roegen, N. [1971] *The Entropy Law and the Economic Process* (Cambridge, MA: Harvard University Press).

Gibbard, A. and Varian, H. [1978] Economic models, *Journal of Philosophy*, 75, 664–77.

Gilboa, I., Postlewaite, A., Samuelson, L. and Schmeidler, D. [2011] Economics models as analogies, *Penn Institute for Economic Research*, working paper 12-001.

Govindan, S and Wilson, R. [2008] Refinements of Nash Equilibrium, in Durlauf, S. and Blume, L. (eds.), *The New Palgrave Dictionary of Economics, 2nd Ed.* (London: Palgrave Macmillan).

Granger, C. [1999] *Empirical Modeling in Economics: Specification and Evaluation* (Cambridge: Cambridge University Press).

Granger, C. [2012] The philosophy of economic forecasting, in Mäki [2012], 311–27.

Greene, W. [2008] *Econometric Analysis, 7th Ed.* (Englewood Cliffs, NJ: Prentice Hall).

Grubel, H and Boland, L. [1986] On the efficient use of mathematics in economics: some theory, facts and results of an opinion survey, *Kyklos, 39*, 419–42.

Guala, F. [2001] Building economic machines: the FCC auctions, *Studies in History and Philosophy of Science, 32*, 453–77.

Guala, F. [2012] Experimentation in economics, in Mäki [2012], 597–640.

Haavelmo, T. [1943] The statistical implication of a system of simultaneous equations, *Econometrica, 11*, 1–12.

Haavelmo, T. [1944] The probability approach in econometrics, *Econometrica, 12 (Supplement)*, iii–115.

Haavelmo, T. [1958] The role of the econometrician in the advancement of economic theory, *Econometrica*, 26, 351–7.

Hahn, F. [1965] On some problems of proving the existence of an equilibrium in a monetary economy, in Hahn, F. and Brechling, F. (eds.), *Theory of Interest Rates: Proceedings of a Conference Held by the International Economics Association* (London: Macmillan), 126–35.

Hahn, F. [1970] Some adjustment problems, *Econometrica, 38*, 1–17.

Hahn, F. [1973] *On the Notion of Equilibrium in Economics* (Cambridge: Cambridge University Press).

Hahn, F. and Negishi, T [1962] A theorem on non-tatonnement stability, *Econometrica, 30*, 463–9.

Hands, D. W. [2001] *Reflection without Rules: Economic Methodology and Contemporary Science Theory* (Cambridge: Cambridge University Press).

Hargreaves Heap, S. and Varoufakis, Y. [1995] *Game Theory: A Critical Introduction* (London: Routledge).

Hargreaves Heap, S. and Varoufakis, Y. [2004] *Game Theory: A Critical Text, 2nd Ed.* (London: Routledge).

Harsanyi, J. and Selten, R. [1988] *A General Theory of Equilibrium Selection in Games* (Cambridge: MIT Press).

Hartley, J. [1996] The origins of the representative agent, *Journal of Economic Perspectives, 10*, 169–77.

Hartley, J. [1997] *The Representative Agent in Macroeconomics* (London: Routledge).

Hausman, D. [1992] *The Inexact and Separate Science of Economics* (New York: Cambridge University Press).

Hayek, F. [1937] Economics and knowledge, *Economica, 4 (NS)*, 33–54.

Heckman, J. [2000] Causal parameters and policy analysis in economics: a twentieth century retrospective, *Quarterly Journal of Economics, 115*, 45–97.

Hendry, D. F. [1980] Econometrics – alchemy or science? *Economica, 47 N.S.*, 387–406.

Hendry, D. F. [2011] Empirical economic model discovery and theory evaluation, *Rationality, Markets and Morals, 2*, 115–45.

Hendry, D. F. and Nielsen, B. [2007] *Econometric Modeling: A Likelihood Approach* (Princeton: Princeton University Press).

Herschel, J. [1830] *Preliminary Discourse on the Study of Natural Philosophy* (London: Longman).

Hey, J. [1981] *Economics in Disequilibrium* (Oxford: Martin Robertson).

Hicks, J. [1939/46] *Value and Capital, 2nd Ed.* (Oxford: Clarendon Press).

Hicks, J. [1956] *A Revision of Demand Theory* (Oxford: Clarendon Press).

Hicks, J. [1976] Some questions of time in economics, in A. Tang, F. Westfield and J. Worley (eds.), *Evolution, Welfare and Time in Economics* (Toronto: Heath) 135–51

Hicks, J. [1979] *Causality in Economics* (Oxford: Basil Backwell).

Hodgson, G. M. and Knudsen, T. [2006] Why we need a generalized Darwinism, and why generalized Darwinism is not enough, *Journal of Economic Behavior & Organization, 61*, 1–19.

Hollis, M. and Sugden, R. [1993] Rationality in action, *Mind, 102*, 1–35.

Honkapohja, S. and Mitra, K. [2006] Learning stability in economies with heterogeneous agents, *Review of Economic Dynamics, 9*, 284–309.

Hoover, K. D. [1988] *The New Classical Macroeconomics: A Sceptical Inquiry* (Oxford: Blackwell).

Hoover, K. D. [2001] *The Methodology of Empirical Macroeconomics* (Cambridge: Cambridge University Press).

Hoover, K. D. [2003] A history of postwar monetary economics and macroeconomics, in Biddle, J., Davis, J. and Samuels, W. (eds.), *The Blackwell Companion to the History of Economic Thought* (Oxford: Blackwell).

Hoover, K. D. [2012] Microfoundational programs, in Duarte, P. G. and Tadeu Lima, G. (eds.) *Microfoundations Reconsidered: The Relationship of Micro and Macroeconomics in Historical Perspective* (Cheltenham: Edward Elgar), 29–61.

Hoover, K. D. and Perez, S. [1999] Data mining reconsidered: encompassing and the general-to-specific approach to specification search, *Econometrics Journal, 2*, 167–91.

Hoover, K. D., Johansen, S. and Juselius, K. [2008] Allowing the data to speak freely: The macroeconometrics of the cointegrated vector autoregression, *American Economic Review, Papers and Proceedings*, *98*, 251–5.

Isaac, M. [1983] Laboratory experimental economics as a tool in public policy analysis, *Social Science Journal*, 45–58.

Jensen, K., Kamath, S. and Bennett, R. [1987] Money in the production function: An alternative test procedure, *Eastern Economic Journal*, *13*, 259–69.

Judge, G. G., Griffiths, W. E., Hill, R. C., Lutkepohl, H. and Lee, T. C. [1985] *The Theory and Practice of Econometrics, 2nd. Ed.* (New York: John Wiley).

Juselius, K. [2006] *Cointegrated VAR Model: Methodology and Applications* (Oxford: Oxford University Press).

Juselius, K. [2011] On the role of theory and evidence in macroeconomics, in Davis and Hands [2011], 404–36.

Kahneman, D. and Tversky, A. [1979] Prospect theory: an analysis of choice under risk, *Econometrica*, *47*, 263–91.

Kaldor, N. [1957] A model of economic growth, *The Economic Journal*, *67*, 594–621.

Kaplan, S., Samuels, J. and Cohen, J. [2013] An examination of the effect of CEO social ties and CEO reputation on nonprofessional investors' Say-on-Pay judgments, presented at the 2013 Ethics Symposium sponsored by the University of Waterloo's Centre for Accounting Ethics, April 18–20.

Kennedy, P. E. [2008] *A Guide to Econometrics, 6th Ed.* (Oxford: Blackwell Publishing).

Keynes, J. M. [1936] *General Theory of Employment, Interest and Money* (New York: Harcourt, Brace and World).

Keynes, J. M. [1937] The general theory of employment, *Quarterly Journal of Economics*, *51*, 209–23.

Kirman, A. [1992] Whom or what does the representative individual represent? *Journal of Economic Perspectives*, *6*, 117–36.

Kirman, A. [2006] Forward, in Colander, D. (ed.) *Post Walrasian Macroeconomics: Beyond the Dynamic Stochastic General Equilibrium Model* (Cambridge: Cambridge University Press).

Kirman, A. [2010] Walras' unfortunate legacy, working paper subsequently published as Kirman [2011].

Kirman, A. [2011] Walras' unfortunate legacy, in Bridel [2011], 109–33.

Klein, J. [2001] Reflections from the age of economic measurement, *History of Political Economy*, *33*, 111–36.

Klein, L. [1957] The scope and limitations of econometrics, *Applied Statistics*, *6*: 1–17.

Klein, L. [1971] Whither econometrics? *Journal of the American Statistical Association*, *66*, 415–21.

Kneale, W. and Kneale, M [1962] *The Development of Logic* (Oxford: Oxford University Press).

Knight, F. [1921] *Risk, Uncertainty and Profit* (Chicago: University of Chicago Press).

Knudsen, T. [2004] General selection theory and economic evolution: The Price equation and the replicator/interactor distinction, *Journal of Economic Methodology*, *11*, 147–73.

Kocherlakota, N. [1998] Money is memory, *Journal of Economic Theory*, 81, 232–51.

Koopmans, T. [1941] The logic of econometric business cycle research, *Journal of Political Economy*, *49*, 157–81.

Koopmans, T. [1947] Measurement without theory, *The Review of Economics and Statistics, 29,* 161–72.

Koopmans, T. [1957] *Three Essays on the State of Economic Science* (New York: McGraw-Hill).

Kreps, D. [1990] *Game Theory and Economic Modelling* (New York: Oxford University Press).

Krusell, P. and Smith, A. [1998] Income and wealth heterogeneity in the macroeconomy, *Journal of Political Economy, 106,* 867–96.

Krusell, P. and Smith, A. [2006] Quantitative macroeconomic models with heterogenous agents, *Advances in Economics and Econometrics: Theory and Applications, Ninth World Congress, vol. 1, Econometric Society Monographs No. 41* (Cambridge: Cambridge University Press) 298–340.

Kydland, F. and Prescott, E. [1996] The computational experiment: an econometric tool, *Journal of Economic Perspectives, 10,* 69–85.

Kydland, F. E. and Prescott, E. [1991] Econometrics of the general equilibrium approach to business cycles, *The Scandinavian Journal of Economics, 93, Proceedings of a Conference on New Approaches to Empirical Macroeconomics,* 161–78.

La Mura, P. [2009] Projective expected utility: a subjective formulation, *Proceedings of the 12th Conference on Theoretical Aspects of Rationality and Knowledge* (New York: Association for Computing Machinery), 184–92.

Lagueux, M. [2010] *Rationality and Explanation in Economics* (London: Routledge)

Lancaster, T. [2004] *An Introduction to Modern Bayesian Econometrics* (Oxford: Blackwell Publishing).

Lawson, T. [1988] Probability and uncertainty in economic analysis, *Journal of Post Keynesian Economics, 11,* 38–65.

Leamer, E. [1983] Let's take the con out of econometrics, *American Economic Review, 73,* 31–43.

Leamer, E. [2010] Tantalus on the road to Asymptopia, *Journal of Economic Perspectives,* 24, 31–46.

Ledyard, J., Porter, D. and Rangel, A. [1997] Experiments testing multiobject allocation mechanisms, *Journal of Economics & Management Strategy, 6, 639–75.*

Leijonhufvud, A. [1997] Models and theories, *Journal of Economic Methodology, 4,* 193–8.

Leijonhufvud, A. [2006] The Uses of the Past, *Discussion Paper No. 3* (lecture to ESHET meetings, 2006).

Leonhardt, D. [2008] Greenspan's Mea Culpa, *Economix, New York Times, 23 October.*

Leontief, W. [1936] Composite commodities and the problem of index numbers, *Econometrica, 4,* 39–59.

Leontief, W. [1947] Introduction to a theory of the internal structure of functional relationships, *Econometrica, 15,* 361–73.

Levin, A. [2010] Nonlinearities, Risks, and the Design of Monetary Policy, paper given November 16, 2010 to the annual meetings of the Argentina Economics Association.

Levine, D. K. [2011] Neuroeconomics? *International Review of Economics,* 10.1007/: s12232-011-0128-7.

Levine, D. K. and Zheng, J. [2010] The Relationship of Economic Theory to Experiments, in Frechette, G. and Schotter, A. (eds.) *The Methods of Modern Experimental Economics* (Oxford: Oxford University Press).

Lichtenstein, S. and Slovic, P. [1971] Reversal of preferences between bids and choices in gambling decision, *Journal of Experimental Psychology*, *89*, 46–55.

Lindley, D. [1987] Thomas Bayes (1702–1761), in Eatwell, J., Milgate, M. and Newman, P. (eds.), *The New Palgrave: A Dictionary of Economics* (London: The Macmillan Press), *3*, 205–6.

Lipsey, R. [2012] Some contentious issues in theory and policy in memory of Mark Blaug, in Boumans, M. and Klaes, M. (eds.) *Mark Blaug: Rebel With Many Causes* (Cheltenham: Edward Elgar).

Lipsey, R. [1963] *An Introduction to Positive Economics* (London: Weidenfeld & Nicolson).

Lloyd, C. [1965] On the falsifiability of traditional demand theory, *Metroeconomica*, *17*, 17–23.

Lloyd, C. [1967] *Microeconomic Analysis* (Homewood, IL: Richard D. Irwin, Inc.).

Lloyd, C. [1980] The Northern Stores Project, in Boland, L., Dean, J., Schoner, B. and Tower, E. (eds.) *The Collected Works of Cliff L. Lloyd* (Burnaby: Simon Fraser University).

Loewenstein, G. [1999] Experimental economics from the vantage-point of behavioural economics, *The Economic Journal*, *109*, F25–34.

Lovell, M. [1983] Data mining, *Review of Economic and Statistics*, *65*, 1–12.

Lucas, R. [1980] Methods and problems in business cycle theory, *Journal of Money, Credit and Banking*, *12*, 696–715.

Lucas, R. [1986] Adaptive behavior and economic theory, *Journal of Business*, 59, 401–26.

Lucas, R. [1989] *Recursive Methods in Economic Dynamics* (Cambridge, MA: Harvard University Press).

Lucas, R. and Prescott, E. [1971] Investment under uncertainty, *Econometrica*, *39*, 659–81.

Lucas, R. and Sargent, T. [1979] After Keynesian macroeconomics, *Federal Reserve Bank of Minneapolis Quarterly Review (Spring)*, 1–16.

Luce, D. and Raiffa, H. [1957] *Games and Decisions* (New York: John Wiley).

Maddala, G. S. [2001] *Introduction to Econometrics, 3rd Ed.* (New York: John Wiley & Sons).

Mäki, U. (ed.) [2012] *Elsevier Handbook of the Philosophy of Science, Volume 13: Philosophy of Economics* (Amsterdam: North Holland).

Makridakis, S. [1986] The art and science of forecasting: an assessment and future directions, *International Journal of Forecasting*, *2*, 15–39.

Makridakis, S. [1991] Forecasting in the 21st century, *International Journal of Forecasting*, *7*, 123–6.

Makridakis, S., Andersen, A., Carbone, R., Fildes, R., Hibon, M., Lewandovvski, R., Newton, J., Parzen, E. and Winkler, R. [1982]. The accuracy of extrapolation (time series) methods: results of a forecasting competition. *Journal of Forecasting*, *1*, 111–53.

Makridakis, S. and Wheelwright, S. [1989] *Forecasting Methods for Management* (New York: John Wiley & Sons).

Makridakis, S., Chatfield, C., Hibon, M., Lawrence, M., Mills, T., Ord, K. and Simmons, L. F. [1993] The M-2 Competition: a real-time judgmentally based forecasting study, *International Journal of Forecasting*, *9*, 5–23.

Makridakis, S. and Hibon, M. [1979] Accuracy of Forecasting: An Empirical Investigation, *Journal of the Royal Statistical Society Series A*, *142*, 97–145.

Makridakis, S. and Hibon, M. [2000] The M3-Competition: results, conclusions and implications, *International Journal of Forecasting, 116*, 451–76.

Mankiw, N. G. [2006] The macroeconomist as scientist and engineer, *Journal of Economic Perspectives, 20*, 29–46.

Mann, H. and Wald, A. [1943] On the statistical treatment of linear stochastic difference equations, *Econometrica, 11*, 173–220.

Mantel, R. [1974] On the characterization of aggregate excess demand, *Journal of Economic Theory, 7*, 348–53.

Marschak, J. [1953] Economic measurements for policy and prediction, in Hood, W. C. and Koopmans, T. (eds.) *Studies in Econometric Method* (New York: John Wiley & Sons), 1–26.

Marshall, A. [1890] *Principles of Economics* (London: Macmillan).

Marshall, A. [1920] *Principles of Economics, 8th Ed.* (London: Macmillan).

Mas-Colell, A., Winston, M. and Green, J. [1995] *Microeconomic Theory* (Oxford: Oxford University Press).

Maxwell, J. [1958] Some Marshallian concepts, especially the representative firm, *The Economic Journal, 68*, 691–8.

McAleer, M. [2011] Are forecast updates progressive? *Kyoto Institute of Economic Research, Discussion Paper No. 762*, 1–24.

McCloskey, D. N. [1994] *Knowledge and Persuasion in Economics* (Cambridge: Cambridge University Press).

Meyer, L. H. [2004] *A Term at the Fed: An Insider's View* (New York: HarperCollins).

Miller, P. [1978] Forecasting with econometric methods: a comment, *Journal of Business, 51*, 579–84.

Mittelhammer, R. C., Judge, G. G. and Miller, D. J. [2000] *Econometric Foundations* (New York: Cambridge University Press).

Morgan, M. [1990] *The History of Econometric Ideas* (New York: Cambridge University Press).

Morgan, M. [1998] Model, in Davis, J., Hands, D. W. and Maki, U. (eds.), *The Handbook of Economic Methodology* (Cheltenham: Edward Elgar), 316–21.

Morgan, M. [2001] Making measuring instruments, *History of Political Economy, 33, Annual Supplement*, 235–51.

Morgan, M. [2008] Models, in Durlauf, S. and Blume, L. (eds.), *The New Palgrave Dictionary of Economics, 2nd Ed.* (London: Palgrave Macmillan).

Morgan, M. [2012] *The World in the Model: How Economists Work and Think* (New York: Cambridge University Press).

Morgan, M. and Knuuttila, T. [2012] Models and modelling in economics, in Mäki [2012], 49–87.

Morgan, M. and Morrison, M. [1999] Models as mediating instruments, in Morgan and Morrison [1999], 10–37.

Morgan, M. and Morrison, M. (eds.) [1999] *Models as Mediators: Perspectives on Natural and Social Science* (Cambridge: Cambridge University Press).

Moore, D., McCabe, G. and Craig, B. [2012] *The Introduction to the Practice of Statistics, 7th Ed.* (New York: W. H. Freeman).

Muth, J. [1961] Rational expectations and the theory of price movements, *Econometrica, 29*, 315–35.

Nash, J. F., Jr. [1951] Noncooperative games, *Annals of Mathematics, 54*, 286–95.

Nelson, R. and Winter, S. [1974] Neoclassical vs. evolutionary theories of economic growth: critique and prospectus, *The Economic Journal, 84*, 886–905.

Nelson, R. and Winter, S. [1982] *An Evolutionary Theory of Economic Change* (Cambridge: Harvard University Press).

Nelson, R. and Winter, S. [2002] Evolutionary theorizing in economics, *Journal of Economic Perspectives, 16*, 23–46.

Neumann, J. von [1937/45] A model of general equilibrium, *Review of Economic Studies, 13*, 1–9.

Neumann, J. von and Morgenstern, O. [1953] *Theory of Games and Economic Behavior, 3rd Ed.* (Princeton: Princeton University Press).

Nikaido, H. [1960/70] *Introduction to Sets and Mappings in Modern Economics* (Amsterdam: North Holland).

Nik-Khan, E. [2008] A tale of two auction, *Journal of Institutional Economics, 4*, 73–97.

Patinkin, D. [1956] *Money, Interest and Prices* (Evanston, IL: Row, Peterson and Company).

Patinkin, D. [1987] Keynes, John Maynard (1883–1946), in Eatwell, J., Milgate, M. and Newman, P. (eds.) *The New Palgrave: A Dictionary of Economics* (London: The Macmillan Press), 3, 19–41.

Pesaran, H and Dupleich Ulloa, M. R. [2008] Nonnested Hypotheses, in Durlauf, S. and Blume, L. (eds.), *The New Palgrave Dictionary of Economics, 2nd Ed.* (London: Palgrave Macmillan). http://www.dictionaryofeconomics.com

Pesaran, M. and Deaton, A. [1978] Testing non-nested nonlinear regression models, *Econometrica, 46*, 677–94.

Plott, C. [1997] Laboratory experimental testbeds: application to the PCS auction, *Journal of Economics and Management Strategy, 6*, 605–38.

Pope, D. and Schweitzer, M. [2011] Is Tiger Woods loss averse? Persistent bias in the face of experience, competition and high stakes, *American Economic Review, 101*, 129–57.

Popper, K. [1963] *Conjectures and Refutations: The Growth of Scientific Knowledge* (London: Routledge).

Popper, K. [1965] *Conjectures and Refutations: The Growth of Scientific Knowledge, 2nd Ed.* (New York: Basic Books).

Price, G. R. [1972] Extension of covariance selection mathematics, *Annals of Human Genetics, 35*: 485–90.

Price, G. R. [1995] The nature of selection, *Journal of Theoretical Biology, 175*: 389–96.

Rabin, M. [1993] Incorporating fairness into game theory and economics, *American Economic Review, 83*, 1281–1302.

Ramsey, F. [1926/31] Truth and probability, in Braithwaite, R. B. (ed.), *Foundations of Mathematics and Other Logical Essays* (London: Routledge and Kegan Paul), 156–98.

Ramsey, Frank P. [1927] A contribution to the theory of taxation, *The Economic Journal, 37*, 47–61.

Richardson, G. [1959] Equilibrium, expectations and information, *The Economic Journal, 69*, 225–37.

Robbins, L. [1928] The Representative Firm, *The Economic Journal, 38*, 387–404.

Robson, A. [2002] Evolution and human nature, *Journal of Economic Perspectives, 16*, 89–106.

Romer, R. [1986] Increasing returns and long-run growth, *Journal of Political Economy, 94*, 1002–37.

Rosenberg, A. [1978] The puzzle of economic modeling, *Journal of Philosophy, 75*, 679–83.

Rubinstein, A. [1991] Comments on the interpretation of game theory, *Econometrica, 59*, 909–24.

Rubinstein, A. [2006] Discussion of 'Behavioral Economics', in Blundell, R., Newey, W. and Persson, T. (eds.) *Advances in Economics and Econometrics, Ninth World Congress* (Cambridge: Cambridge University Press), 246–54.

Rubinstein, A. [2008] Comments on neuroeconomics, *Economics and Philosophy, 24*, 485–94.

Russell, B. [1945] *A History of Western Philosophy* (New York: Simon and Schuster).

Samuelson, L. [2002] Evolution and game theory, *Journal of Economic Perspectives, 16*, 47–66.

Samuelson, L. [2005] Economic theory and experimental economics, *Journal of Economic Literature, 43*, 65–107.

Samuelson, L. and Robson, A. [2010] The evolutionary optimality of decisions and experienced utility, presented at the SFU workshop on the *biological basis of behavioural economics*, 14 May.

Samuelson, P. [1947/65] *Foundations of Economic Analysis* (New York: Atheneum).

Samuelson, P. [1948b] Consumption theory in terms of revealed preference, *Economica, 15 (NS)*, 243–53.

Samuelson, P. [1948a] *Economics* (New York: McGraw-Hill).

Samuelson, P. [1953] Consumption theorems in terms of overcompensation rather than indifference comparisons, *Economica, 20 (NS)*, 1–9.

Santos, A. C. [2011] Experimental economics, in Davis and Hands [2011], 39–60.

Sargent, T and Wallace, N. [1976] Rational expectations and the theory of economic policy, *Journal of Monetary Economics, 2*, 169–83.

Sargent, T. [1979] *Macroeconomic Theory* (New York: Academic Press).

Sargent, T. [1984] Autoregressions, expectations and advice, *American Economic Review, 74, Papers and Proceedings*, 408–15.

Sargent, T. [1993] *Bounded Rationality in Macroeconomics: The Arne Ryde Memorial Lectures* (Oxford: Clarendon Press).

Sargent, T. [2004] *Recursive Macroeconomic Theory* (Cambridge, MA: The MIT Press).

Sargent, T. [2008] Evolution and intelligent design, *American Economic Review, 98, Papers and Proceedings*, 3–37.

Saul, J. R. [1995] *The Unconscious Civilization* (Toronto: House of Anansi Press).

Savage, L. [1954] *The Foundations of Statistics* (New York: Wiley).

Schumpeter, J. [1933] The common sense of econometrics, *Econometrica, 1*, 5–12.

Selten, R. [1975] The Chain-Store Paradox, *Theory and Decision*, *9*, 127–59.

Sent, E.-M. [1997] Sargent versus Simon: bounded rationality unbound, *Cambridge Journal of Economics, 21*, 323–38.

Sent, E.-M. [2004] Behavioral economics: How psychology made its (limited) way back to economics, *History of Political Economy, 36*, 735–60.

Shackle, G. [1967] *The Years of High Theory* (Cambridge: Cambridge University Press).

Shackle, G. [1972] *Epistemics and Economics* (Cambridge: Cambridge University Press).

Shubik, M. [1959] *Strategy and Market Structure* (New York: John Wiley).

Shubik, M. [2012] What is a solution to a matrix game, *Cowles Foundations Discussion Paper No. 1866*.

Simon, H. [1947] *Administrative Behavior: A Study of Decision-Making Processes in Administrative Organization* (NewYork: Macmillan).

Simon, H. [1955] A behavioral model of rational choice, *Quarterly Journal of Economics, 69*, 99–118.

Sims, C. [1980] Macroeconomics and reality, *Econometrica, 48*, 1–48.

Sims, C. [1996] Macroeconomics and methodology, *Journal of Economic Perspectives, 10*, 105–20.

Sims, C. [2010] But economics is not an experimental science, *Journal of Economic Perspectives, 24*, 59–68.

Smith, V. K. [1969] The identification problem and the validity of economic models: a comment, *South African Journal of Economics, 37*, 81.

Smith, V. L. [1962] An experimental study of competitive market behavior, *Journal of Political Economy, 70*, 111–37.

Smith, V. L. [1976] Experimental economics: Induced value theory, *American Economic Review, 66*, 274–9.

Smith, V. L. [1982] Experimental economics: Induced value theory, *American Economic Review, 66*, 923–55.

Smith, V. L. [1992] Game theory and experimental economics: Beginnings and early influences, *History of Political Economics, 24, Supplement*, 241–82.

Smith, V. L. [2002] Method in experiment: Rhetoric and reality, *Experimental Economics, 5*, 91–110.

Smith, V. L. [2008] *Rationality in Economics: Constructivist and Ecological Forms* (New York: Cambridge University Press).

Solow, R. [1956] A contribution to the theory of economic growth, *Quarterly Journal of Economics, 70*, 65–94.

Solow, R. [2008] The state of macroeconomics, *Journal of Economic Perspectives, 22*, 243–9.

Solow, R. [2011] Macroeconomics and the uses of general equilibrium, in Bridel [2011], 98–101.

Sonnenschein, H. [1972] Market excess demand functions, *Econometrica, 40*, 549–63.

Spanos, A. [2008] Statistics and economics, in Durlauf, S. and Blume, L. (eds.), *The New Palgrave Dictionary of Economics, 2nd Ed.* (London: Palgrave Macmillan) 1129–62. http://www.dictionaryofeconomics.com

Spanos, A. [1995a] On theory testing in econometrics: modeling with nonexperimental data, *Journal of Econometrics, 67*, 189–226.

Spanos, A. [1995b] On normality and the linear regression model, *Econometric Reviews, 14*, 195–206.

Spanos, A. [1999] *Probability Theory and Statistical Inference: econometric modeling with observational data* (Cambridge: Cambridge University Press).

Spanos, A. [2009] The pre-eminence of theory versus the European CVAR perspective in macroeconometric modeling. *Economics: The Open-Access, Open-Assessment E-Journal, 3*, 2009–10. http://www.economics-ejournal.org/economics/journal articles/2009-10

Spanos, A. [2010a] Theory testing in economics and the error-statistical perspective, in Mayo, D. and Spanos, A. (eds.) [2010] *Error and Inference: Recent Exchanges on Experimental Reasoning, Reliability and the Objectivity and Rationality of Science* (Cambridge: Cambridge University Press), 202–46.

Spanos, A. [2010b] Statistical adequacy and the trustworthiness of empirical evidence: Statistical vs. substantive information, *Economic Modelling, 27*, 1436–52.

Spanos, A. [2011] Revisiting Haavelmo's structural econometrics: Bridging the gap between theory and data, paper presented at the Trygve Haavelmo Centennial Symposium, December 13, 2011, in 'Gamle festsal', Domus Academica, Oslo.

Spanos, A. [2012] Philosophy of econometrics, in Mäki [2012], 329–93.

Starmer, C. [1999] Experiments in economics: should we trust the dismal scientists in white coats? *Journal of Economic Methodology, 6*, 1–30.

Stigler, G. [1954] The early history of empirical studies of consumer behavior, *Journal of Political Economy, 62*, 95–113.

Sugden, R. [1998] The role of inductive reasoning in the evolution of conventions, *Law and Philosophy*, 377–410.

Sugden, R. [2008] The changing relationship between theory and experiment in economics, *Philosophy of Science, 75*, 621–32.

Sugden, R. [2013] Review of Morgan [2012], *Erasmus Journal for Philosophy and Economics, 6, 108–14.*

Summers, L. [1991] Scientific illusion in empirical macroeconomics, *Scandinavian Journal of Economics, 93*, 129–48.

Swamy, P. A. V. B. [1970] Efficient inference in a random coefficient regression model, *Econometrica, 38*, 311–23.

Swamy, P. A. V. B., Conway, R. and von zur Muehlen, P. [1985] The foundations of econometrics – are there any? *Econometric Reviews, 4*, 1–61.

Vajda, S. [1956] *The Theory of Games and Linear Programming* (London: Methuen & Co.).

Valavanis, S. [1959] *Econometrics: An Introduction to Maximum Likelihood Method*, edited from manuscript by A. Conrad (New York: McGraw-Hill).

Varian, H. [1992]. *Microeconomic Analysis, 3rd Ed.* (New York: Norton).

Varian, H. [2006]. *Intermediate Microeconomics: A Modern Approach, 7th Ed.* (New York: Norton).

Vromen, J. [2004] Conjectural revisionary economic ontology: Outline of an ambitious research agenda for evolutionary economics, *Journal of Economic Methodology, 11*, 213–47.

Vromen, J. [2006] Routines, genes and program-based behavior, *Journal of Evolutionary Economics, 16*, 543–60.

Vromen, J. [2012] Ontological issues in evolutionary economics: The debate between Generalized Darwinism and the Continuity Hypothesis, in Mäki [2012], 737–63.

Wald, A. [1936/51] On some systems of equations of mathematical economics, *Econometrica, 19*, 368–403.

Walker, D. A. [1996] *Walras's Market Models* (Cambridge: Cambridge University Press).

Weintraub, E. R. [1979] *Microfoundations* (Cambridge: Cambridge University Press).

Winter, S. [1971] Satisficing, selection, and the innovating remnant, *Quarterly Journal of Economics, 85*, 237–61.

Witt, U. [2012] Evolutionary economics and psychology, Lewis, A. (ed.), *Cambridge Handbook of Psychology and Economic Behavior* (Cambridge: Cambridge University Press) 493–511.

Wolfe, J. [1954] The representative firm, *The Economic Journal, 64*, 337–49.

Woodford, M. [1999] Revolution and Evolution in Twentieth Century Macroeconomics, presented at the conference Frontier of the Mind in the Twenty-First Century, Library of Congress, Washington, D.C.

Wray, R. [2011] The dismal state of macroeconomics and the opportunity for a new beginning, in Davis and Hands [2011], 452–69.

Zaman, A. [1996] *Statistical Foundations for Econometric Techniques* (San Diego: Academic Press).

Zarnowitz, V. [1967] *An Appraisal of Short-term Economic Forecasts* (New York: Columbia University Press).

Zellner, A. [1978] Folklore versus facts in forecasting with econometric methods, *Journal of Business*, *51*, 587–93.

Name index

Subject index

Printed in the United States
By Bookmasters

Printed in the United States
By Bookmasters